Play and Learning in Early Childhood Settings

International Perspectives on Early Childhood Education and Development

Volume 1

Early childhood education in many countries has been built upon a strong tradition of a materially rich and active play-based pedagogy and environment. Yet what has become visible within the profession, is essentially a Western view of childhood preschool education and school education.

It is timely that a series of books be published which present a broader view of early childhood education. This series, seeks to provide an international perspective on early childhood education. In particular, the books published in this series will:

- Examine how learning is organized across a range of cultures, particularly Indigenous communities
- Make visible a range of ways in which early childhood pedagogy is framed and enacted across countries, including the majority poor countries
- Critique how particular forms of knowledge are constructed in curriculum within and across countries
- Explore policy imperatives which shape and have shaped how early childhood education is enacted across countries
- Examine how early childhood education is researched locally and globally
- Examine the theoretical informants driving pedagogy and practice, and seek to find alternative perspectives from those that dominate many Western heritage countries
- Critique assessment practices and consider a broader set of ways of measuring children's learning
- Examine concept formation from within the context of country-specific pedagogy and learning outcomes

The series will cover theoretical works, evidence-based pedagogical research, and international research studies. The series will also cover a broad range of countries, including poor majority countries. Classical areas of interest, such as play, the images of childhood, and family studies will also be examined. However the focus will be critical and international (not Western-centric).

Ingrid Pramling-Samuelsson · Marilyn Fleer
Editors

Play and Learning in Early Childhood Settings

International Perspectives

 Springer

Editors

Prof. Ingrid Pramling-Samuelsson
Göteborg University
Dept. Education
SE-405 30 Göteborg
Sweden
ingrid.pramling@ped.gu.se

Prof. Marilyn Fleer
Monash University
Fac. Education
Frankston VIC 3199
Australia
marilyn.fleer@education.monash.edu.au

ISBN: 978-1-4020-8497-3   e-ISBN: 978-1-4020-8498-0

DOI 10.1007/978-1-4020-8498-0

Library of Congress Control Number: 2008927209

Printed on acid-free paper

9 8 7 6 5 4 3 2 1

springer.com

Foreword

This book represents the outcome of the joint activities of a group of scholars who were concerned about the lack of international research in play for children from birth to 3 years. The authors are members of the Organisation Mondiale pour l'Èducation Préscholaire (OMEP). For further information, see http://www.omep-ong.net/.

The idea of carrying out a research project internationally was born at the OMEP's World Congress in Melbourne, Australia 2004. All member countries were invited and 10 countries decided to participate, of which three have withdrawn during the process. The reason for this might be that in these countries only one person was working with the project, while other seven countries have been working in a team of two or more persons. The countries that have carried out research and contributed to this book with a chapter each are Australia, Chile, China, Japan, New Zealand, Sweden and USA (Wisconsin). For more information about the participating countries and their corresponding addresses, see Appendix I.

This book project started in Melbourne with a discussion about what is general in early childhood education globally, and what is culturally specific. The discussion was inspired by one of the keynote speakers, Nazhat Shameem (2004), judge in the supreme court in Fiji, when she said: "If we all think we are so different and specific in each culture, the role of human rights has no value anymore."

We formulated three questions:

- What is the meaning of play and learning, for 0 to 3?
- How do teachers work to support this?
- What are the families' views of play?

We decided to use Barbara Rogoff's socio-cultural theory as a framework for our interpretations. We used her three foci of analysis: intrapersonal, interpersonal and cultural/institutional.

We also agreed on making an empirical study including at least five children, aged from birth to three, from five different early childhood education settings, typical for each country. Some countries have collected data from more children. Each child is observed by video recordings during one whole day, and the child's teacher and parents are interviewed. The empirical data should be seen as case studies, and can never represent each country on a more general level. However, we are convinced that different national ethos become visible in these few case studies.

Children aged from birth to three as a target group has received very limited attention in research all over the world. This age group, is increasingly becoming part of the early childhood education system in many countries, and from what we know from the Organisation for Economic Co-operation and Development (OECD) evaluation (OECD, 2001), the staff taking care of the children in this age group seem to be those with the lowest education. What does that mean for young children's experiences in everyday life in early childhood education? We hope you as a reader of this book will enjoy reading this book as much as we who have in worked with the studies documented in the forthcoming chapters.

Göteborg   Ingrid Pramling-Samuelsson
Melbourne   Marilyn Fleer

Contents

Contributors

Verónica Aedo
Teacher in the Pontificia Universidad Católica de Chile, Vice-president of OMEP
Chile, e- mail: vaedog@puc.cl

Leonor Cerda
Director of the early childhood Education Program, Universidad Católica del
Maule, e-mail: lcerdad@ucm.cl

Louis Chicquette
2121 N. Nicholas Street, Appleton, Wisconsin 54914, USA,
e-mail: CHICQUETTELOUI@aasd.k12.wi.us

Patricia Dintrans
Teacher of the Early Childhood Education Program, Universidad Católica Raúl
Silva Henríquez, e-mail: pdintrans@ucsh.cl

Fiona Ellis
Dunedin Collage of Education, PO Box 56 Dunedin, New Zealand,
e-mail: Fiona.Ellis@dce.ac.nz

Marilyn Fleer
Monash University, POS Box 527 Frankston, Victoria, 3199, Australia,
e-mail: marilyn.fleer@education.monash.edu.au

Mamiko Ishizuka
Kindergarten Attached Kamakura Women's University, Japan,
e-mail: tanpopo@kamakura-u.ac.jp

Hui Li
Assistant Professor, Faculty of Education, The University of Hong Kong, Pokfulam
Road, Hong Kong, e-mail: huili@hku.hk

Amiria O'Malley
Te Wananga o Aotearoa, 63, Te Wananga O Aotearoa 1861, Gisborne and
Northland. 64, Korowai Manukura (Sch of Ed), 07 872 0330,
e-mail: Amiria.O'Malley@twoa.ac.nz

Ana Cristina Mantilla
Key Research Assistant, Monash University, PO Box 527 Frankston, Victoria, 3199, Australia, e-mail: Ana.Mantilla@Education.monash.edu.au

Mari Mori
Department of Human Sciences, Toyo Eiwa University, Yokohama, Japan, e-mail: mamo@toyoeiwa.ac.jp

Tomomi Naito
Faculty of Child Studies, Kamakura Women's University, Japan, e-mail: dzf05027@nifty.com

Akiko Nezu
Department of Early Childhood Care and Education, Toyoko Gakuen Women's College, Japan, e-mail:akiko.n@toyoko.ac.jp

Mirna Pizarro
Teacher of the Early Childhood Education Program, Universidad de Magallanes, e-mail: mirnapizarro@hotmail.com

Nirmala Rao
Faculty of Education, The University of Hong Kong, Pok Fu Lam Road, Hong Kong, e-mail: nirmalarao.is@gmail.com

Silvia Redón
Director of the Early Childhood Education Program, Universidad Católica de Valparaíso, e-mail: silvia.redon@ucv.cl

Corine M. Patricia Rivalland
Key Research Assistant, Monash University, PO Box 527 Frankston, Victoria, 3199, Australia, Dunedin Collage of Education, PO Box 56 Dunedin, New Zealand, e-mail: Corine.Rivalland@education.monash.edu.au

Jean Rockel
University of Auckland, Faculty of Education (Epson), Private Bag 92601, Symonds Street, Auckland, New Zealand, e-mail: j.rockel@auckland.ac.nz

Verónica Romo
Director of the Early Childhood Education Program, Universidad Central of Chile, President of OMEP Chile, USA, e-mail: vromol1@yahoo.es

Chikage Samizo
e-mail: samizo@duc.ac.jp

Ingrid Pramling-Samuelsson
Göteborg University, Department of Education, Box 300, SE-405 30 Göteborg, Sweden, e-mail: Ingrid.Pramling@ped.gu.se

Sonja Sheridan
Göteborg University, Department of Education, Box 300, SE-405 30 Göteborg, Sweden, e-mail: Sonja.Sheridan@ped.gu.se

Sue Stover
Auckland University of Technology, PO Box 92006, Auckland 1142, New Zealand,
e-mail: sue.stover@aut.ac.nz

Holli A. Tonyan
Lecturer, Monash University, PO Box 527 Frankston, Victoria, 3199, Australia,
e-mail: holligaj@gmail.com

Meripa Toso
University of Auckland, Faculty of Education (Epson), Private Bag 92601 Symonds
Street, Auckland, New Zealand, e-mail: m.toso@auckland.ac.nz

Jayne White
Victoria University of Wellington: New Zealand, e-mail: jayne.white@vuw.ac.nz

Lenore Wineberg
University of Wisconsin Oshkosh, 800 Algoma Blvd., Oshkosh, Wisconsin 54901,
USA, e-mail: wineberg@uwosh.edu

Chapter 1
A Cultural-Historical Perspective on Play: Play as a Leading Activity Across Cultural Communities

Marilyn Fleer

Introduction

Across the international community, early childhood professionals have generally privileged the place of *play* within both practice and curriculum documentation (Wood, 2004). The term play is almost synonymous with early childhood education (Ailwood, 2003). Yet, there is much debate around what constitutes play, and the theoretical perspectives which drive how play is talked about and made visible to professionals (Fleer, 1999).

Although play is very important in the discourse, theory and practice of early childhood education, much of the foundational research which has informed current practice in Western heritage communities (and more recently Eastern countries) (Cooney, 2004; Fleer, 1996; Haight, Wang, Fung, Williams & Mintz 1999), are now very dated (Dockett & Fleer, 1999). Many of the children who had participated in the early studies of Piaget, Parten and Smilansky (to name a few very influential theorists) have grown up or have died. The socio-political contexts of children and their families are very different to those of Parten's subjects, as the life experiences of children today are diverse, global and technological (see Kaliala, 2006).

In addition, research into play has tended to concentrate upon the play activities of 4-year-old children, with less research effort directed towards how babies and 2-year olds play (Dockett & Fleer, 1999). Similarly, research into play has privileged contexts which have been constructed (e.g. laboratories), as apposed to research in more naturalistic settings, such as homes and early childhood centres (see Wood, 2004).

Research into play has also been framed in ways which privilege European heritage cultural practices, rather than seeing play as culturally specific (Cooney, 2004; Fleer, 1996; Gaskins and Göncü, 1988; Göncü, Mistry, & Mosier, 2000; Haight et al., 1999; Rettig, 1995). Gaskins and Göncü (1988) argued that 'Cultural and individual variations in quantity and quality of symbolic play (that they noticed in their cross-cultural research) raise questions about the origins, developmental

M. Fleer
Faculty of Education, Frankston, Victoria, 3199 Australia
e-mail: marilyn.fleer@education.monash.edu.au

I. Pramling-Samuelsson, M. Fleer (eds.), *Play and Learning in Early Childhood Settings*, DOI 10.1007/978-1-4020-8498-0_1,
© Springer Science+Business Media B.V. 2009

outcomes, and functions of play' (p. 107). More recently, Göncü et al. (2000) have noted in their empirical work that 'it is not warranted to assume that all communities value and provide comparable play opportunities for their children' (p. 321). They have found 'community differences in frequency of both the numbers of children who played, as well as differences in children's play partners' noting that 'occurrence of social play presents cultural variations' (p. 325). They suggest that in the past, 'an overlap between Western researchers' conceptualizations of play and the play of children from other communities, often generating misrepresentations of non-Western children's activities as lacking if they did not have the pretend features of Western children's play' (p. 323).

It is timely that an international study of the play activities of children aged 1–3 years be undertaken. In this book, seven studies of the play activities of infants and toddlers are presented, with a view to not only update what we know about very young children's play, but also to gain a more international perspective on how play is framed, sanctioned, theorized, and built into the discourse and documentation of early childhood education across seven countries.

Defining Play

Although most professionals speak about play as though it were a single entity, play has been defined and theorized in many different ways. For instance, Fromberg (1992) suggests that play is characterized by thinking and activity that is symbolic, meaningful, active, pleasurable, voluntary, rule-governed and episodic. Bateson (1972) suggests that play is evident when participants frame events, through attitude, pretence, vocalization and other metacommunicative cues. Göncü et al. (2000) suggests that play is evident when there is a sense of playfulness and fun, but also that we should look carefully across cultures for variations. These examples illustrate the diversity of views on how play is defined. This is not simply a contemporary challenge, but rather something that has been with us as a profession for a long time. For instance, Hutt et al. (1989) found in their review of children's activities, 'some fourteen distinct categories of behaviour were identified, all of which, in one or another context, have been labelled as "play"' (p.10). What is particularly interesting about their review of the literature at that time is that the 14 categories actually represented almost all children's behaviour. In essence, play could be viewed in its broadest sense as describing almost all the activities that young children engage in. This literature suggests that there is no standard definition for play, and that most of the behaviours and activities young children engage in can be termed as play by one theorist or another.

Historically, different theories have been developed to explain the activities of children. For instance, Mitchell and Mason (1948) suggested that play was a way of 'blowing off steam'. Their surplus energy theory explained that play was undertaken when humans had excess energy. In contrast, Lazarus (1883) put forward the Recreation theory of play, whereby children restore their energy levels by playing.

After extensive investigations of human and animal behaviours, Groos (1898) suggested that through play, children practised the skills they needed in adult life. He termed this the Instinct-practice theory of play. Hall (1906) also recognized instinct as an important dimension in play, suggesting that play was important for human evolution. The recapitulation theory of play put forward by Hall (1906) suggests that children enact the stages of human evolution through play. Play has also been explained as an opportunity for the safe expression of pent-up emotions (see Carr, 1902; Claperde, 1911).

The diversity of explanations for play, discussed by these classical theorists of play, can also be mirrored in more recent theorization of play. For example, Psychoanalytical theories of play, based on the work of Freud and his colleagues, and advanced by Klein (1932), support the use of play for helping children deal with emotional problems (e.g. play therapy). Play therapy has a firm place within contemporary early childhood education, and this literature is drawn upon for justifying the place of dramatic play within programmes (Dockett & Fleer, 1999).

Cognitive theories of play, such as those of Piaget (1962) and Smilansky (1968), and social theories of play, as put forward by Parten (1932, 1933), are more widely known and used by early childhood professionals in most European heritage communities (see Main editors note for Fleer, 1999). These important works have informed researchers and educators interested in young children. Scholars such as Bruce (1991), Gaskins (2005), Göncü et al. (2000), Hutt et al. (1989), Kaliala (2006), Moyles (1994), Paley (1990), Wood (2004), and Wood and Attfield (1996) have drawn upon these works in their support or critique of play within early childhood education. Contemporary researchers have also used these traditional theories of play to frame their studies (e.g. Ailwood, 2003; Clements, 2004; Hagan, Anderson, & Parry, 2001; de Haan, 2005; Lofdahl, 2006; Michalopoulou, 2001; Vejleskov, 1995).

Many of these contemporary scholars have used the foundational research and theorization of Parten (1932, 1933) and Smilansky (1968) to inform their writings and research on early childhood education. For instance, Bruce (1991) in drawing upon the work of Göncü (1987) has espoused a view of play known as 'Free-flow play':

> Free-flow play is sometimes called 'imaginative play', 'free play', 'fantasy play', 'pretend play' or 'ludic play'. It is not structured play, guided play, games play, practice play or exploratory play (Bruce, 1991, p. 7).

Beardsley and Harnett (1998) use the terms 'pretend play', 'role play', 'fantasy play', 'imaginative play', 'free-flow play', 'dramatic play' and 'sociocramatic play' in defining the play activities of children in their writings. As a result, we are now seeing a substantial body of literature on play (Vygotsky, 1966), most of which draws upon foundational research undertaken some time ago, and predominantly with European heritage children (notable exceptions are Cooney, 2004; Fleer, 1999; Gaskins, 2005; Göncü, 1998, 1999; Göncü et al., 2000; Miller & Harwood, 2002; Tamis-LeMonda & Bornstein, 1992; Tobin, Wu, & Davidson, 1999). The theories and research that have amassed over time represent a complex and variable set of

designs, findings, theories and definitions. As Wood and Attfield (1996) suggest,
play is:

> ...infinitely varied and complex. It represents cognitive, cultural, historical, social and phys-
> ical interconnections between the known and the unknowing, the actual and the possible,
> the probable and the improbable. It is a dialogue between fantasy and reality, between past,
> present and future, between the logical and the absurd, and between safety and risk. Given,
> these complexities it is hardly surprising that play has defied neat tidy definitions (p. 4).

In this particular publication, a cultural–historical perspective has driven the framing
of the research, and the analysis and write up of the findings across the seven countries. It is through a range of cross-cultural contexts that the complexity and richness
of the activities of children can be assembled – albeit in only seven countries, with
multiple contexts being illuminated. Nevertheless, the cultural–historical framing
of this research allows for a more connected view of play to emerge, as the cultural
contexts frame what is possible for children and what is valued by communities.

A Cultural-Historical Perspective on Play

A legacy of Vygotsky's writing has been the interest generated in understanding the
social, cultural and historical contexts in which children and adults find themselves
today. Of significance is Vygotsky's view that in order to understand the individual,
one must also understand the cultural–historical context in which the individual
resides. Cultural–historical theory foregrounds those contexts which shape social
relations, community values and past practices which have laid the foundations of
what participants pay attention to in their communities. In this book, the social,
political and historical contexts of the different countries are detailed as an important
dimension in understanding the way play is spoken about, researched and positioned
within the early childhood profession.

Although Vygotsky wrote very little on the nature of play, we can learn a great
deal about his views if we examine his seminal article *Play and its role in the mental
development of the child* (Vygotsky, 1966) within the context of his theorization as
articulated in *The collected works on L.S. Vygotsky* (Volumes 1–6). Of particular
interest for this discussion on play is his writing on development (Volume 5), higher
mental functions (Volume 4) and concept formation (Volume 1).

One of the central defining features of Vygotsky's (1966) writing on play is his
view that play provides a space for the conscious realizations of concepts. For instance, he gives the example of two children who in real life are sisters, and who play
out being sister. He argues that the sisters have an everyday concept of 'being sisters', but may not have a scientific concept of sibling relationships. Vygotsky (1966)
states that in the play context, that a space is created in which children can bring
together their everyday concept of 'being sisters', with the scientific concept of
'sisterhood'. Through play, the children consciously focus on the concept of 'sisters', thus paving the way for concept formation. He states: 'What passes unnoticed
by the child in real life becomes a rule of behavior in play' (p. 9). It is these rules for

behaviour in everyday life that are acted out through play. Vygotsky (1966) argues that, in this way, a zone of proximal development is generated through play.

In Volume 1 Vygotsky (1987) discusses how everyday or spontaneous concepts, such as using language, lay the foundation upon which the study of language (e.g. grammar) can take place. The academic or scientific concepts (e.g. studying language at school) cannot take place without the everyday concepts (of using language) being enacted through life or practice. Similarly, he argued that to only ever study a new language for example, without ever practising it in everyday contexts (i.e. speaking it), meant that concept formation was limited. He suggested that everyday concepts move their way upwards, and scientific concepts moved their way downwards. He argued that through the interlacing of everyday and scientific concepts, that children became conscious of their everyday practice (scientific concepts in practice), thus transforming their everyday practice. For example, knowing to put on a jumper when you are cold (an everyday concept) does not help you when you wish to go surfing and want to keep warm. However, knowing about insulation (scientific concept) will transform how you may go about buying a wet suit to keep you warm in the water. Vygotsky (1966) argued that in play, children are positioned as having to move outside of everyday concepts, and begin to consciously consider the behaviours of everyday practice. Rather than acting unconsciously when 'being a sister', in play children must actively think about the concept of a 'sister' in order to play. Vygotsky's theoretical ideas on play within the context of everyday and scientific concept formation (Volume 1) are very powerful for us as researchers and professionals grappling with how to define play or when debating the value of play. If play provides a conceptual space for the dialectical relations between everyday concept formation and scientific concept formation, then we have at our disposal a whole new way of thinking about play and learning.

> I think that in finding criteria for distinguishing a child's play activity from his (SIC) other general forms of activity it must be accepted that in play a child creates an imaginary situation (Vygotsky, 1966, p. 8).

Taking a cultural–historical perspective on play means that we look to define play when we notice that preschool children place themselves into an imaginary situation, with rules, and children act out the behaviours that are associated with those rules (e.g. being a mum or a sister in play). However, Vygotsky (1966) stressed that preschool children do not put themselves in an imaginary world (that would be a delusion), or that children simply copy the real world that they observe. He argues against the strongly held view that play is the child's work, but rather he suggests that play is a leading activity and not the predominant activity of young children.

He suggested that children under three tend to focus on objects and their action is in relation to the objects in their environment. He argued that children under three are constrained by what is visible only. That is, a door suggests you open it, a toy phone suggest you call someone on it. He argued that over time the child begins to act differently in relation to what it sees. Preschool children tend to substitute objects with meaning, such as a stick becoming a horse. Through play, the child is also liberated from real actions – for example, the child makes eating movements with its hands to represent eating. A child under three is more likely to use actions to explore, such as sucking on fingers or stroking or manipulating objects. Preschool children are not constrained by objects or real actions. Objects are substituted by meaning, and actions are substituted by meaning as the child develops. According to Vygotsky (1966, p. 12) 'play is a transitional stage' in which a separation from an object can take place. He argues that 'It is terribly difficult for a child to sever thought (the meaning of a word) from object.'

Vygotsky (1966) argued that 'whenever there is an imaginary situation in play there are rules, not rules which are formulated in advance and which change during the course of the game, but rules stemming from the imaginary situation' (Vygotsky, 1966, p. 10). He argues that 'In play the child is free. But this is an illusory freedom' (p. 10), because the rules dictate how play is enacted.

Vygotsky also argued that whilst imaginary situations have concealed rules of how to behave in that imaginary situation, that for older children who play with explicit rules, that an imaginary situation is created. Vygotsky (1966) suggested that through playing chess, a school-aged child has to engage with an imaginary world. This is particularly evident in board games, such as Monopoly or Hangman.

Vygotsky's (1966) work on play highlights the differing capacities of children of different ages, for instance:

> I think that play with an imaginary situation is something essentially new, impossible for a child under three; it is a novel form of behavior in which the child is liberated from situational constraints through his activity in an imaginary situation (p. 11).

Vygotsky's (1966) theory raises many questions about the nature of play and the development of thinking in play. In this book, contemporary snap shots of play with children under the age of three reveal many contradictions, both with respect to Vygotsky's theory on the role of play in mental development for children under 3 years and also play across cultures. Nevertheless, Vygotsky's (1966) sociocultural–historical work lays important foundation for understanding play across cultures.

Another important theoretical idea that Vygotsky put forward was the zone of proximal development. For Vygotsky (1966) play created a zone of proximal development. As such, play is important in the development of higher mental functioning (see Volume 4). Vygotsky (1966) stated that 'In play a child is always above his (SIC) average age, above his daily behavior; in play it is as though he were a head taller than himself' (p. 16). Vygotsky's (1997) writings on higher mental functioning were founded on a belief in the dialectical relations between natural or biological development and historical or cultural development. In Volume 4, he argues that biological development and cultural development are essentially two sides of the same coin. He suggests that biological development makes available to children new ways of interfacing with their environment, such as walking or speaking. However, he also argues that through social relation with people and things biological development is also significantly influenced. In play, children have at their disposal biological and cultural tools that interact to generate development. Understanding the social contexts in which children play is particularly important for interpreting development in and through play. Vygotsky (1997) states that 'higher mental functioning cannot be understood without sociological study' (p. 18). As such, this book seeks also to interpret how staff and families who support children's learning through play understand and value play. Many of the authors of chapters in this book have analysed teacher and family perspectives on play in order to better understand the development of higher mental functioning within the context of play.

> As in the focus of a magnifying glass, play contains all the developmental tendencies in a condensed form; in play it is as though the child were trying to jump above the level of his normal behavior. (Vygotsky, 1966: 16)

In Volume 5 Vygotsky (1998) discusses his theory of development, notably the crisis points that emerge as a result of the dialectical relations between biological and cultural development in young children. In the background of Vygotsky's (1966) theory on play lies his thinking on crisis points. For instance, Vygotsky (1966) speaks strongly about the interests, incentives and motives of children to act. These motives and needs are the foundations to his crisis points.

> At preschool age special needs and incentives arise which are highly important to the whole of the child's development and which are spontaneously expressed in play (Vygotsky, 1966, p. 7).

Vygotsky (1998) presents progression of critical periods, interspersed with crisis points. For example, there is the crisis of the newborn, followed by infancy (2 months–1 year). At the age of one is a crisis point, as the motives and interests of the infant change. Vygotsky labels the period from 1 to 3 years as early childhood. A crisis appears at the age of three. This is followed by a period known as the Preschool age (3–7 years), with a crisis point at 7 years (see Vygotsky, 1998, vol. 5, p. 196). Vygotsky (1966) has argued that 'Play is the source of development and creates the zone of proximal development' (p. 16). For Vygotsky (1966) play was the 'leading activity which determines the child's development' (p. 16).

> The play-development relationship can be compared to the instruction-development relationship, but play provides a background for changes in needs and in consciousness of a much wider nature (Vygotsky, 1966, p. 16).

Vygotsky (1966) argues that 'As play develops, we see a movement toward the conscious realization of its purpose' (p. 16). Vygotsky (1998) suggests that changes in consciousness are evident at given age levels. The motives, interests and incentives change as a result of the dialectical relations between cultural and biological development. He warns that play should not be viewed completely as an intellectual activity, as motives, interests and incentives of children shape the nature of play. Of significance in Vygotsky's writings is the social situation of development.

> The social situation of development represents the initial moment for all dynamic changes that occur in development during the given period. It determines wholly and completely the forms and the path along which the child will acquire ever newer personality characteristics, drawing them from the social reality as from the basic source of development, the path along which the social becomes the individual. Thus, the first question we must answer in studying the dynamics of any age is to explain the social situation of development (Vygotsky, 1998, p. 198).

The social situation of a child is determined by the society and cultural context in which the child is embedded. The motives, interests and incentives will be different across cultures, thus influencing the nature of development. If play is the leading activity for the development for young children, and play represents action within an 'imaginative sphere, in an imaginary situation, the creation of voluntary intentions and the formation of real-life plans and volitional motives' (Vygotsky, 1966, p. 16) then examining play across cultures within the birth to 3 years is vitally important.

Participating Countries

In this book seven countries participated in the study of the play activities of children from birth to 3 years. In Chapter 2, play in Aotearoa New Zealand is detailed. The significance of the Maori, Pasifika and Pakeha (British immigrants) history is shown within the context of early childhood curriculum development and professional learning of teachers (all professionals working with very young children are given this title). The nomenclature and specializations within early childhood education is depicted by White et al., through the Playcentres, Education and Care services, Te Kohanga Reo, Pasifika language nests, Home-based education and care, Playgroups and Kindergartens.

In Chapter 3, the Australian socio-political context is given, with the mix of public and private institutions for early childhood education, each being uniquely defined within the seven states and territories of Australia. The culturally and linguistically diverse background of the Australian population, and the previous structural division between care and education, provide for a unique context to understand the nature and discourse of play within early childhood education. Staff in education settings have university qualifications and most programmes which are labelled as care have technically qualified staff. This is consistent with the staffing profiles found in Chile, as discussed in Chapter 4 by Aedo et al. In Chile, enormous political support is given to early childhood education, with politicians believing in the importance of the early years for fostering major educational outcomes for the whole community. Curriculum in Chile is focussed on the birth to six sectors with a special curriculum in place for infants and toddlers. Play is the main methodology for supporting learning in early childhood in Chile.

Early childhood education in Hong Kong China, is also structurally divided between care and education, as is shown in Chapter 5. Nirmala Rao and Hui Li show how the historical context and political belief system of families and authorities shape the way in which play is framed and enacted within early childhood education. Like Aotearoa New Zealand, Hong Kong China has different institutions for the care and education of young children, and like Australia they are administered by either Health or Education Government Departments.

In Chapter 6, Mori et al. give the socio-political background of early childhood education and care in Japan. In Japan early childhood education is organized as Yochien (Preschool/kindergarten), Hoikusho (day nursery/chid care centre) and

Nintei Kodomoen (combination of Yochien and Hoikusho). Like other countries with this split in education and care systems, Japan has university-qualified staff in Yochien and a Day nursery licence for Hoikusho. Curriculum for 0–3 years children is play oriented, with a focus on supporting the child to 'form one's character'.

Early childhood education in Sweden is detailed in Chapter 7. Unlike Australia, Chile and Japan, most staff working in early childhood education in Sweden are qualified. Ingrid Pramling-Samuelsson and Sonja Sheridan provide rich examples of play in action in Swedish Preschools, many of which exemplify the Swedish National Early Childhood Curriculum. In Chapter 8, Lenore Wineberg and Louis Chicquette discuss their Wisconsin early childhood education in the context of recent Government policies of 'No Child Left Behind', the NAEYC accreditation system, and the theoretical writings of Vygotsky and Piaget.

The diverse cultural and geographical landscape provides a complex picture for the findings detailed in subsequent chapters. The cultural–historical context of each of the participating countries, provides a rich and interesting backdrop to understanding the nature of play for children aged birth to 3 years. Much can be gained from an analysis of the data gathered in the seven participating countries. In Chapter 9, Ingrid Pramling-Samuelsson and Marilyn Fleer brings together the similarities and the uniqueness of how play is defined, enacted and theorized for very young children across the participating countries. It is through a cultural–historical study of play that we gain a better understanding of how play is discussed, shaped and privileged internationally within the field of early childhood education.

Methodological Framework for Cross-Cultural Research

Each of the chapters that follow have framed their research following a sociocultural–historical perspective. Vygotsky's seminal work has focussed attention on the study of the dialectical relations between individuals and their communities. His work has been instrumental in both broadening the research lens, but also in introducing theoretical complexity, as the biological child is considered only in relation to cultural–historical contexts. In order to understand how a child plays, we must also study the sociohistorical and cultural context in which play can occur – that is the institutions, the social and cultural systems, the political and historical practices and activities of particular communities which give rise to or which shape how play may be enacted. The complexity of studying children's play within a range of cultural communities requires a systematic approach to framing and analysing research data. Vygotsky's work has laid the foundations for moving the unit of analysis beyond the individual and into the dynamic region between the individual and the society in which the individual lives. Through this process, the child is transformed, but he/she also contributes towards and shapes society. Rogoff (2003) has provided a useful approach for framing the analysis of such dynamic contexts and processes – as first articulated by Vygotsky (see his collected works). All the researchers who contributed to this book were inspired by

Rogoff's analytical framework (see Rogoff, 1998, 2003) to help them to formulate their study designs. Some researchers closely followed her conceptual framework for analysis, whilst others worked more broadly within the principles of cultural–historical theory. However, each researcher sought to investigate the play activities of children aged birth to 3 years within a cultural–historical context. A sample of five children or more was set as the target for the cross-cultural comparison. Each child was videotaped in their early childhood setting (however defined or organized). Filming occurred immediately on arrival in their early childhood setting and concluded when the child was collected by their family and taken home. All the experiences of the target children were captured on videotape. Families and staff were also invited to participate in the study. Although slight variations in interview questions were noted across the studies, most researchers interviewed families and teachers in relation to their beliefs and practices on play. The overall analytical framework that has guided the preparation of this particular book has drawn upon the work of Rogoff (1998, 2003), in particular her three planes of analysis.

Rogoff's diagrammatic representation (shown in Figs. 1.1–1.6) show how her three planes of analysis are constructed. The three lenses illustrate how play can be analysed across cultures (Figs. 1.4–1.6).

Fig. 1.1 Individual plane of analysis (Rogoff, 2003, p. 53)

Fig. 1.2 Image of the child and 'separate images of the children in the context demonstrated' (Rogoff, 2003, p. 53)

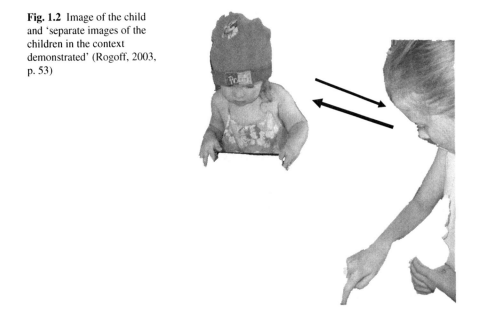

In the first image, Fig. 1.1 the focus is on the child's hand. This is a traditional approach to observing a child – the solitary individual. Information about the context or purpose of the activity has not been included in the observation. The interactions the child is having with her peers or the teacher has also been removed or simply not recorded.

The role of the other child in that context when the observation was made may well be represented as separate observations for each of the children (see Fig. 1.2). This approach to observing fits closely with developmental psychology, whereby you 'study "*the child*" apart from other people, who are studied separately even

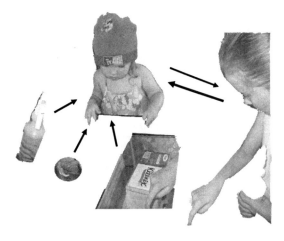

Fig. 1.3 Separate images of the children and the context influencing each other (Rogoff, 2003, p. 55)

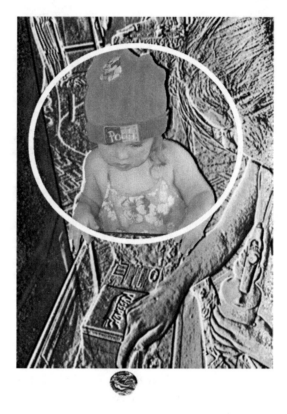

Fig. 1.4 Transformation-of-
participation – intrapersonal
focus of analysis
(Rogoff, 2003, p. 57)

when they are engaging in the same event. Then the "*social influences*" are examined through correlating the characteristics of actions of the separate entities'
(Rogoff, 2003, p. 54).

Similarly, Rogoff (2003) argues that the cultural features are often treated as
separate entities. She argues that what is studied is the influence of culture on the
individual child. This is noted in Fig. 1.3 by drawing attention to the artefacts,
and the other individual children in the image. These approaches are common, but
Rogoff (2003) argues that they are not adequate for understanding sociocultural
processes.

However, when we take all of the elements detailed in Figs. 1.1–1.3 and put
them together (as shown in Fig. 1.4), we see quite a different image or observation –
richer, interdependent and culturally embedded. As Rogoff argues:

> The child is foregrounded, with information about him (or her) as an *individual as the*
> *focus of analysis*. At the same time, interpersonal and cultural-institutional information
> is available in the background. A general sense of interpersonal and cultural-institutional
> information is necessary to understand what this child is doing, although it does not need to
> be attended to in the same detail as the child's efforts (Rogoff, 2003, p. 56).

Rogoff (2003) has argued that if we wish to study the interpersonal relationships
between the children, then we bring all the different players into focus, as is shown

Fig. 1.5 Interpersonal focus
for analysis (Rogoff, 2003,
p. 59)

above in Fig. 1.5. In the example we would be interested in knowing about how they were supporting each other, how one child introduced the ideas.

Rogoff (2003) argues that 'the distinctions between what is in the foreground and what is in the background lie in our analysis and are not assumed to be separate entities in reality' (Rogoff, 2003, p. 58). We can better understand the individuals when the individual is thought of as participating in social relations and cultural activities.

Finally, Rogoff (2003) has also shown the importance of cultural features in making sense of our data. Rogoff (2003) has termed this the cultural–institutional focus of analysis. In Fig. 1.6 it is evident that the children and their relationship with each other are put into the background, and cultural/institutional features are foregrounded. For instance, knowing the staff are all qualified (as in the case with Sweden), or knowing that the Centre is a Pacifika Language Nest (as in New Zealand) shape the way the data are understood. In the example of the child studying the snail, it is important to know that the teacher has in place a comprehensive environmental education program, one that is supported by Early Childhood Australia (a National professional association for teachers and carers of young children).

Using three lenses (personal, interpersonal, cultural–institutional) for observing children is fundamental to documenting how play is enacted across countries. If

Fig. 1.6 Cultural–
institutional focus of analysis
(Rogoff, 2003, p. 60)

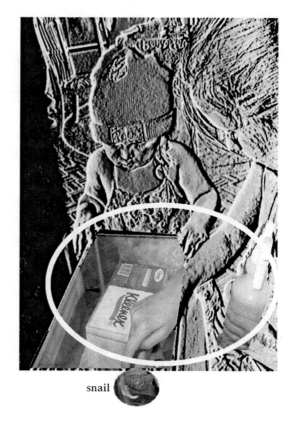

snail

we are to have meaningful observations of children at play, we need to employ
all three lenses for observing children. In this book, the researchers have used
Rogoff's (2003) lenses to help them to analyse and frame their observations of
young children at play. Using a cultural–historical framework for the study of children aged birth to 3 years has allowed for richer and new interpretation of play
across cultures.

Conclusion

Vygotsky's (1966) theory of the role of play in the mental development of children
provides powerful new directions for re-thinking how we have conceptualized play.
Considering play as the leading activity in the development of young children is different to thinking about play as the 'child's world' or the 'child's work'. A cultural–
historical study foregrounds the motives, needs and interests of children alongside
of the cultural contexts which privilege and value specific practices. Rogoff's (2003)
three planes of analysis allow for rich analysis across cultures and time, thus allowing for a contemporary view of play to result, and for a new theoretical perspective
to emerge.

References

Ailwood, J. (2003). Governing early childhood education through play. *Contemporary Issues in Early Childhood, 4*(3), 286–298.

Bateson, G. (1972). *Steps to an ecology of mind.* New York: Ballantine.

Clements, R. M. (2004). An investigation of the status of outdoor play. *Contemporary Issues in Early Childhood, 5*(1), 68–80.

Cooney, M. H. (2004). Is play important? Guatemalan Kindergarteners' classroom experience and their parents' and teachers' perceptions of learning though play. *Journal of Research in Childhood Education, Summer, 18*(4), 261–277.

Dockett, S., & Fleer, S. (1999). *Play and pedagogy in early childhood: Bending the rules.* Harcourt Brace: NSW.

Fromberg, D. P. (1992). A review of research on play. In C. Seefeld (Ed.), *The early childhood curriculum: a review of current research* (2nd ed., pp. 42–84). New York: Teachers College Press.

Beardsley, G., & Harnett, P. (1998). *Exploring play in the primary classroom.* London: David Fulton.

Bruce, T. (1991). *Time to play in early childhood education.* London, UK: Hoddler and Stoughton.

Carr, H. H. (1902). *The survival value of play.* Investigation of the Department of Psychology and Education: University of Colorado.

Claperde, E. (1911). *Psychologie de l'Enfant et Pedagogie Experimentale* (M. H. Holman, Trans.). New York: Longman, Green and Co.

Fleer, M. (1996). Theories of 'play': Are they ethnocentric or inclusive? *Australian Journal of Early Childhood, 21*(4), 12–18.

Fleer, M. (1999). Universal fantasy: The domination of Western theories of play. In E. Dau & E. Jones (Eds.), *Child's play: Revisiting play in early childhood settings* (pp. 67–80). Sydney, Philadelphia and London: MacLennan and Petty.

Fromberg, D. P. (1992). A review of research on play. In C. Seefeldt (Ed.), *The early childhood curriculum: A review of current research* (2nd ed., pp. 42–84). New York: Teachers College Press.

Gaskins, S. (2005). *The cultural relativity of Vygotsky's theory of play.* Unpublished paper presented as part of an invited symposium on "Play and Culture," ISCAR 2005, Sevilla.

Gaskins, S., & Göncü, A. (1988). Children's play as representation and imagination: The case of Piaget and Vygotsky. *The Quarterly Newsletter of the Laboratory of Comparative Human Cognition, October, 10*(4), 104–107.

Göncü, A. (1987). Toward an interacional model of development changes in social pretend play. In L. Katz (Ed.), *Current topics in early childwood education, 7,* 108–126.

Göncü, A. (1998). Development of intersubjectivity in social pretend play. In M. Woodhead, D. Faulkner, & K. Littleton (Eds.), *Cultural worlds of early childhood* (pp. 117–132). New York: Routledge.

Göncü, A. (Ed.). (1999). *Children's engagement in the world: Sociocultural perspectives.* New York: Cambridge University Press.

Göncü, A., Mistry, J., & Mosier, C. (2000). Cultural variations in the play of toddlers. *International Journal of Behavioral Development, 24*(3), 321–329.

Groos, K. (1898). *The play of animals.* New York: D. Appleton and Co.

Hagan, B., Anderson, H., & Jones Parry, J. (2001). Insiders and outsiders: Observing and assessing at play. *New Zealand Research in Early Childhood Education, 4,* 155–163.

Haight, W. L., Wang, Z., Fung, H. H., Williams, K., & Mintz, J. (1999). Universal, developmental, and variable aspects of young children's play: A cross-cultural comparison of pretending at home. *Child Development, November/December, 70*(6), 1477–1488.

Hall, G. S. (1906). *Youth.* New York: D. Appleton and Co.

de Haan, D. (2005). Social pretend play: Potentials and limitations of literacy development. *European Early Childhood Education Research Journal, 13*(1), 41–55.

Hutt, S. J., Tyler, S., Hutt, C., & Christopherson, H. (1989). *Play, exploration and learning: A natural history of the preschool.* New York: Routledge.

Kaliala, M. (2006). *Play culture in a changing world.* Open University Press: UK.

Klein, M. (1932). Studying children's social play through a child cultural approach: Roles, rule sand shared knowledge. *Advances in Early Education and Day Care, 7,* 179–211.

Lazarus, M. (1883). Uber die Reize des Spiels. Germany: F. Dummler.

Lofdahl, A. (2006). Grounds for values and attitudes: Children's play and peer-cultures in pre-school. *Journal of Early Childhood Research, 4*(1), 77–88.

Michalopoulou, A. (2001). A spatio-pedagogical approach to symbolic pay as kindergarten activity in early childhood. *European Early Childhood Education Research Journal, 9*(2), 59–68.

Miller, A. M., & Harwood, R. L. (2002). The cultural organization of parenting: Change and stability of behaviour patterns during feeding and social play across the first year of life. *Parenting Science and Practice, 2*(3), 241–272.

Mitchell, E. D., & Mason, B. S. (1948). *The theory of play.* New York: Barnes and Co.

Moyles, J. (Ed.). (1994). *The excellence of play.* Bucks, UK: Open University Press.

Paley, V. (1990). *The boy who would be a helicopter: The uses of storytelling in the classroom.* USA: Harvard University Press.

Parten, M. B. (1932). Social participation among preschool children. *Journal of Abnormal Psychology, 27,* 243–269.

Parten, M. B. (1933). Social play among preschool children. *Journal of Abnormal Psychology, 28,* 136–147.

Piaget, J. (1962). *Play, dreams and imitation in childhood.* New York: Norton.

Rettig, M. (1995). Play and cultural diversity. *The Journal of Educational Issue of Language Minority Students, 15*(Winter), 1–8. (www.ncbe.gwu, edu).

Rogoff, B. (1998). Cognition as a collaborative process. In W. Damon (chief Ed.), D. Kuhn & R. S. Siegler (Volume Eds.), *Cognition, perceptions and language: Handbook of child psychology* (5th ed., pp. 679–744). New York: John Wiley & Sons Inc.

Rogoff, B. (2003). *The cultural nature of human development.* Oxford: Oxford University Press.

Rogoff, B., Mosier, C., Mistry, J., & Göncü, A. (1998). Toddlers' guided participation with their caregivers in cultural activity. In M. Woodhead, D. Faulkner, & K. Littleton (Eds.), *Cultural worlds of early childhood* (pp. 225–249). London, UK: Routledge.

Smilansky, S. (1968). *The effects of sociodramatic play on disadvantaged pre-school children.* New York: Wiley.

Tamis-LeMonda, C. S., & Bornstein, M. H. (1992). Language and play at one year: A comparison of toddlers and mothers in the United States and Japan. *International Journal of Behavioral Development, 15*(1), 19–42.

Tobin, J. J., Wu, D. Y. H., & Davidson, D. H. (1999). *Preschool in three cultures. Japan, China and United States.* USA: Yale University.

Vejleskov, H. (1995). A study of children's acts and interactions during play with different play materials. *European Early Childhood Education Research Journal, 3*(2), 43–65.

Vygotsky, L. (1966). Play and its role in the mental development of the child. *Voprosy psikhologii, 12*(6), 62–76.

Vygotsky, L. S. (1987). Thinking and speech. In L. S. Vygotsky (Ed.), *The collected works of L.S. Vygotsky, Vol. 1, Problems of general psychology* (pp. 39–285). R. W. Rieber & A. S. Carton (Eds.); N. Minick (Trans.). New York: Plenum Press.

Vygotsky, L. (1997). *The collected works of L.S. Vygotsky, Vol. 4, The history of the development of higher mental functions.* Translated by Marie J. Hall (Editor of the English Translation: Robert W. Rieber). New York: Kluwer Academic/Plenum Publishers.

Vygotsky, L. S. (1998). *The collected works of L.S. Vygotsky, Vol. 5, Child Psychology.* Translated by Marie J. Hall (Editor of the English Translation: Robert W. Rieber). New York: Kluwer Academic/Plenum Publishers.

Wood, E. (2004). Developing a pedagogy of play. In A. Anning, J. Cullen, & M. Fleer (Eds.), *Early childhood education: society and culture* (pp. 19–30). London: SAGE Publications Ltd.
Wood, E., & Attfield, J. (1996). *Play, learning and the early childhood curriculum.* London. UK: Paul Chapman Publishing.

Chapter 2
Play and Learning in Aotearoa New Zealand Early Childhood Education

Jayne White, Fiona Ellis, Amiria O'Malley, Jean Rockel, Sue Stover and Meripa Toso

The Context for Play in Aotearoa New Zealand

A small island nation of about four million people, Aotearoa New Zealand[1] is located in the south-west Pacific. Originally inhabited by Māori, a Polynesian people, the country was colonized by the British who in 1840 signed the Treaty of Waitangi/*Te Tiriti o Waitangi* with many Māori chiefs.[2] This treaty is widely regarded as the founding document for a bicultural society as it gives unique status to Māori as the indigenous *tangata whenua*.[3]

In the early 21st century, there is a wide range of people of different ethnicities in Aotearoa New Zealand. As well as a fast-growing population of Pasifika peoples (from Samoa, the Cook Islands, Niue, Tokelau, Tonga, Tuvalu and Fiji), an increasing Asian, Indian and European population adds to the ethnic diversity of Aotearoa New Zealand. In 2001 15% of New Zealanders identified themselves as Māori; 7% Pasifika; 7% Asian and 79% European (Statistics New Zealand, 2004). It is significant that, because of intermarriage and inter-cultural adoption, many New Zealanders identify themselves as belonging to more than one ethnic group.

Within this diverse cultural landscape and alongside comparative educational research indicating both high performance and low equity (see OECD, 2004), early childhood education has taken an increasingly prominent position in national education policy. Developed in consultation with the early childhood sector, the government's 10-year early childhood strategic plan *Pathways to the Future/Nga Huarahi Arataki* (Ministry of Education, 2002) is being implemented to raise quality, and to address inequitable access for Māori and Pasifika families.

J. White
Victoria University of Wellington, New Zealand
e-mail: jayne.white@vuw.ac.nz

[1] The authors use 'Aotearoa New Zealand' to label their country as it includes the Maori name for these islands and indicates to readers the authors' commitment to acknowledging Maori culture and heritage.

[2] For information about the Treaty of Waitangi/*Te Tiriti o Waitangi*, see www.treatyofwaitangi.govt.nz

[3] A glossary of Maori words and phrases is at the end of this chapter.

I. Pramling-Samuelsson, M. Fleer (eds.), *Play and Learning in Early Childhood Settings*, DOI 10.1007/978-1-4020-8498-0_2,
© Springer Science+Business Media B.V. 2009

Government priorities are to be achieved through effective teaching and learning; collaborative learning processes and participation for all (Ministry of Education, 2005b). Amongst the goals are:

- by 2007, 20 hours per week of free care and education for 3- and 4-year olds in "teacher-led" services;[4] and
- by 2012, qualified and registered teachers[5] (in "teacher-led" services).

Increased government funding for early childhood education services has been budgeted to support the achievement of these and other strategies.

Not only do these developments support the increasing professionalization of the early childhood education sector in Aotearoa New Zealand but they also respond to the government's agenda both to:

- support families through substantial paid parental leave for women in employment (currently amounting to 14 weeks); and
- ensure women have opportunities to participate in the workforce.

Alongside a heightened profile of early childhood education service provision through childcare subsidies and increased funding, quality early childhood education is clearly a high priority for the New Zealand government and a valued option for New Zealand society.

Parents are increasingly using early childhood services for their very young children. Although numbers of children enrolled in early childhood education services are regularly increasing year by year, the number of children under 3 years has increased significantly (see Table 2.1).

As well as unlicensed playgroups which are often organized in community centres, a wide range of licensed services is available to families of very young children; these reflect ethnic diversity as well as a long history of philosophically distinct services.

Table 2.1 Children aged 3 and under in early childhood services, 2004

Birth to 12 months	9,388
12–24 months	23,627
24–36 months	35,850

Source: Ministry of Education (2005a).

---

[4] Ministry of Education distinguishes between 'teacher-led' and 'parent-led' services. In 'teacher-led' provisions, teachers provide education and care. In 'parent-led', parents, whanau or caregivers provide education and care. (See Ministry of Education, 2005a).

[5] Initially government policy was to require all early childhood teachers to have completed at least a three year diploma course. However, the requirement has relaxed enough that centres can include amongst their teachers a small percentage of teachers who are either in training, or who provide cultural mana and/or language fluency.

The licensed, government-subsidized early childhood education options for children under 3 years old are:

- "Playcentres" (parent-led co-operatives);
- "Education and care" (childcare);
- "Home-based education" (care and education offered by caregivers in their own homes under the supervision of a fully-qualified early childhood teacher);
- Immersion services, including:

    o Māori language (many but not all Māori immersion centres are affiliated to Te Kohanga Reo Trust)
    o Samoan language (such as A'oga Amata[6])

(See Table 2.2).

Families are also able to select hours of provision ranging from 2–3 hours per week to 40+ per week. In most cases the period of time is negotiated, rather than predetermined. Families may also choose to access more than one service in any week for the education of their infant, toddler or young child. For example, each week, a toddler could participate in two Playcentre sessions (along with a parent or caregiver), as well as regularly attending "care and education centre" (without a parent or caregiver) several days a week.

Adult–child ratios within the education arrangement are established through minimum standards. These standards are currently outlined in the Early Childhood Regulations (Ministry of Education, 1998) although many services achieve levels of quality beyond these minimum requirements.

What is Play in Aotearoa New Zealand?

Play as an approach to children's learning gained credibility in the 1940s with government policy supporting both Frobelian-inspired kindergartens (which are for 3- to 4-year olds and operated through kindergarten associations) and playcentres (locally developed parent co-operatives). May's historical research revealed earlier commitment to play as an appropriate way of learning for very young children. This approach, however, was not maintained – compulsory public education starting in the latter part of the 19th century resulted in more regimented styles of provision (May, 2005).

However, amongst Māori, play was traditionally seen as a mechanism for acquiring skills required for cultural survival (Smith & Smith, 1993). Since the 1980s when Te Kohanga Reo became widespread, play is understood as an appropriate means of supporting appropriate way of transmitting culture and language (Royal-Tangare, 1997).

---

[6] A'oga Amata are early childhood education services that provide education and care from a Samoan perspective, with Samoan language used throughout the day.

Table 2.2 Numbers of children enrolled by service and age, 2004

Service	Total number of children aged 3 years or younger	Number of children aged 3 years	Percentage of children aged under 3 years	Number of children aged under 1 year	Number of children aged 1 year	Number of children aged 2 years
Playcentre	15,440	8,520	55.1	1,567	2,866	4,087
Education and Care	81,096	35,390	43.6	3,366	12,059	19,965
Te Kohanga Reo	10,418	4,841	46.4	471	1,159	2,411
Home-based Education	9,922	5,980	60.2	1,145	2,395	2,440
Playgroups	20,707	13,675	66.0	2,811	4,702	6,162

Source: Ministry of Education (2005a).

Play as a "game" or leisure activity features highly in contemporary New Zealand culture. Ferguson (2004) sees play in the context of sport. He highlights the way a game of rugby influences the lives of young New Zealand males and females in relation to expression and identity. As part of its promotion for a "push play" initiative, the government's Sport and Recreation Council is pushing for New Zealanders to become the most active nation in the world by providing national support for physical activity as play SPARC (2004). This initiative is based on the belief that active bodies encourage active minds.

Within New Zealand's education community, play is closely associated with ideas about freedom; "freedom of expression" and "creativity" are linked to play. Historically, play was linked to the notion of "free kindergarten" – referring to the freedom of access to early education (i.e. "free" in the sense of costing no money); as well as to "free play".

However, the pressures of modern society on families, coupled with a market-driven push for formal learning, have resulted in early childhood education professionals playing a strong advocacy role for the rights of children to play as it provides the most appropriate platform from which learning can take place. Play is therefore viewed as both purposeful and exploratory with the ultimate intention of increasing learning.

What children learn, and what learning is valued in New Zealand society, reflects the diverse cultural, ethnic and philosophical views of individuals, communities. However, with the advent of a national early childhood curriculum, *Te Whāriki* (Ministry of Education, 1996), play has been strongly positioned within the context of learning. *Te Whāriki* adopts the metaphor of a woven mat to convey the interrelated nature of learning and teaching. The "warp" of the weaving are the four principles of *Te Whāriki*:

- Family and community;
- Holistic development;
- Empowerment; and
- Relationships.

These principles are closely aligned to the principles of the Treaty of Waitangi, and signal a sociocultural approach to teaching and learning.

The "weft" of *Te Whariki* comprises five learning strands:

- Well-being;
- Belonging;
- Communication;
- Contribution; and
- Exploration.

These strands weave together the most important aspects of early childhood education (that are shared across all early childhood education services) through both planned and spontaneous learning experiences with "people, places and things" (Ministry of Education, 1996, p. 11). Hence, learning is viewed as a relationship, or interaction, between the child, adults, the setting and cultural artefacts such as toys or resources. Play, therefore, can be interpreted in this curriculum as "resourceful action in and across settings" (Edwards, 2005, p. 58) that underpins appropriate learning for very young children.

Te Whāriki advocates for teaching and learning experiences that are culturally appropriate to the child, their family and community. These will be different for diverse communities, yet are underpinned by the premise that children are central to learning and that their rights are paramount. The role of the adult (teacher or parent) is to support learning by gaining insights into the world of the child, and responding appropriately. However this process is reciprocal and involves the mediated co-construction of learning – captured best in the Māori term "*ako*" (Pere, 1994).

Play is subtly woven into *Te Whāriki*. As a means of promoting learning, the role of adults is to support play by selecting from a repertoire of appropriate and relevant teaching strategies that will enhance learning. This selection is based on observational knowledge of the child and their family, gained through assessment processes that "notice, recognize and respond" accordingly (Ministry of Education, 2004, p. 6). Where assessment is seen as an integral part of the curriculum, adults need to be attuned to the child as a learner within the context of play.

For government funding, centres are required to ensure that:

> Educators [should] plan, implement and evaluate curriculum for children in which ... children's play is valued as meaningful learning and the importance of spontaneous play is recognised... (Ministry of Education, 1998).

Te Whāriki positions the child as life-long learner, and advocates for the critical role of family and community in the learning process. In accordance, the New Zealand curriculum aspires that:

> ... all children will grow up as confident and competent learners, healthy in mind and body, and spirit, secure in their sense of belonging and in the sense that they make a valued contribution to society (Ministry of Education, 1996, p. 9).

Te Whāriki is written for infants and toddlers as well as young children. In recognizing the unique characteristics of infants and toddlers the curriculum suggests that this younger age group has "particular needs and capabilities" (Ministry of Education, 1996, p. 18). However the document also emphasizes the fluctuating nature of learning, individual variation, and different cultural views on learning dependent on the child, their family and the context of the wider world.

Te Whariki recognizes and values play that is both purposeful, as well as a source of enjoyment and pleasure. Play is upheld as a means of exploration and a way of acquiring knowledge. In *Te Whariki* play is not bound by one definition. *Te Whariki* recognizes that services and communities will have different perspectives on the relationship between play and learning as well as the way it is approached. It was within this context that we approached the study of six children across Aotearoa New Zealand.

The sociocultural nature of the research methodology for the play project (i.e. through Rogoff's analytical framework) was therefore entirely consistent with the national and local New Zealand approach to play as a socially and culturally constructed phenomena. Rogoff's three lenses provided the researchers with an opportunity to explore play through the perspectives of the individual child, the child as part of a network of relationships, and the wider community and societal values and associated practices which impacted on the way play was seen by the researchers themselves. The emphasis on individual, local and national was evidenced through data such as the everyday play activity (seen in the footage); interviews about the activities with parents and teachers (through the stimulated recall interviews) and the wider institutional and societal values of the national and local landscape (through an exploration of each service's unique philosophy, and the overarching influence of a national early childhood curriculum). Using Rogoff's framework enabled an investigation of both a personal and a professional view of play across the diverse cultural and contextual landscape of early childhood education in Aotearoa New Zealand. Further, the collaborative nature of the research project, across geographical, cultural and contextual spaces, meant that the interpretations of the researchers themselves became central to the analysis process (for further discussion of the methodology see White, Rockel, & Toso, 2007).

Method

The Aotearoa New Zealand study focused on six children in five early childhood services: Playcentre; mainstream "Education and Care"; Māori immersion; Samoan immersion centre (A'oga Amata), and "Home-based Education" service. This range of services was chosen to reflect the diversity of early childhood education provision for birth to 3-year old infants and toddlers in Aotearoa New Zealand (Table 2.3).

   In this study, each child was videoed for one typical day[7] in their early childhood education experience by researchers/videographers who lived in the location and were familiar with the context and culture of the services involved. A maximum of 1 hour of the footage was then shared with the child's teacher/educator/kaiako and family independently. The discussions that took place between participants contributed to the data that were gathered in an effort to try to make sense of play from a contemporary local perspective. Final analysis of the footage, including the transcripts of discussions, was then undertaken by the five researchers working collaboratively across the country.[8]

How Do Children Play in Aotearoa New Zealand?

The children in each of the services were keen participants in play and were observed to be extremely confident within (and in several cases – beyond) the early

---

[7] In the case of Ana, the video covered a normal Playcentre session – $2\frac{1}{2}$ hours.
[8] With numerous ethical issues to work through, this research process took $1\frac{1}{2}$ years to complete. (See White et al., 2005).

Table 2.3 Description of participants in the study

Child's name: service attended (region)	Child's age	Child's gender	Child's ethnicity	Hours per week child spends in service	Service's ratio of adults: children	Service's age composition
ANA Playcentre (Auckland)	26 months	Female	Samoan	5 hours ($2 \times 2\frac{1}{2}$ hours)	1:3	Mixed – 0–5 years
ISOBEL Care and education centre (Dunedin)	19 months	Female	European	$42\frac{1}{2}$ hours (full time)	1:4	Single age – 0- to 2-year olds
LEILANI A'oga Amata (Auckland)	16 months	Female	Samoan	45 hours (full time)	1:3	Mixed – birth-5 years with separate area for under 2-year olds
JOVAN and HINEWAIRUA Māori Immersion Centres (Auckland and Hamilton)	Both 19 months	Jovan – Male; Hinewairua Female	Both Māori	$42\frac{1}{2}$ hours (full time)	1:3	Mixed – birth-5 years with separate area for under 2-year olds
CAMERON Home-based education (Wellington)	19 months	Male	European	16 hours (2×8 hours)	1:4 (no more than two under 2 years olds)	Mixed – 0–5 years old

childhood education service environment. They actively explored their environment, making choices to participate in a wide range of learning experiences. They knew the routines of the setting; they knew where and how to access tools and props required (such as a painting apron); or signalling the need for support from an adult and persevering until that support was given.

Although each child was active and would move from place to place frequently, they also spent considerable periods of time at one or more experience that captured their interest. For example, Ana explored the dramatic play associated with a telephone, rehearsing her role as communicator; Isobel tipped chalk from containers of different sizes as she explored measurement properties for an uninterrupted period of 15 minutes; and Leilani read a book that she had chosen with her teacher (and later sat under a tree to read alone). In this way, each child was able to develop social scripts, and literacies that were compatible with their interests.

During a regular outing to the local sports field and playground, Cameron explored his ongoing interest in "the BIG green tractor" (see Fig. 2.1). Cameron's discovery of the tractor is a weekly ritual – one that is reinforced through the provision of picture books and equipment in the home base and surrounding community. His interest is shared by the educator and other children in the home-based setting.

The videos demonstrated how each child would observe other children and events in order to decide where they placed themselves and their play. With adults close by, the children could rely on someone attending to their basic needs at all times.

Fig. 2.1 Cameron and the BIG green tractor

Adults (whether the "primary"[9] teacher, parent, the parent/educator or the other staff) offered a base from which each child could explore new ideas or revisit familiar experiences.

Teachers and parents spoke about the way each child was prepared to try things out, and the interests each child showed in learning by watching others or in presenting ideas from other aspects of their world. In the footage of Cameron there were several occasions where he initiated game playing such as the "Oh no" game of throwing crayons on the floor, or flicking water on his peer and laughing raucously as the action was retaliated by a cupful of water thrown in his face!

While watching the video, some parents and teachers were surprised at such spontaneous and sophisticated levels of play. Jovan's mother (who was also his *kaiako*) described it as "all these eureka moments in one day whereas in a week I usually catch one or two". Similarly Cameron's educator said "I'm absolutely amazed at the things I didn't notice that were going on". She described Cameron as "an Einstein of the future". For Isobel's teacher there was a similar revelation as she responded to the video footage by suggesting ways that she might have been able to extend the learning experience, with the benefit of hindsight.

All six of the children were seen to replicate in play what they had seen earlier. For example, Hinewairua participated in the routine of brushing the sand off everyone's legs before they went inside, as she had seen her *kaiako* do. Isobel watched the actions of her peers and the adult carefully before participating in play by pretending to fly like an aeroplane. Leilani was able to cuddle the baby in the same way as her teacher modelled for her, climb up high like her older peers and participate in physical activities such as kicking a ball in the school playground with her older brother. Cameron watched his older peers carefully and took up their cues in exploring ideas such as placing sticks down the drain at the park, or reading the popular book "Maisie's Bus" that was rediscovered at the library during their outing. These experiences contributed to the children's identity as members of the group – with shared experiences and interests. Cameron's educator described this as a feature of Cameron's role within the home-based family grouping.

The reciprocity of relationships between peers was evident in the play of these children. Nurturing behaviours, when observed in play episodes, were highly valued by the families watching the video. For Leilani's parents and teachers, nurturing younger peers was viewed as a natural part of her evolution into the mixed age group – as she grows up, this role will increasingly become an expectation. Cameron was observed being hand-fed morning tea by an older child when the caregiver was out of sight. For children of this age it was viewed as a positive sign of things to come. The Māori immersion *whānaui* described this nurturance trait in play as *tuakana-teina*. For example, while watching Jovan's interactions with another

---

[9] That is, the teacher who has a primary role for this particular child.

younger child, Jovan's father observed, "He's a *tuakana* to the other child but he's a *teina* himself. He goes on and gives all the *aroha* back".

Ana's parent and educators saw the mixed age family-orientated Playcentre environment as supporting Ana's repertoire of play and consequential learning. This was also described by her mother in relation to Ana's developing social literacies:

> So she is wanting to interact and her language skills are building up at the moment too so it will probably get more and more that she will want to interact with… more and more children. She does like the older children, like wanting to be on the swing and do the same things that they do. She does tend to follow. She really likes E. (an older child), she uses E.'s name quite a lot. And F. is her other little friend, she is more her age.

The provision of group learning experiences (such as shared eating times or morning prayer), not only supported the children in experiencing group membership but also gave ample opportunities for solitary or parallel play experiences. The opportunities to participate in shared experiences offered "punctuation marks" (or pauses) to the child's day. Times where these occurred were frequently associated with transitions (such as arrival, farewell, sleeping or eating).

In the home-based setting, these "punctuation marks" were provided by the ritual of going to the park and kicking a ball, buying hot chips for morning tea and visiting the library. Cameron could choose to sit in the buggy or lie on the cushions in the library. Because this ritual allowed Cameron to predict events, he could rely on these features in his day. Similarly, in the earlier part of his morning, once the other children had arrived, Cameron could access the musical instruments with the full expectation that there would be singing and dancing before morning tea time. His educator describes these routines as being especially important for children of this younger age.

In services where children attended on a sessional basis, such as Playcentre, "punctuation marks" still existed (for example, Ana was gently encouraged to participate in a shared, but not compulsory, group snack time), but were less necessary because of the relatively short period of time children spent in the centre. However for the A'oga Amata and the Māori immersion service, these moments were viewed as additional opportunities to transmit the language through chants, *waiata* or prayer. On the day of videoing Jovan stood up of his own volition and shared his first *mihimihi* with other members of the group – much to the delight of the adults around him.

As well as supporting learning through exploration, imitation and discovery, play fulfilled an emotional function for the child and their learning. For example, Leilani was feeling mildly unwell on the day of the video. Play was actively used to settle her into the A'oga Amata environment when her parents left. As a result, Leilani became interested in and involved in familiar activities such as patting sand cakes and singing the birthday song. (See Fig. 2.2)

The readily available lap of her teacher, and other physical expressions of touch alongside explanations and demonstrations guided and supported Leilani's

Fig. 2.2 Leilani recapturing a special birthday event

transition in to play. This was further enhanced through cultural expression of language, songs and protocols as well as the teacher's knowledge of a familiar event (in this case a recent birthday event) that could create a catalyst for play. The evident closeness in establishing a secure attachment relationship supported Leilani's self awareness and assisted her developing identity as a learner. For all of the children in this study such moments of closeness were available whenever needed, and created a base from which play could occur.

In What Ways Is the Space Arranged to Facilitate Play?

Physical, emotional and conceptual space was a central feature of the children's experience of play, and their ability to have their play preferences upheld. Children moved in and out of spaces according to their interest and needs. Each of the children made personally informed decisions to move from one space to another (although there were expectations that they would participate in certain cultural rituals at parts of the day). The children moved around the environment(s) with a clear expectation that their play preferences would be upheld by others around them. For example, Isobel frequently played hide-and-seek with nobody in particular but always with the expectation that someone would be there to reciprocate with a "BOO" when she emerged from her hiding place! For Isobel this was not only a way of inviting play, but also a link to familiar play scripts from her home, as described by her parents in their interview (see Fig. 2.3).

All six children had access to extensive spaces; for several children these spaces included "adult spaces". For example, children in the Māori immersion service had regular opportunities to join adults in rehearsing for cultural events as part of the *Wananga* with which the early childhood service was associated. In these contexts play took place amidst the activity of an adult world. An example was the learning

Fig. 2.3 Isobel plays
peek-a-boo with no one in
particular

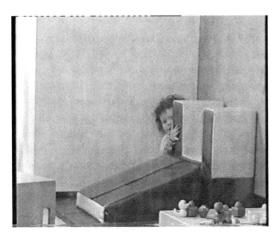

of the *poi* movements for Hinewairua during adult *kapa haka* practice at the campus
gallery next door to the early childhood centre. (See Fig. 2.4.)

Within this context, the play was described as "passive" and the teacher's associated role as being "an accountability and responsibility to nurture that which is
already there". In this context, the *kaiako* was seen to be in a state of guardianship
for the emerging person they have been tasked with teaching.

A similar role was fulfilled by Cameron's educator in a range of different learning sites in the "adult world" – including the educator's car which offered further
opportunities for Cameron to pursue his interests in vehicles. Describing Cameron's
learning as being "like a sponge", his dad said: "Sometimes it doesn't even look like
he's paying attention, but then all of a sudden he'll mimic you two or three minutes
later exactly as you've done it".

Fig. 2.4 Hinewairua's
movements with *poi* are
purposeful

The flow between each aspect of the child's day through the provision of a range of play opportunities was seen as a feature of learning. In the A'oga Amata, space was used to support children in the under two area to play with older children in the shared *fale*.[10] Leilani was able to enter in and out of this space according to her interests and needs but also supported by cultural rituals (such as prayer time). The space facilitated an ebb and flow within the learning environment and supported a smooth transition in and out of play contexts both indoors and outdoors. The teachers at this service strongly believe that this process is of great benefit in the transition each child makes across the under-two and over-two environments, and that transitions in themselves are a feature of learning. This belief is supported by their experiences as part of a centre within a school complex with frequent interactions between the centre and the wider school community.

Children had ready access to a wide range of experiences such as play dough, water, paint, family play with dolls, musical instruments, heuristic play items (placed on a large mat to display the materials), other manipulative items, natural resources and always an ample supply of books. The fluid provision of play experiences in the A'oga Amata environment was described by the parent as being "almost like a change of scenery; every day it's something different and what they do is set up little play centres."

The outdoor spaces provided in all the services offered ample opportunity for children to experience the sensation of outdoor sounds and fresh air; the textures of grass, bushes and sand, as well as exposure to a repertoire of other learning experiences. Each service provided opportunities for a wide range of large motor experiences such as movement, climbing, jumping and running for these children, facilitated both adult promptings and by the child's own initiative and independent access. The familiarity each child shared with the spaces, both in terms of routines, cultural rituals and access to equipment, meant that they knew where things were located and could predict events. Items of special significance to the child were able to be transported around the learning environment, and at times, protected from peers. For example, Jovan had a particular interest in the bead apparatus, which he often carried with him (and had taken home with him at nights on occasion). His interest in this resource was evidenced by the amount of time he spent returning and investigating the apparatus.

The equipment in each of the services reflected local environment and culture. Cultural artefacts were always readily available (for example, *poi* in the Māori immersion setting, hand drums in the A'oga Amata). They also provided important cues about the emphasis placed on play as a vehicle for exploration. For example Ana had regular access to, and made use of, carpentry equipment including real hammers, saws, drills, nails and vices.

---

[10] A *fale* is a traditional Samoan house that is supported by poles. The *fale* is also used metaphorically to convey a secure base for learning.

Fig. 2.5 Ana engages in risky carpentry

For all the children in this study, equipment was used to promote exploration based on the teacher's knowledge of the child's interests. Therefore different teacher-initiated experiences were offered at different times, depending on what was happening. For example, the teacher in the A'oga Amata selected leaves for Leilani to play with because she had "noticed her interest in them" earlier.

Consideration was also given to the importance of creating spaces for resting times, and a balance of routine and special activity throughout the day. This feature was particularly important in the full day services, where children spent longer periods of time in the early childhood education setting. There was a careful and deliberate balance between planned and spontaneous learning experiences, indoor and outdoor activity, and exploration of the wider world. Teachers were quite purposeful in their provision of equipment, which included a strong emphasis on exploring the natural world through the provision of resources that the child could investigate in play. The video footage showed the A'oga Amata teacher reinforcing Leilani's sense of wonderment at natural resources such as flax and leaves, Jovan's mother/*kaiako* stepping back to allow him to investigate water in a bucket and Cameron exploring a range of vessels for holding water then diving into the water-trough on a hot day.

In each of the videos children were observed to use large expanses of physical space at varying times of the day. For some children, there were vast expanses of land the children could explore freely. Children were able to run fast down the hill and hide behind trees within the expanse of space offered in the outdoor environment

of the centre. In addition there were times where the wider world could be accessed –
such as Cameron in his local community. The spaces enabled these children to take
calculated risks in their play, and experiment with ideas. For example, Jovan pushed
a rather large trike up a ramp and was able to calculate how fast he needed to go
to avoid crashing. Cameron showed an intense interest in a rugby ball that was
perched on a nearby picnic table at the park, negotiating temporary possession of
it from its owner. Cameron proudly announced to his educator "Rugby ball – BIG
rugby ball", as he threw the ball across to her. In circumstances such as these, intervention occurred only when there was a safety concern or a direct response. This
and other similar experiences reinforced the adult view of the child as "confident
and competent" as well as the importance of "trying things out".

Ana's educator advocated for the child's right to take risks as a means of "assertive" expression:

> I think if you don't give children the opportunity to take risks then I think they are almost
> suffocated. ...You can eliminate risks, you can narrow risks, you can take safe risks, step-
> ping outside your comfort zone and I think you feel more empowered when you step outside
> your comfort zone, like doing the bungy jump for instance. Why do people bungy jump?
> Because it's exhilarating... So I think that if you don't let people feel the power within
> them, then you end up with a society that is squashed ... into thinking about rules all the
> time, and not being able to think outside the square, because you might not be *allowed* to
> think outside the square. Whereas we want children to grow up to be forward thinkers, to
> be able to express how they feel, whether it be happy feelings or sad feelings. You want
> them to grow up to be able to stand up and say "That's not right!" and "I'm not going to
> accept that!"

Adults across all services believed that play and learning took place in a range of
environments, such as:

- within the local context, for example:

  - participation in the weekly gatherings of the *wananga*;
  - easy access to the school playground which offered space and greater oppor-
    tunity for risk;

- within the wider community, for example:

  - walking to access facilities;
  - excursions in the car;
  - real life experiences with animals.

Movement between environments took different forms. For example, Ana and
Leilani had continuous access to the outdoor area. In other settings, specific times
were allocated for such movement (such as Jovan's attendance at the *wananga* and
Cameron's movement within his local community).

Approaches to routines varied from individualized times for eating and sleeping
to established times for play and morning tea times. For example, Ana was gently
called to leave her water play and to participate in a shared morning tea, Hinewairua
was called to morning tea by a process of *karanga* and similarly Cameron could predict the encroaching morning tea time by the predictable sights, sounds and smells

offered along the journey – such as the local fish 'n chip shop and its associated aromas.

The contexts in which play took place were aligned to the service philosophy and function. For example, the home-based service had a strong philosophy that valued "real life" experiences; so while walking to the library, Cameron's "need to know" led to time at a bookshop searching for books about tractors.

Space was seen as central to the experience of play across all settings, and meant that the learning environment embraced the wider world of the child and their community. Jovan's mother/*kaiako* described this movement between spaces as an important feature of learning.

What Is the Role of the Teacher in Play?

The teachers (called "*kaiako*" in the Māori immersion service, "educator" in the Playcentre setting and "educator/visiting teacher" in the home-based setting) were very clear about their intentions for children in play. Developing an identity through language and cultural transmission were prominent features of discussion surrounding the intended outcomes of play for both A'oga Amata and Māori immersion. But within "mainstream" centres, teachers and parents also encouraged culturally appropriate identities with, for example, an emphasis on qualities such as independence, assertive behaviours and learning to be part of a "team". All services shared a similar emphasis on learning through play within relationships with people, places and things.

With the exception of the Playcentre educator,[11] the teachers in this study were trained to Diploma of Teaching level (or above). All of the teachers had made strong connections with the families of the child both through information sharing and ongoing reciprocal relationships. On several occasions, teachers spoke about experiences the child brought from home, and which they had attempted to support and extend upon in the early childhood education setting. Their knowledge of the child in other settings was used to inform the provision of play and associated interpretations of the learning that was taking place. For example, Isobel's teacher described the interests of the child alongside her knowledge of what happened at home:

> So she is very keen to help with the garden, I think they do a lot of that at home, and music.
> I know that they go to the beach a lot, and they go for walks a lot. Because that is what
> Mum told me at the beginning, they are quite active people.

While three of the five services had clear policies identifying "key" teachers, centre practices varied. For example, while not an exclusive relationship, Leilani's key teacher aimed to provide her with a sense of security in their relationship,

---

[11] The Playcentre educator had completed several years of Playcentre supervisors' training which is recognized within Playcentre by the Ministry of Education, but does not automatically equate to a transferable qualification such as a Diploma of Teaching.

which enabled her to confidently interact with all the other teachers and the environment. Conversely, Isobel's teacher did not spend a great deal of time with her on the day of filming. In watching the video her teacher commented on the way Isobel went to different adults at times of the day – "But you notice she goes to D. [another teacher] a lot and she goes to various teachers, just for that contact."

In Jovan's setting, his ability to interact with other *kaiako* was seen as particularly important (as his mother was one of the teachers in the centre). For Ana there was also shared responsibility – this time between parents at different stages of training. The purpose of the Playcentre – to support both the child *and* the parent – meant that a collective approach was taken to learning. The video footage showed Ana's mother and the educator "on duty" interacting independently with Ana throughout the session. This mother valued the interactions of the educator and the fact that she "played" with the children: "I've noticed her play with other people's kids a lot . . . and I can just see the look on Ana's face that she was enjoying being with her".

Kaiako in the Māori immersion setting saw their role very differently. They spoke about their responsibility in "setting the stage for play". This involved maintaining the environment in ways that facilitated choice, but also in offering cultural cues. For *kaiako* this was also associated with Jovan and Hinewairua's participation in the real world, and the children's responsibility as long-term transmittersof culture.

Similarly, in the home-based setting, the educator described her role as supporting play that enables children to develop working theories. For her, important features of play were the notion of "play as work" and the importance of trying out new ideas:

> Play *is* learning – if children were allowed to play more often and for longer in their education experience, they would have less trouble learning later in life. Five years of age is too early for formalised learning experiences.[12] I absolutely believe that play is the best possible way for children to learn and that from birth to three lay the foundations for all future learning and successes.

The task of the various teachers was to offer sufficient experience for the children to draw upon but also to follow the children's interests and take advantage of the "teachable moment". To achieve this, teachers had diverse approaches – ranging from Leilani's teacher who continuously moved about the environment with her; to Isobel's teacher, who played a much more low key role. *Kaiako* described their role as guardian, based on the concept of *kaitiakitanga*. In practical terms this meant that, before intervening in play, the *kaiako* waited for the cues to come from the child.

Isobel's teacher also believed that when children were playing, they were also learning. She described as an "observer of life" and explained:

> I think that the whole time that they are playing they are learning. (Isobel) does watch people and other children all the time. So she is watching what they are doing and she gives things a try. She has always got her eyes open. She knows when you put water outside she is there. Because she keeps an eye open all the time and likes to join in.

---

[12] In New Zealand children start school at age 5 years.

This teacher described how she would provide experiences that had a huge interest in, such as painting and music. She spoke of how there should be those things available for her and encouragement to play with them if that is what Isobel wanted to do.

This was echoed by teachers in the other settings also. For example, the home-based educator said:

> I think about what I'm doing all the time. I record in the children's diaries any activities they persist with, exhaust themselves working on, or just enjoy; and that clarifies things for me. I think "what next?", "where to from here?" and see a next step. I don't always get it right but that's OK – I'm still learning and being challenged.

The notion of the child as a "keen observer" was supported by Isobel's parents who noted how much of what she knew she had learnt by watching others.

There was little or no pressure placed on children of this age, in any of the settings, to engage in a specific play experience unless the child chose to join in. Where settings provided regular times for everyone to come together, there was an expectation of participation, and the children willingly responded showing that the experience was clearly a source of enjoyment. There was often a tolerance of the need for these children to come to the experience through play, and such experiences were reinforced outside of the group times – either by singing, playing music, tapping rhythms or the repetition and promotion of language.

A feature of play for all of the children in this study was the effort teachers had gone to in providing natural materials within the setting or within the wider world that the child engaged with as part of their early childhood experience. These ranged from presenting a collection of leaves and a very large sand area, to special attention in caring for a bird (in a cage) in the A'oga Amata setting. In the home-based setting such resources were readily available in the regular outings into the community, as well as the home environment where there were chickens to be fed, plants to be watered and trees to be climbed. These resources were used to engage children in experiences of wonderment, such as the tactile experience of examining the leaves and experiencing the lightness of weight in throwing them; the many aspects of learning such as sorting, ordering and understanding quantity through sand play; and for promoting care of the environment through caring for the bird and cleaning out the bird cage together. Other play experiences were featured across all of the settings, such as playdough, painting, manipulative materials, climbing indoors and out and, of course, music. They were intentionally utilized to promote learning through play.

In all settings, music was strongly evident (embedded in rhythms and songs) as well as in group experiences such as prayers, greetings and action songs. For the Māori immersion centres and A'oga Amata, singing, chanting and movements offered cultural cues as well as language acquisition.

In the Māori immersion centre,

- *waiata* was used to invite children to participate in a group experience;
- *karanga* was used to signal changes in the routines; and
- *karakia* was used to bless the food.

Waiata was also intentionally used to support the acquisition of Māori language –
during rituals and routines, as well as in periods of independent activity (on the
tape recorder). Teachers in the Māori immersion service described the purpose of
these activities as "capturing *reo*". They also saw cultural rituals as opportunities to
rehearse aspects of the real world.

Jovan's dad was proud when he watched the video footage of Jovan engaged with
the *haka*, stating "He's been watching the All-Blacks.[13]"

Similarly, it was Cameron's father who noticed him doing the *haka* with a rugby
ball – saying "That's my boy!" Leilani's teacher said "The language – it's about the
language, the singing ... singing all the time, I think that's how they easily pick up
the language." Hence, through play, important cultural messages are transmitted.

Underneath the spontaneity of experiences in these learning environments, teachers were clearly purposeful – not only in the provision of experiences but also in
the intentionality of their interactions with children. For example, Ana's educator
articulated her role in play as provoking learning as preparation for real-life experiences. (See Fig. 2.5.) In the shop-scene she describes what she was trying to achieve
through her interactions:

> I was trying to get her to recognise the things that were in the shop, to be able to give me
> things that might be familiar to her and to role play the shop as a shop would be. That you
> go into a shop and you ask for things and you're given things, and you pay for things, and
> then sometimes you get interrupted by other people coming into the shop, and that there
> are always people that are coming and going. And so I tried to get her to interact with L.
> At one stage, I said to her "L's got some money for you" and she took it but that was the
> end of that, she wasn't interested in interacting with him. And he wasn't really interested in
> interacting with her either. And I also tried to get her to interact with me on a different level
> with the telephone, but she didn't quite switch into that either. But I was trying to extend
> her within the shop. I thought that at the beginning she was in the shop but she wasn't quite
> sure about what she was meant to do in the shop. So I felt like asking her for something that
> may prompt her. . .

The intentionality of teacher interactions in play was also described by Ana's key
teacher: "I strive to extend their thinking about what they are doing". This required
a great deal of observation, and a balance between intervening and stepping back to
build on the cues of the child. In the A'oga Amata these strategies were also evident
throughout the day. However the teacher stayed close by for a larger proportion
of the time – yet sufficiently withdrawn so as to enable the child to explore the
environment in their own way. An example is seen on the video where Leilani was
invited to jump, and a hand was held out to support this. Leilani did not take the hand
but chose to stand on the box and experience the sensation of height. This choice
was respected by her teacher, who supported her to stand on the box whilst enabling
other children to move past her to jump. Eventually the teacher brought a plank for
Leilani to use instead, as an alternative way of getting down. Throughout intervals

---

[13] The All-Blacks are the New Zealand national rugby team who begin each game with a *haka*.
The *haka* is a tradition that is based on challenging visitors to reveal their intentions prior to entry
into the community.

such as this there seemed to be little need for speech, with a lot of interaction taking place nonverbally.

This standing back was also evident across other services. For example, Cameron's interest in the parked cars on the road was supported by his educator who made careful judgements about her level of intervention in relation to safety. The approach was deliberate. Teachers described the importance of allowing time for the child to respond without being overwhelmed by instructions or other agendas that may misunderstand or detract from their learning.

Other teaching strategies that were apparent in all services included modelling – subtly inviting children to try out new challenges (often with humorous interchanges). For example, in the outdoor area, Isobel's teacher moved beyond a facilitation role to one of playing *with* the children. The strategies to use in each moment were informed by the teacher's intimate knowledge of the child, and their ongoing observation of was happening in play.

"Refuelling" moments were facilitated by teachers either through the provision of spaces for children to go for solitude, observation or rest (such as the tree for Isobel or the couch for Jovan); or physical engagement such as rocking or cuddling (this was especially noticeable in the A'oga Amata). The familiarity shared between child and teacher afforded high levels of exploration and autonomy. Not only did this support exploration but it also created a shared understanding of what was valued by the child in play:

> It is very important to leave children, in this case Leilani, to explore for herself through play – she is learning many things about herself. She is very independent. She also takes her time. I just observe her but I know that she is quite capable. . . when Leilani needs my aid she calls for me or she comes to me.

In most cases the daily programme was carefully planned, however there was also an acceptance that things might change. When this occurred, the teacher was required to be prepared to shift direction in response to the child. A responsibility of the teacher was, therefore, to be responsive at all times. The Playcentre educator described this as "child-initiated play":

> So the children will implant something in my head, and I will bring something new along or try and extend what we've already got. I think the children's ideas are more important than the adult's ideas in this particular play situation, because our philosophy is child-initiated play and the children are free to do what they want to do and the adults' role is to extend (the child's play). So I feel that the children's ideas are more important than the adults' ideas.

After watching the video footage of Cameron, his educator recognized that both direct and indirect experiences influenced the nature of play:

> . . .an enormous amount of social development is happening while I'm "cleaning and preparing". The children are negotiating, nurturing, resolving conflicts and enjoying their relationships far more than I realised!! Maybe being a role model is just as important as planning and observing and my relationship with their parents is of paramount importance.

Hence learning through play was derived from the cues offered by child in direct and indirect relationships with their peers, family and the wider community. This approach to learning is consistent with *Te Whāriki* (1996) and with the recently developed *Kei tua o te pei* which provide assessment exemplars (Ministry of

Education, 2004). With a heavy emphasis on play as a prime vehicle for learning, assessment is a key responsibility of the teacher in the New Zealand context. It is also an essential bridge between play for play's sake, and play for learning.

Although assessment was a consistent feature of the child's day – evident through ready access to children's portfolios, and the intimate knowledge of each child that the teachers were able to draw upon to promote learning, it did not feature as a central discussion point during the interviews. However, viewing the footage, in itself, was seen as an opportunity for teachers to reflect deeply on their practice. These reflections conveyed a desire to extend on the child's learning, and highlight the interpretive aspect of the teaching role where play is seen as a prime vehicle for learning.

What Is the Meaning that Families Give to Play in Aotearoa New Zealand?

For the families involved in this study, play for their children was seen as a "given", described as the "only way" by Isobel's parents. There was, therefore, no question that play was essential for learning at this young age. At Playcentre – for those who, for the purposes of this study, identified themselves as "educators" and for those who identified themselves as "parent", play was seen as basic to how children learn. They believed that play took place through daily interactions with family and others. When asked to discuss play, Ana's mother said:

> I just assumed that was how children learned. I suppose children can get drilled and things, but that would be horrible and boring. You can teach them anything, counting and all sorts of things while you are doing things *with* them, and I think they enjoy it.

For the A'oga Amata parents, play was also an opportunity to teach children how to interact socially. These parents described how they had learnt so much about learning through play by watching the teachers:

> ...they're really lovely how they deal with that and they don't do this big punishment of the one who's hit, they just make a huge big fuss of the one who didn't hit – and they go "oh [child] is brave" ... You can see they're teaching the kids to do that. They'll actually take their hand and make them go [stroking movement]. It's a really nice way of teaching them to interact.

Cameron's parents recognized the complex learning that took place through the skilled facilitation of the educator, and the value of play as a medium for learning to occur:

> (It is) very subtle and you can see the way that R. [educator] facilitates it ... She's directing everything through play, but at the same time she's actually getting little messages across to him and so I think that's really clever and so she's knocking up a whole range of skills just in one little activity and I just think that's great because at the end of the day these kids are kids, very young, the language is limited and so the routines and the fun and the way she interacts and has dialogue with them and ...it's just outstanding...it really is...I mean he benefits hugely from it.

Fig. 2.6 Jovan takes the
stance of his tupuna

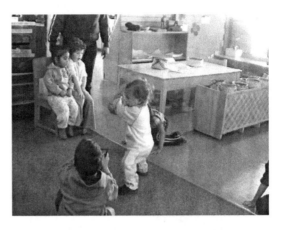

The Māori immersion whānaui described play in relation to the concept of *whakawhanaungatanga*, thus making connections between the physical and spiritual aspects of the whole child. When a child entered the early childhood environment they brought with them their *whakapapa*, their history and the hopes their family had for them in the future. In this way child's play was viewed as a "connecting link" between the centre and other dimensions of the child. The *whānau* saw play as essential in nurturing the potential of each child for their shared future. This meant that play involved exploration in cultural rituals and events as well as immersion in the *reo*.

Jovan's father became quite emotional when he watched Jovan spontaneously demonstrate the *haka*, saying "I felt like crying". When Jovan completed the *haka* by holding a drum in a *taiaha* stance (see Fig. 2.6), his father said "I am so proud of my son;" whereupon Jovan's mother leaned over and said "... and of ourselves". For these parents, Jovan's connection with the *taiaha* in play was associated with his developing sense of identity as a Māori, and as a future leader.

The Playcentre parent also saw the significance of play as a way of linking closely into the child's "world" – that it was a way to deal with interesting, routine or perplexing aspects of daily life. She believed that play allows children to explore the adult world at their own pace:

> I see as a child exploring their world in whatever they do, whether it be play as what we adults determine it to be play, or play as in what adults sometimes express as being work. ...In play I think they get to explore at their own pace. I think children learn through their own play in their own time what they choose to play with, i.e. the sand pit. You know nobody is saying to them you have to do it this way or that way, they can just explore it at their own pace at their own time.

A similar view was held by the A'oga Amata parents, who said:

> Everything's explorative in the environment. She's (the teacher) always inventing these different things and they all get interested in what she's doing. . ... They've got *lotu* (prayer) in the morning where they make all the kids come sit down ... and that's routine. But then the rest of the day they've got all these other things they can do – what interests them.

Isobel's parents also saw play as the best way for learning – particularly at this younger age. They went on to say that everything is play – "apart from getting dressed and that, on reflection, even that was play". They believed that play gave Isobel opportunities to do things she wants to learn on her own terms instead of just watching and doing what adults are doing and trying to emulate. In play, they said, there were fewer constraints, and gave the example that "in play you can stack things up crazily or smash them all down – which is not generally the way in everyday life". They believed play facilitated much more self-direction by the child than other forms of learning, and was therefore the most appropriate way for this younger age group to learn.

Several of the parents saw play as an opportunity to explore physical or social boundaries. They valued the fact that their child could make choices, and have preferences upheld. The fact that there were fewer barriers in the centre than at home, made this a desirable feature of the service. Isobel's parents commented:

> She sees no barriers to just going over and doing something … It is the same as going around all the instrument – is there a particular reason she just can't go over and grab D's (the teacher) drum and bang it? There is … no barrier there.

Cameron's parents aligned play closely to the notion of game playing. On several occasions through the interview his father made comments about Cameron's role as a New Zealand male; for example, "Get the legs round boy. . .get the legs round. . .you can do it!"; or "Good old kiwi kid".

A keen rugby fan himself, Cameron's father was thrilled to discover elements of game playing throughout Cameron's day. He believed that "life is a game" and that the lessons learnt through Cameron's early childhood education experience – even the difficult ones – would assist him throughout life:

> Take rugby – there's the team thing going on. Well, in the real world you've got to get on with people… Unfortunately unless you live up in the Himalayas somewhere, there's not much hope of you being isolated by yourself. There's a whole lot of time factor in it – sometimes you've got limited time; sometimes you have to extend yourself because time isn't going quick enough. There's when you're knackered; there's when things don't go the right way; there's the referee blowing the whistle and so you have to follow the laws and the rules; there's consequences; there's rewards of winning, sometimes you lose….

The Playcentre parent believed that children should be able to take risks and challenge authority through play. The video revealed an incident where Ana was asked not to go up the slide because of the risk to the other children coming down the slide. However, Ana waited a while and then climbed up the slide when there were no children sliding down. Watching the video, Ana's mother expressed her belief that it was important for Ana to explore her ideas:

> … when she's hell bent on doing something, she almost needs to do it to settle her otherwise that'll be her focus. I think … what I saw was – she wanted to walk up the slide, that was what the whole thing was about … and she was happy once she had done it, and she only needed to do it once to prove she could do it maybe, or to see if she could do it herself.

Regardless of how they interpreted play, all the parents saw it as the primary way their children could learn about their world and themselves. The overwhelming emphasis on social interaction and developing sense of self as part of society was a feature of all the interviews and supported a sociocultural view of learning where the child is in relationship with people, places and things (Ministry of Education, 1996).

The parents of these children also commented on the importance of the transmission of learning to and from the spaces between home and early childhood service. Effective transition was facilitated by open communication between the adults in both settings – as they shared experiences of play with one another and compared these. The relationship between home and service was reflected in the planning and delivery of learning experiences that were clearly considered in relation to the aspirations of the parent for their child. Together with an intimate knowledge of the child and their preferences, the provision of play was seen as a springboard for learning. The episodes of most intensive play were associated with the captive interest of the child in aspects of the environment and the people within it. Such episodes were often recognized by these parents because they were transferred between the home environment and the early childhood education context – facilitated by a partnership approach to learning.

What Role Do Parents Play?

All of the families in this study were highly involved in the education of their children to the point that it was sometimes difficult to position them outside of the domain of "teacher". Parent involvement included:

- the parent also being one of the teachers (in the Māori immersion service);
- the parent being fully involved in the programme as both parent and educator and regularly interacting with her own child (and other children) during the session (in the Playcentre programme);
- the parent popping in at lunchtimes to join in the play (in the Education and Care service or Home-based Education settings);and
- the parent contributing ideas and information to the teachers that would support the programmes provided.

Each family recognized the significance of their involvement in their child's learning. This involvement was seen as necessary in creating links between the world of the early childhood education service, and the wider world of the child. Through reciprocal information sharing, parents largely believed play would be encouraged that was consistent with their aspirations for the future of their child.

Parents frequently discussed the importance of the teacher as coming to understand and know their child in relation to play. For them, information (both documented and communicated verbally) played an important part in the learning and teaching experience for their child. It created a confidence that the staff knew what they were doing, and that they were watching out for their child, described by Isobel's parents as follows:

> We know a little bit from lunchtime visits. And we know a little bit from, the interaction at the end of the day with the staff, because they will tell us a bit about what they are doing, and they usually put a written A4 sheet about what activities have happened that day. I don't always read that though. It is more a verbal interactions. And then I think I learn a lot with books that come home periodically... And they record it in quite a lot of detail and they have a photo and they seem quite insightful actually. You know usually you get a sense that they do really know our kids. Well I certainly feel that when I read, I kind of feel comforted that she is not just going and wandering around being a little lost soul [with] no one really keeping an eye on her. When you read the stories you can tell that they understand her being a real character.

Jovan's parents valued documentation as a "surprise" for them in that it offered new insights into the play their son was engaged in. For Jovan's father, who was unable to spend long periods of time in the centre, access to photographs and other portfolio information offered reassurance that the *mana* of his son (and through his son, the wider *whānau*) was upheld through play.

Through watching videos of their children at play, parents recognized their children were engaging in familiar learning experiences. On numerous experiences, they commented that their children were involved in similar activities at home (such as bubbles in the sink, music, running, and playing games like "hide and seek"). Ana's mother described experiences in both the home and Playcentre environment that were aligned, such as "making pretend cups of tea" and joining in with her older brother with building blocks.

Similarly Cameron's parents were able to make links between settings saying "Ah – now I know why he does that" or "Oops, that's my fault". They also noted play interests that they had not previously been aware of, commenting "We must get Cameron a tennis racquet"; and "I never thought of trying that!".

For Isobel's parents, outdoor experiences and opportunities to engage in real-life experiences were valued feature of play in both settings. They talked about sorting the plants to be watered and feeding the chickens. The children's interests that were illuminated through play were seen as transferable between both environments. Such connecting links between experiences at the service and in their own home through play was important for all the parents. In this way, parents viewed play and learning in the early childhood education environment as complementary to the experiences at home.

Leilani's parents strongly endorsed the way learning took place at the A'oga Amata. Her father described the teachers as people who "upgrade themselves all the time". The respect and admiration Leilani's parents had for the teachers in the A'oga Amata meant that the parents could learn from them. In this way the teachers provided them with ideas for working effectively with their child through play:

> I've learned lots watching them, and what they do if the kids are needy or demanding – they'll sit on the floor with them rather than pick them up. So they'll sit down on the floor and have a cuddle and then play with the child.

For Leilani's parents, the relationship they shared with the teachers at the A'oga Amata was not only sustained by their teaching but also by the way they supported

Leilani's family to feel as if they had a valued contribution to make. Her mother recognized that this was fostered even before Leilani was born:

> It was really nice, when I went down when I was pregnant with her and I enrolled her. The doctors, then the A'oga! They were so lovely, they were all giving me hugs and crying. It was really nice to be part of the A'oga community.

The support parents were, in turn, able to give to play in the early childhood education setting enabled them to recognize and value play as it occurred in other settings too. The reciprocal nature of the role of parents and teachers in supporting children at play meant that learning took place for adults as well as children. Even when families were unable to spend time in the early childhood setting, teachers invested time and effort into sharing information through documentation. This recognition of the importance of family in children's learning was a consistent feature of play in this study.

Conclusions

The results of this study demonstrate a commitment to play as a legitimate and appropriate vehicle for learning through exploration for these very young children. As parents and teachers of older children have not been asked their views on play in New Zealand, it is difficult to know to what extent perceptions of play may differ for children in older age groups. Certainly for these children play was seen as a right – not only tolerated but encouraged. In the context of early childhood education, play therefore formed the basis for learning. Through interactions, guardianship and the provision of "refuelling" moments, these children were supported to engage in meaningful, purposeful play experiences which reflect the values and beliefs of their family and society. In this way, the value of play was strongly aligned to the development of children's identity as Māori, Samoan, as members of a rugby nation, a team player, or as risk-takers and policy-makers of the future.

The purpose of play was strongly aligned to developing identity. Through play these young children were able to explore their place in society. Adults talked about play as a vehicle for creativity and risk-taking, and play as a means of cultural transmission. They also saw play as a natural way of nurturing the uniqueness of each child, by upholding their preferences and interests without interference. Several teachers believed that children of this age learn passively and actively, through being part of an active and nurturing environment. As a result, nurturance and experience in rituals as well as interactions with the wider community were as much a part of the play and learning experience. There was a recognition that there are times for contact and times for stepping back, thus allowing for refuelling, private exploration and re-establishing a base from which to explore.

Play took place in the adult's domain beyond the early childhood service. Areas of encounter offered places where play was a "given" with little or no associated expectation for these children. Rather, the ebb and flow of the environment, with its unhurried pace, set the scene for children to explore freely. Children moved in and out of spaces and played in their own world alongside others, supported by periodic cultural cues that served as a "punctuation mark" to the day. The children occasionally returned to familiar spaces and used these as a base from which to explore. Adults were always close by and keen to respond to the child when they were invited into their world.

The adult in play was described as a "guardian" of the child; in practice this often meant the adult only intervened if invited by the child. On other occasions the adult facilitated play through the provision of experiences, and by intentional teaching practices such as modelling, or scaffolding particular play experiences. These opportunities were often embedded within cultural rituals and events, and were underpinned by strong beliefs about how and what children should learn. The way adults interpreted their role in supporting play was also influenced by their long-term goals for children as participants in the society. As such, play was seen not only as a right but also as a rite of passage into the adult world. The role of teachers, therefore, was to be in tune with the aspirations held by families for their child. Their task was to ensure that exchanges of information were facilitated in ways that upheld the cultural and societal expectations of families. In play this meant being attuned to each other, and to the child, through careful observation and interpretation.

The experience of watching the video offered teachers and parents an opportunity to reflect further on their practice. Whilst teachers were able to talk about their role in supporting and extending play, they also recognized aspects of the children's play that could have elicited a different response from them. Noticing opportunities for extending learning through play (described by one *kaiako* as "eureka moments") were facilitated by standing back from the busyness of the early childhood day.

In creating opportunities to stand back, there were additional ways of finding out what interests each child. With this knowledge, adults were able to learn more about the way the child engaged in play and to plan appropriate ways of responding. In this way the notion of guardianship is broadened to embrace responsiveness so that the teacher is attuned to the educational needs of the child as well as nurturing their well-being.

Throughout this chapter, the wider national agenda for children as citizens of New Zealand, as espoused through the four principles of *Te Whāriki*, are evident:

- *Family and community* was evident in the way families played a central role in play through active involvement and mutual exchanges of information.
- *Empowerment* was seen in the manner with which the child was supported to make meaningful play choices. For toddlers, who do not always have a shared language, this is particularly relevant through the mechanism of play. Coupled with a recognition that learning can take place passively, the toddler has freedom to explore their world in their own way, and at their own pace.
- *Holistic development* was evident in the way the emotional, social, physical, cognitive and spiritual dimensions of the child were cared for through the combination of a guardianship role and provocateur of learning on the part of the adult.

- *Relationships* were evident:

    o through mutual exchanges of information between parent and teacher (where parent information was highly valued and used to inform the further provision of play);
    o between children and teachers (including the sensitive use of a repertoire of strategies);
    o between child and child (evident in the *tuakana–teina* relationship); and
    o between the child and their environment (shown in numerous ways through interactions with the environment, the wider world, the use of space and provision of resources).

Play supported these principles, and brought about learning that mirrored the child's interest and innate desire to explore their world. In this way play served as a natural vehicle for transmitting the values and beliefs of a society, and culture. Such an approach to play is not bound by one definition or moment in time. Instead, play presents as a means of creating and reconstructing knowledge in relationships with others. Hill (2005) suggests that this re-constructive process is critical in shifting from a view of play as a New Zealand tradition to seeing play as an opportunity to learn more about the complex world of the child, and to respond appropriately.

For a society as diverse as Aotearoa New Zealand, play can best be described as our greatest hope for the future – the *right* to express oneself within dynamic spaces and the *rite* of passage into the complex and diverse world that will comprise the future for these children.

Acknowledgments The researchers would like to thank and acknowledge the children, families, *whanau*, teachers, educators and *kaiako* who participated in this study. Special acknowledgement to Victoria University of Wellington for their practical and ethical oversight of the project as well as the OMEP National Executive (2003–2005). Thanks also to University of Auckland, Auckland University of Technology, Te Wananga o Aotearoa, Dunedin College of Education and Victoria University of Wellington for supporting each of the individual researchers in completing their part of the project.

Glossary of Māori (and Some Samoan) Words and Phrases

Aotearoa: "Land of the long white cloud"; the Māori name for New Zealand.
Ako: A Māori concept that the learner and teacher roles are reciprocal – so that the teacher is also the learner and the learner is also teacher. Ako is closely aligned to the socio-cultural concept of "co-construction" which positions learning within shared processes and joint goals.
Aroha: Love (in its broadest sense).

Faiaoga:	Teacher in Samoan language.
Kaiako:	Teacher.
Kaitiakitanga:	The practice of being a guardian, a nurturer.
Kapa haka:	Māori cultural performing arts – usually songs, chants, *poi* and dance.
Karakia:	A prayer.
Karanga:	The call traditionally used to call visitors on to the *marae* (meeting house).
Mana:	A person's worth. *Mana* refers to the way a person is perceived by others and treated accordingly; to have *mana* is to receive respect and honour.
Matua:	Parents in Samoan language.
Mihimihi:	A formal way of introducing oneself. In mihimihi the child learns to orate publicly by sharing their links to land, hāpu, iwi (tribal groupings) as well as ancestry.
Poi:	A small ball on a long cord. A traditional Māori activity involving rhythmic swinging of a ball which is usually performed by women in Māori presentation, but which was earlier an activity for warriors to improve co-ordination.
Reo:	Language.
Taiaha:	A traditional spear-like wooden weapon used in some *haka*.
Tamaitiiti:	Children in Samoan language.
Tangata whenua:	"People of the land"; the indigenous people.
Te Kohanga Reo:	"Language nest"; the whānau-based Māori language immersion service which began in the 1980s.
Tuakana-teina:	Older sibling – younger sibling. This relationship is based on the notion that the *tuakana* takes responsibility for the caring, teaching, guiding of the *teina*.
Tupuna:	Ancestor
Waiata:	Song. *Waiata* typically convey important cultural messages and stories.
Wananga:	A place of learning; a Māori-focused tertiary institution.
Whakapapa:	Geneology. For many Māori, *whakapapa* can be traced back to the creation of the Māori world.
Whakawhanaungatanga:	Creating family. Practices that bond and strengthen the kinship ties of *whānau* to their ancestral lands, to the past, present and future (Pere, 1994).
Whānau:	Family, including extended family Faiaoga – teacher; matua – parents, children – tamaitiiti.

References

Edwards, A. (2005, Mar.). Let's get beyond community and practice: The many meanings of learning by participating. *The Curriculum Journal 16*(1), 49–65.

Ferguson, G. W. (2004). *"You'll be a man if you play rugby": Sport and construction of gender.* Auckland: Dunmore Press.

Hill, D. (2005). Curriculum: Challenges of context and complexity in early childhood settings. *The First Years Nga Tau Tuatahi New Zealand Journal of Infant and Toddler Education, 7*(1), 21–26.

May, H. (2005). *School beginnings. A 19th century colonial story.* Wellington: New Zealand Council of Educational Research.

Ministry of Education. (1996). *Te Whāriki: He Whāriki Mātauranga mo ngā Mokopuna o Aotearoa/Early childhood curriculum.* Wellington: Learning Media.

Ministry of Education. (1998). *Quality in action: Implementing the revised statement of desirable objectives and practices.* Wellington: Learning Media.

Ministry of Education. (2002). *Pathways to the future: Ngā huarahi arataki: A 10-year strategic plan for early childhood education.* Wellington: Author.

Ministry of Education. (2004). *Introduction to Kei Tua o Te Pae: Assessment for learning – Early childhood exemplars.* Wellington: Learning Media.

Ministry of Education. (2005a). *Statistics.* Retrieved 10 May 2005 from www.minedu.govt.nz

Ministry of Education. (2005b). *Educate: Ministry of Education statement of intent 2005–2010.* Wellington: Author.

OECD. (2004). *Learning for tomorrow's world: First results from PISA 2003.* Paris: OECD.

Pere, R. (1994). *Ako : Concepts and learning in the Māori tradition.* Wellington: Te Kohanga Reo National Trust Board.

Royal-Tangare, A. (1997). *Māori human development theory.* In P. Whaiti, M. MaCarthy, & A. Durie (Eds.), *Mai I Rangiatea: Māori wellbeing and development.* Auckland: Auckland University Press.

Smith, L. T., & Smith, G. H. (1993). *Traditional Māori education.* Unpublished Paper, Research Unit for Māori Education, The University of Auckland, Auckland.

SPARC. (2004). *SPARC invests $1 million in active communities.* Retrieved 13 February 2005, from www.sparc.org.nz

Statistics New Zealand (2004). http://www.stats.govt.nz/people

White, E. J., Stover, S., Ellis, F., O'Malley, A., Rockel, J., & Toso, M. (2005, December). Collaboration in an international early childhood education research project: Perspectives of the New Zealand OMEP research project. *Paper presented to the OMEP Asia-Pacific Conference "The Youngest Citizen: Community, culture and curriculum",* OMEP Aoteaora New Zealand with Victoria University of Wellington School of Early Childhood Teacher Education, 2–3 December, Wellington, New Zealand.

White, J., Rockel, J., & Toso, M. (2007). Reflecting on a research project on play through sociocultural eyes: Eureka moments. *Australian Research in Early Childhood Education 14*(2), 47–60.

Chapter 3
Play and Learning in Australia

Marilyn Fleer, Holli A. Tonyan, Ana Cristina Mantilla,
and Corine M. Patricia Rivalland

Introduction

Early childhood education in Australia has generally been considered to be inclusive
of children from birth to 8 years of age (Fleer, 2000). However, in practice we find
that some state or territory authorities consider only the period prior to school to be
under their jurisdiction. The variability in how early childhood education is framed
is also evident in the naming of institutions. In Australia there is no universal term
to label the educational setting immediately prior to schooling. For example, in the
Australian Capital Territory and in New South Wales the year immediately prior to
the first year of school is called Kindergarten. In Victoria and Tasmania it is called
Preparatory (or prep), in Queensland it is named as preschool, in South Australia
it is called Reception, in the Northern Territory it is known as Transition and in
Western Australia it is called preprimary.

There are also a range of educational settings for young children within Australia. In addition to the mandated education settings (kindergarten and school) the
sector also includes: Family Day Care; Long Day Care Centres; Multifunctional
Aboriginal Children's Services; Multifunctional Children's Services; Mobile Children's Services; Occasional Care Centres; Outside School Hours Care; Playgroups;
Preschools and Schools; toy libraries; and Maternal and Child Health Centres.

Diversity in how these educational settings are physically located, jurisdic-
tional responsibility and their relationships to each other also exists. For instance,
preschools may be located within schools, stand-alone centres or integrated within
long day care centres. There is a mixture of public, non-government not-for-
profit, private for-profit and private not-for-profit organizations, as well as involvement from State Governments, local government and the nonprofit sector (Press &
Hayes, 2000).

As such, it is possible to see that developing a working knowledge of early
childhood education in Australia is problematic. This chapter introduces the social

M. Fleer
Monash University, Frankston, Victoria 3199, Australia
e-mail: marilyn.fleer@education.monash.edu.au

I. Pramling-Samuelsson, M. Fleer (eds.), *Play and Learning in Early Childhood
Settings*, DOI 10.1007/978-1-4020-8498-0_3,
© Springer Science+Business Media B.V. 2009

and political context of early childhood education in Australia in order to better understand the social construction of play within early childhood education. Secondly, the theoretical and practical dimensions of early childhood education and care are discussed with a view to understanding the socio-historical dimensions of play within early childhood education in Australia. This is followed by the study design, findings and conclusions drawn as a result of investigating the play activities of children aged birth to 3 years.

The Social, Political and Economic Context of Early Childhood Education in Australia

Australia is a federation of states and territories. As such, responsibility for governing the country is shared between the Australian Government and State/Territory governments. In the care and education contexts, the Australian Government funds health and wellbeing services, whilst states/territories have primary responsibility for funding education (Press & Hayes, 2000). This split in governing means that policy and funding have been separated into care and education portfolios. That is, the Australian Government has responsibility for childcare, and states and territories have responsibility for early childhood education. The institutionalizing of care and education within different Departments has meant that working across sectors is difficult. However, recent trends in adopting a "whole of Government" approach has meant that policy developers from different departments are actively informing each other of policy changes, are planning together in a more systematic way, and have constituted committees with a brief to bring together policy and funding across Governments whenever possible. For example, at the Australian Government level, two major Departments have worked together to prepare policy directions for early childhood education and care. The Department of Education, Employment and Workplace Relations, and the Department of Family and Community Services have written an important document entitled: *Towards the Development of a National Agenda for Early Childhood* (2003). This document was released in 2003 alongside a series of public consultations within each state and territory. This initiative was designed to signal to the community that Government was working more collaboratively. The publication also documented Government priorities (literacy, numeracy and inclusive education). A recent National Government change has meant that early childhood staff formally in the Department of Family and Community Services have now moved their function to the Department of Education, Employment and Workplace Relations. Thus signaling a major structural change in Australia, where early childhood care and education have been formally brought together.

Compulsory schooling begins at roughly age six, although cut-offs for defining compulsory attendance vary across states and tables (see Table 3.1). In addition, all states and territories have programmes for children starting from around age four. By contrast, starting ages, costs and availability vary widely. Some have specific start and end cut-off points whereas others have continuous entry. In sum, although

Table 3.1 Comparison of ages for entry into school-based programmes in Australia (Adapted from Press & Hayes, 2000, p. 64)

State/Territory	Entry age into programme 2 years before Year 1	Entry age into programme 1 year before Year 1	Entry age into Year 1	Compulsory starting age
Western Australia	4 by 30 June	5 by 30 June	6 by 30 June	From the beginning of the year the child turns 6 years and 6 months
New South Wales	4 by 31 July	5 by 31 July	6 by 31 July	Sixth birthday
Victoria	4 by 30 April	5 by 30 April	6 by 30 April	Sixth birthday
Queensland	4 by 31 December	5 by 31 December	6 by 31 December	Sixth birthday
South Australia	Continuous entry after fourth birthday	Continuous entry into Reception class after 5th birthday	Single entry in January after two to five terms in Reception depending on initial entry	Sixth birthday
Tasmania	4 by 1 January	5 by 1 January	6 by 1 January	Sixth birthday
ACT	4 by 30 April	5 by 30 April	6 by 30 April	Sixth birthday
Northern Territory	Continuous entry after fourth birthday	5 by 30 June Continuous intake after fifth birthday into transition	Continuous entry after minimum of two terms in transition	Sixth birthday

all children will encounter formal schooling at age six, *some* children will have had up to 3 years of preparatory experiences of varying types with varying combinations of care arrangements.

Similar variability exists in the qualifications required for professionals working across these early childhood settings. In Australia, all state and territory education authorities require that teachers working in Australian schools with children aged 5 years and older must have tertiary teaching qualifications (3 or 4 years of a university Bachelor of Education is required). However, variability in qualifications is noted for children in early years education settings for children of 5 years and younger, with notable variation along the education and care division of policy and governance. For programmes regulated as providing "care", the Australian government requires only 2 years of technical education related to caring for children. Here, we see a wide variation. In Australia approximately half of staff working in long day care centres have formal qualifications. In family day care schemes approximately one-fifth of caregivers and the majority of coordination unit staff hold formal qualifications. Of those staff who hold formal qualifications, only about one-fifth have a teaching qualification. Most have a Child Care Certificate (1 year technical qualification) or Diploma of Child Care (2 years technical qualification) and some have a nursing qualification (this was the base qualification, but is being phased out – nurses are required to upgrade their qualifications to include education). Similarly, state and territory governments require staff who teach in school preparatory programmes during the years prior to mandatory school (prepri-mary, preschool, kindergarten or transition, preparatory, reception) to have tertiary teaching qualifications of either a 3-year or a 4-year degree.

Socio-Historical Connections: Theory and Practice Dynamics in Australia

Most teachers in Australia are very experienced. The Senate Enquiry into early child-hood education in Australia calculated the average age to be 48 years (Senate Employment, Education and Training Committee, 1996). However, this also means that most teachers completed their tertiary education qualifications 25 years ago, when the theoretical emphasis was grounded in interpretations of Piaget's theory of development. This legacy must be taken into account when examining contemporary early childhood theory and practice within Australia.

During the 1980s, early childhood education in Australia was strongly influenced by the work of Sue Bredekamp. Her early work on developmentally appropriate practice (DAP) (1987), and her later additions to this on culturally appropriate prac-tice (Bredekamp & Copple, 1997) have informed professional development and cur-riculum and policy directions in Australia for at least a decade. As a result, a critical mass of teachers have a strong grounding in the work of Piaget and Bredekamp. For example, many early childhood programmes feature individual children's inter-ests, with staff recording individual observations of young children and undertaking analyses in accordance with the social, emotional, physical, cognitive and language domains. The dominant discourse surrounding early childhood education practice in Australia is informed by DAP, and grounded in Piaget's stage-based theory on child development within the context of an active hands-on pedagogy. As a result, child-centred ideology enacted through individual observations and planning within Frobelian children's gardens (e.g. blocks, puzzles, construction kits, collage trolleys, child-sized home corner or dramatic area, child-sized tables and chairs, trestles and planks, slides, jumping mattresses, etc.) is what is seen in many early childhood centres within Australia.

However, since the mid-1990s DAP has been re-examined by scholars in the USA (Lubeck, 1998) and in Australia (Clyde, 1995; Cross, 1995; Fleer, 1996). Australian researchers in early childhood education have asked whose develop-ment is being privileged (MacNaughton, 1995), considered cultural variations which make this worldview problematic (Fleer, 1996; Fleer & Kennedy, 2000) and ques-tioned previously accepted staged-based research as being the dominant perspective underpinning the theoretical and practical directions in early childhood education (Clyde, 1995). As a result of this work, challenges to the status quo of early child-hood practice and theory have been forthcoming in recent years.

As noted by Edwards (2003a), sociocultural theory has led the charge in debunking DAP as the dominant theoretical informant in Australia. This is in line with a general worldwide trend in education:

> There is a growing interest in what has become known as 'sociocultural theory' and its near relative 'activity theory'. Both traditions are historically linked to the work of L.S. Vygotsky and both attempt to provide an account of learning and development as mediated processes (Daniels, 2001, p. 1).

Sociocultural theory and activity theory have both provided researchers and practitioners with "methodological tools for investigating the processes by which social, cultural and historical factors shape human functioning" (Daniels, 2001, p. 1). In the context of these theoretical perspectives, development is not seen as unfolding, but rather development is inseparable from the social, cultural, social and political contexts in which humans reside. Rogoff (2003, p. 3) has recently used the phrase "[t]he cultural nature of development" and Daniels (2001, p. 14) urges a view of development within the context of "'mediation' which opens the way for the development of a non-deterministic account in which mediators serve as the means by which the individual acts upon and is acted upon by social, cultural and historical factors".

The legacy of Vygotsky's work has seen a burgeoning body of theoretical writing and new opportunities for pedagogical research in early childhood education. As Daniels (2001, p. 2) suggests:

> These developments in social theory are creating new and important possibilities for practices of teaching and learning in schools and beyond. They provide us with theoretical constructs, insights and understandings which we can use to develop our own thinking about the practices of education.

In Australia, early research into mediation processes by early childhood teachers drew upon Vygotsky's theory on the social formation of mind and Bruner's work on scaffolding (see Fleer, 1992). This research actively examined the role of the adult in children's learning and focused on documenting scaffolded interactions over time in childcare, preschool and the early years of school.

Research undertaken by Edwards (2003a, b) into how early childhood teachers think about and enact their beliefs on curriculum has shown that there is a growing realization among early childhood teachers that DAP and the work of Piaget have not fully supported them in dealing with the complexities of teaching in the 21st century, particularly when catering for the diversity of children who attend their settings. Edwards (2003b) found that many teachers expressed ideas which illustrate a working knowledge of sociocultural theory, but used the dominant discourse or conceptual tools available to them (DAP; Piaget) to talk about curriculum. Edwards also interviewed teachers who used the principles of Reggio Emilia to inform their work with young children. In Australia, there is a small but growing number of scholars and practitioners who have visited Reggio Emilia Italy and have brought back new ideas, principles and future directions to support early childhood practice (see Millikan, 2003). Edwards found that those teachers in her sample who subscribed to the beliefs and principles of Reggio Emilia had at their disposal a broader set of conceptual tools for articulating their beliefs about curriculum.

Alongside of these theoretical discussions and ongoing research, have been postmodern critiques of early childhood education. Postmodern perspectives have become increasingly influential, sparking much debate in the field and encouraging early childhood educators to question existing and taken-for-granted practices. In particular, critiques of the foundations of early childhood education (Dahlberg et al., 1999) have generated focused conferences and papers on the reconceptualization of early childhood education. Blaise (2005) argues that poststructuralism "offers the field of early childhood education a way of producing new knowledge by using poststructural theories of language, discourse, subjectivity, and agency to understand how power is exercised in the classroom" (p. 15).

Similarly, the mounting evidence from three decades of cross-cultural studies on young children and their families (Göncü, 1999; Rogoff, 1990, 1998; Woodhead, 1998) has provided further evidence of the shortcomings of the theoretical foundations of early childhood education. The ethnocentric nature of theories of play (Dockett & Fleer, 1999; Fleer, 1996), the domination of a universal framework for the development of all individuals in our culturally and linguistically diverse communities (Dahlberg et al., 1999; Fleer & Williams-Kennedy, 2002; Siraj-Blatchford & Clarke, 2000) and an entrenched Western belief in the individual over the sociocultural collective (Rogoff, 1998) have all been foregrounded and questioned.

Early childhood education in Australia is currently in a phase of change. Whilst the dominant discourses surrounding the domains of learning and DAP have enshrined in quality assurance processes a particular worldview (see Fleer & Kennedy, 2000), sufficient disquiet exists for teachers to consider new theoretical perspectives (Blaise, 2005; Edwards, 2003b). The principles of Reggio Emilia and the introduction of sociocultural theory have both generated change in the field. As recently noted by Edwards (2003b), early childhood education in Australia is currently undergoing a paradigm shift. How these new theories and principles play out in practice within an Australian context is yet to be determined. What these new themes mean in relation to existing understandings and views on how play is framed and used for learning is not well understood, particularly in relation to infants and toddlers.

Introduction to the Empirical Study

Participants

Three groups of participants formed part of this study: the target children, their primary caregivers and siblings, if any, and the early childhood professionals.

Researchers contacted a university-based childcare centre located in Southern Victoria. Explanatory statements and letters of invitation were distributed to families. Eight families agreed to participate in the project and signed and returned informed consent forms indicating their level of involvement in the project and authorising their child to be videotaped for one full day while at the centre. Eight target children, three boys and five girls took part in the study. Three of the children were from the 1- to 2-year-old group, two were from the 2- to 3-year-old group and three were from the 3- to 4-year-old group. Ages ranged from 12 to 38 months.

Six early childhood professionals took part in the study. The three room leaders had Technical and Further Education (TAFE) qualifications and two of the three assistants had had many years of experience working with children, but no formal qualifications. One assistant was currently undergoing her TAFE qualification.

Methods of Data Collection

In order to capture the daily reality of the different participants within the early childhood context, the target children and teachers were filmed for one full day following a method used by Tobin, Wu and Davidson (1989).

Prior to the full day video observation, the camera operator spent one and one-half days in the centre thus allowing the children to familiarize themselves with the equipment and the new person within their context with the view to minimize any disruption to natural the field. During the formal video recording, the camera operator situated herself in an inconspicuous area of the room or the garden and used the zoom function to film from a distance. She did not intervene in any of the activities. One target child from the three rooms was followed for one full day, two pairs of children were filmed on the same day and one child was filmed for approximately 4 hours. A total 25 hours of video data were gathered.

Videotaping was conducted over 1 month from October to November 2005. These are spring months in Australia. Most of the days were both sunny and warm which influenced the amount of time children spent outside and children's play opportunities.

After the completion of all video recording, a time and date convenient to the centre's management and teachers was set for the viewing of tapes and interview times. The room leaders were interviewed on the early childhood centre premises. Each participant was asked to view the videos and record episodes that were representative or showed a different dimension of children's play. To keep track of the data, teachers were given a proforma for each episode, including prompts for a name for their chosen episode, a start and end time, and a few notes that would help them jog their memory during the interview. While the participants were reviewing the tapes and writing notes, the assistant researcher was available for assistance or to answer questions but did not intervene at any time. Each time an episode was identified, the participant shared their thinking about the episode with the research assistant. The review sessions were audiotaped and transcribed.

Some of the questions and prompts that guided the interview were:

1. What is your philosophy about play and education in relation to play?
2. You have identified these different kinds of play, what has informed your philosophy?
3. Do you recall where you learnt that?

Room leaders were also invited to view a selection of play episodes that had been chosen by the main researcher. During this viewing time teachers were asked questions inspired by Rogoff's (2003) writing on the three lenses:

1. What can you see that is happening here? (personal lens, Rogoff, 2003).
2. If you were to show this episode at an information night to new/prospective parents, without explanation, what would they see? (interpersonal lens; Rogoff, 2003).
3. There are many everyday practices shown. What are the things you hardly even notice anymore? What are the things that didn't surprise you? (institutional lens; Rogoff, 2003).

The same questions and methods were used with the assistants. However, due to staff and time constraints linked to the complexity of the early childhood context, we had only one hour to interview the assistants. In order to maximize this time, these teachers were invited to view the main researcher's preselected segments and take part in an audio-recorded interview.

All interviews were transcribed by an experienced transcriber. These transcribed interviews, the episodes selected by the teachers, episodes selected by the main researcher and the video observation of the eight target children formed the bulk of the data related to the early childhood context.

Findings: The Children's World and Experience

Daily Routine

For our eight target children, the child care centre is the place where they share daily routines and activities in the company of other children their age and a few adults (usually two) that they all seem to know well and feel close to. Some children come to the centre once or twice a week while others come everyday. Most of them stay in the centre for at least five consecutive hours during which they follow a recurrent schedule framed by their arrival and departure, meals, rest, and indoor/outdoor activities.

Most children arrive to the Centre between 7.30 and 9.00 a.m. Children from all ages (6 weeks to 5 years old) gather in the room for children 1–2 years old that the centre uses as the "family room" at this time of the day. Two to three early childhood professionals focus their attention on the children who seem to be upset when their parents leave as their goal is to ensure that the children have easily settled in the centre.

Children are taken to their rooms by an early childhood professional soon after 9.00 a.m. Once the children are divided, children can only play either inside or outside depending on the weather and the room leader's choice for the day. Free play is interrupted by the adults when it is time for morning tea. All children sit around a table with the early childhood professional(s) and are encouraged to wait for their turns and use the words "please" and "thank you". Older children are also encouraged to wash their hands before sitting down, to make their own choices about food and, sometimes, to serve themselves. All children in the 1–2 and 2–3 rooms are gathered at the same time making meals one of the few assembly times that take place in these rooms. Children in the 3–4 room are not necessarily gathered at the same time and other assembly times seem to be more relevant than meal times.

In all rooms, morning tea is followed by free inside or outside play. Children's play is interrupted again a couple of hours later (times vary according to children's age) in order to get ready for lunch. The lunch meal in the 1–2 and 2–3 rooms is similar to that described above for morning tea.

There is a separate routine around the lunch meal for children in the 3–4 room. Prior to lunch, the room leader for children in the 3–4 room asks children to sit in a circle and to join her for a set of activities. The 3–4 assembly time typically includes enacting and singing songs, a story read aloud, and finally, a song using the children's names to acknowledge who is in the room that day (as was also observed in Sweden) and to help children take turns to stand up and wash their hands. All children in the 3–4 room are then asked to make a line and walk outside the room together to gather in a dining room set up near the kitchen. Children in the 3–4 room are asked to fulfil additional responsibilities like collecting plates and cutlery, scraping and so on. For the 3–4 room, lunch is followed by an additional assembly time where all children sit down on the carpet at the centre's foyer and sing songs before returning to the room.

After lunchtime, children play for a short while and then are asked to get ready for nap time. In general, younger children are undressed by early childhood professionals who change their nappies and take them to their cots in a separate room. Older children sleep on mattresses that are set on the floor. These children need to have a quiet time on their mattresses but do not necessarily need to fall asleep. Early childhood professionals sit close to them (sometimes between the beds of the more active children) while taking observations, filling out documentation and/or planning. Children wake up or stand up after a couple of hours, get dressed and have afternoon tea. Most children are picked up soon after this meal and hence the ambience in all rooms seems to be marked by a feeling of expectation and anxiety as children start seeing their peers being picked up and wait for their own parents/guardians to arrive. Departure is always a joyful time with children showing their excitement and readiness to say good-bye and leave.

Children's Play in Three Rooms

The materials available for the children's play, the children's interaction with peers and adults, and their themes of play, varied between the three rooms studied, as is noted in this section.

Children in the 1–2 Room: Inside Play

Early childhood professionals in the 1–2 room have noticed that if the adult is present inside the room, and continues to,

> ...*keep walking about and doing things, the children, don't really sit and do much ah they follow you, but if you sit down, you can watch it if you sit down you can guarantee, they'll all go off, and play. They might come back to you but, but if you walk around and you stand there long that this is what they tend to do, they tend to sort of hover around you.* (Carla)

It was evident that the three early childhood professionals in the room have decided to stay on the floor with the children as much time as they possibly could while they were inside. It was very clear when observing the videos that most children – not all – tended to follow them around the room while they were standing up and until they sat down; they first start exploring objects that can be easily reached and finally start wondering around farther. They are, however, very attentive to any adult-initiated activity. If any of the adults brings out an object or starts a game/activity with any child, it does not take long for other – if not most – children to gather around them and start participating. This is clearly seen when,

> Christian gives Michelle a book that he has found on the floor. Michelle opens it and reads one of the words; three children turn around and start walking towards them. Christian finds his way onto Michelle's lap while the other children sit down in a circle around Michelle. Michelle has to stop reading as children continue arriving and going over others to find their way closer to the book. Michelle stops and stands up, waits for children to settle and then sits down and reads them the story.

These observations fit with Vygotsky's (1987) statement that children of this age are "constrained by what is visible only" (see Fleer, Chapter 1). Children in this room are seen moving things around the home corner and sitting for short periods of time on a small sofa; sitting around or on top of a wooden trough and throwing blocks on the floor; going through a colourful tunnel and exploring colourful objects placed on the floor or on low shelves. In sum, children used their actions to explore and used all the objects that were available to them in their environment.

There were a few episodes of imaginary play and they were all limited to the use of objects. The most common imaginary situation was done by most children in the room throughout the day and is described as undertaken by George:

> George grabs a colourful plastic telephone and places it on his left ear. He walks around the room holding the telephone in the same position. He then sits on a chair and relaxes while babbling on the phone.

Role play was also shown by different children using blankets and fabrics to cover baby dolls and walking them around the room or putting them in their cots. There was also some evidence of children bringing experiences from home and enacting them at the home corner in the centre.

In general, most children tended to explore objects and move around by themselves. This was described by most of these early childhood professionals as "solo play". However, *they will have little conversations we do see that in the 1 to 2 room occasionally where you'll see and it's really cute to see it where there cause they're at the same level and they're having a little ? (laugh) and they walk off cause they're quick. (laugh)* (Louise)

Moreover, one on one interactions between children and adults were frequently seen. Interactions usually included singing or games which involve tickling or some sort of physical play (see also, Göncü, Mistry, & Mosier, 2000)

Finally, children in this room also engaged and participated in some sporadic adult-directed games and activities. In this sense, singing, dancing and/or playing musical instruments, and reading books seemed to be the most recurrent themes. Early childhood professionals in this room seemed to be quite proud of the fact that the children of this young age could sit down and listen to stories, sometimes for a long period of time:

if we're going to have a story we all need to sit down and it's a learning experience. Um cause I've worked in other centres where you can see, oh, they don't do this, because it's a nightmare to get them all to sit down. (I-hm-hm) And so it's a beautiful thing I think C, has brought this in to us, cause C's been in the field for many many many years and um we've kind of taught M that this is a great idea [...] and it's just beautiful, because we get them all sitting and then they learn and then when they go up to the next room, [...] you just say 'okay everybody who wants a story and they just put down the things where they're supposed to be and they all come down and sit just (clicks finger) like that. (Louise)

Children in the 1–2 Room: Outside Play

When outside, the early childhood professionals in the 1–2 room,

tend to take a step back or we try, to take a step back, because we really want them, to try and, and get involved themselves we really want them to take the initiative and say '[inaudible] I'm going to do this now I'm going to do that', it's I [inaudible] really rather not want to tell them, alright you're going to play with this now because you're just wandering around but sometimes I mean they're tired or, you know just, are wandering around aimlessly so they do need that encouragement um and then that takes yeah our role is to, encourage them occasionally we'll give them two choices like we'll point to the bike or sandpit sometimes [inaudible] but sometimes they'll, they'll choose which one they want to do [inaudible] oh yeah I can do that sometimes I just need that little bit of motivation [inaudible] just like adults sometimes we think, ah, what colour am I going to write with today or anything like that you just think 'oh I don't want to think about it' and you just get someone to say 'oh just do that' oh okay yeah that's easy. (Michelle)

This meant that early childhood professionals tended to change their positioning as soon as they left the room. While inside, they tried to sit down as much as possible whereas outside they did not seem to have a preference for standing or sitting and they interacted a lot less with the children. They were observed walking around the garden with or without children, talking to each other and other workmates through the fence, sitting down by themselves and, occasionally, undertaking a special activity with children.

Similar to previous findings, children of this age continued showing their focus on objects. Hence, their actions were limited to the materials set up by teachers in this particular area and the "natural" resources of this environment. Children were seen using buckets and shovels at the sandpit, riding tricycles (definitely a favourite!), throwing and kicking plastic balls, and walking around the garden. There was however one main difference between these children's inside and outside play:

> Outside you find they don't stay around your [adults] knees so much they're all, you know off they go and they do explore much much more outside ... they probably do interact a lot more together [...] they sort of pass each other so they actually, interact a lot more (Carla-okay) when they're outside and even in the sandpit they do, they do interact with each other more outside than inside. [...] (Carla)

It was no surprise that a few imitative play episodes were observed. One of them is described below.

> Illana lays down on the sandpit and stays still. A boy arrives and lays down beside her. They both smile and giggle. Illana moves her upper body up and the boy copies her. They laugh and lay down again. The boy moves upwards and Illana copies. They giggle again and continue doing this for a short while.

Finally, although adults tended to step back while playing outside, there were some adult-directed activities. In one of them

> Carla starts marching over the bridge and children start following her. Carla goes around and tells them what to do. She goes over some tyres that she uses as obstacles and encourages the children to copy her. She goes back to the bridge and continues marching. Eventually, most children from the room are following her. Carla stops marching when children start moving away.

Children in the 2–3 Room

The early childhood professionals in this room chose to play outside most of the day while the observations were being filmed. There were therefore only a few episodes to analyse inside this room.

Different from the 1–2 room explained above, early childhood professionals in this room were seen moving around (e.g. organizing the room, setting up materials on table, etc.) the room without needing to sit down close to the children for them to start exploring or engaging in play. Early childhood professionals seemed to act as facilitators of activities. They described themselves as

> ...well, sometimes we call ourselves teachers, sometimes because... hmm, to be there I suppose to support and assist when they need it and to extend their learning when needed. Often, asking open ended questions, spontaneous singing, spontaneous planning of objects, of what they are doing, actions, that sort of thing. So there is a support sort of person for the day. Does that make sense? (Aimee)

Some imaginary play episodes with objects occurred, mainly in the home corner. One example is described below:

> Justin moves around the home corner and grabs some kitchen utensils. He puts something in the oven and waits until it is ready. He takes it out and gives it to a friend that is passing by. He goes back to the oven and makes sure that it is empty.

Role play was only observed once inside the room when one of the target children imitated an adult (a mother) when waking one of her friends up after sleep time at the Centre. This same episode could act as evidence of children bringing experiences from home and enacting them at the centre, as the child adopted the role of a mother waking her child up by saying "It's time to wake up!" and then saying "Do you want mummy?" and moving closer saying "it's OK, you are OK" when she notices that her friend looks sad.

Adult–child interactions were not observed inside the room and only one adult-directed activity took place:

> N calls the children and tells them that she is going to play some music so that they can all sing and dance. The children gather in the middle room and look at her. The music starts and N begins to sing. The children sing along and dance. N claps her hands and moves around. The children follow.

Children in the 2–3 Room: Outside Play

Similar to the early childhood professionals in the 1–2 room, staff in the 2–3 room were observed walking around the garden with or without children, talking to each other and other workmates, and sitting down outside. They were also seen undertaking small group activities and very rarely, leading a special activity for a big group of children.

When outside, children in this age group continued showing their preference for using objects for playing. Therefore, their most common activities were based on the use of the materials set up by the early childhood professionals: one swing, one ladder, one wooden obstacle course, buckets, shovels and a pretend oven in the sand pit, and tricycles (a big favourite among children in the 2–3 room as it was for children in the 1–2 room). Similar to children in the 1–2 room, most of the children in this room tended to manipulate and explore objects. However, a significant amount of the observations in this room showed a more complex play taking place; there were more social play episodes than in the 1–2 room and frequent nonliteral ("as if") situations where children brought imagination and imitation into their play were observed. Therefore, in contrast with Vygotsky's writing and our observations of the children in the 1–2 room, 2–3 year old children were capable of using imaginary situations in their play.

Some of the imaginary situations observed included a child skiing (putting a pretend seat belt on and then "skiing" around the sand pit saying "ski, ski…" and singing some songs), children making a cake out of sand and singing happy birthday, and many episodes of role play. One of the episodes of role play that is worth mentioning was undertaken by Tara:

> Tara is playing on the short obstacle course with Justin. Tara walks from one side to the other and Justin lies on one side. Justin pretends he is falling down and asks Tara for help. Tara starts saying "coming, coming" as she balances along. She holds Justin's hands and pulls him. They both smile. Tara then decides to act as the mum. She tells Justin that mum is going to work and that she will be back soon. She continues balancing. She comes back to where Justin is and pulls his hands again. She then tells Justin to stay there because

she is going to work and will come back later. She grabs a tricycle and rides away saying "good-bye, mummy going work".

This and other episodes showed how children brought ideas from home into their play at the centre. Another good example is described by an early childhood professional:

> Tara was pretending to talk to mum and dad and talk about them, about going to the shops to buy watermelon, hmmm... and the way I've liaise this to the home is that I have noticed her mum sometimes says they often go to Safeway on the way home to buy something, she really loves going to Safeway. So I think that's where it is coming to her play there. (Aimee)

Throughout the day children in the 2–3 room imitated each other doing different activities (e.g. riding the tricycle and stopping behind the child that "leads" at certain places, following another child on the obstacle course, running behind each other and so on). These children seemed to enjoy each other's company and seemed more curious about each other's actions than in the children observed in the 1–2 room. This was acknowledged by the early childhood professionals working in this room who said that children were starting to interact with each other a lot more. They therefore included labels like "parallel play" and "cooperative play" while describing the children's play. In general, they labelled episodes where children were "doing their own things" (Aimee) as "solo play" and episodes where they were "chatting and interacting with [another friend] but just more playing and allowing [the friend] to follow [them] around" (Aimee) as "parallel play"; they also mentioned some short instances of cooperative play (as on the episode where Tara pushed a boy on the swing) to describe the times when "they designate some roles and role playing, maybe turn taking if you are lucky, that sort of thing which is more the cooperative play." (Aimee)

In sum, there seemed to be visible differences in the amount of imaginary play situations observed and the duration of these episodes when comparing 1–2 year olds and 2–3 year olds. This was explained by an early childhood professional from the 1–2 room who has recently moved to the 2–3 room and has noted the following differences in the children's play:

> Ahh probably a lot a lot more role playing going on in the [2 to 3] room. Where they're like, they'll get a horse and go 'ddddd' and put them together and make little voices, because they're more vocal than cause we do, like, [inaudible](7.27) whereas this age group [1 to 2] they tend to bang things and knock things over and, and they [...] lose interest very quickly and will move to the next whereas in the 2 to 3 room they can stay with something a lot longer (I-okay) and get more intense in what they're doing. (Louise)

Early childhood professionals were not seen having many one-on-one interactions with children outside. If they were interacting with children, they were usually with at least two children at the same time. They generally listened to the children and let them choose what they were doing and how. They asked questions and tried to have conversations with them. However, there were a couple of episodes where adults either initiated or directed the children's play. One involved a pair of children and an adult. The adult was seen helping Tara settle down inside the room and then having a short conversation on the veranda. The adult (Danielle) told Tara to go to the sandpit with her to bake cookies. They walked together and sat down near each other. Justin was already sitting at the sandpit and observed what they were doing. Danielle directed Tara into mixing the ingredients in a plastic bowl, making the shapes and putting them in the oven. Tara followed her directions while Justin continued observing. Tara put the biscuits in the oven and started pushing buttons and saying "not ready yet". Suddenly, she opened the oven door and brought the biscuits out. Danielle told her that they were hot and they both blew. Justin blew as well. Danielle asked questions about the biscuits' flavour and about the people they were going to share them with. Tara gave Danielle a biscuits and offered Justin some too. They all smiled and the children giggled.

Children in the 3–4 Room: Inside Play

Similar to early childhood professionals in the 1–2 room, staff in the 3–4 room stated that

> when you sit down with the children, they tend to gravitate to you, um if you, want them to engage in construction play then all you have to do is sit down in the construction area and, start making something and they'll all come over. (Joanna)

However, staff in the 1–2 room seemed to prefer sitting down in order to help the children settle, relax and to facilitate the children's engagement in play, whereas staff in the 3–4 room seemed to selectively choose to join or gather a group of children in specific activities and used conversations and/or actions to help them focus, prolong their play and extend their thinking. This was described by the room's leader in the following way:

> ...my role just by being there is just to encourage them, really to stay at what they're doing, and um, you know praise them for you know for what they've made or, you know encourage them to talk about what they're doing or what they're making or whether they can make it a little bit different if it's not working, ah we'll try it this way. [...] your presence helps them to focus on what they're doing, and your encouragement tends to maybe, um, push them a little bit further to actually making something and actually finishing, what they're making rather than, um just have a fiddle and move away. (Joanna)

Although this could be interpreted to suggest that these early childhood professionals get involved and direct children's play, she clearly clarified that she sits just for

> ...encouraging the different things that are happening, um you know just extending on, um what a child is saying or doing but, I very much tend to just, sit back and it's more encouragement rather than, you know saying 'you do this, you do that' or 'try this, try that' it's just, going with the flow like you know trying to extend maybe their language encouraging them to talk about what they've made or what they're doing, or, what they're thinking about when they're making it. (Joanna)

The use of objects continued being important for this age group. Yet, objects did not appear to be used for manipulation or exploration (like in the 1–2 and 2–3 rooms); they were used in a more creative and complex manner. Blocks and colorful plastic shapes were used to construct fences or zoos for toy animals, as well as for building tall towers. Kitchen sets in the home corner were used for having pretend meals, tea, etc. with a group of friends or with toys. Play dough was used to make monsters, to pretend to share chocolate with friends, to make fossils or to hide objects (e.g. shells or marbles) inside. Headphones were used to listen to music and the activity usually motivated children to sing, dance, shake their hands and/or imitate other children who were doing the same activity. Finally, books were selected by children who tended to sit down on a small sofa to "read" by or to other children.

One early childhood professional provided some ideas about why the children's play might have been different for this age group. She mentioned that children's play becomes more complex as they get older and also the fact that children this age are able to "distinguish between fact and fantasy". In addition, although the early childhood professional did not explicitly link her approach to planning to the changes in children's play, the way that they play in this room could be a consequence of the importance she attributed to open ended activities and the value that she seemed to give to children's free choices. In her own words,

> . . .*some people believe that you have to leave the same activity in the same place, you know especially when they've got part time children so they know it's there, it's familiar and they can go to it but I find that children become bored with that. So I'm constantly moving things around, and rather than put out, ah for instance you know play dough and shells and cutters and things, I've just got a shelf with, a lot of open ended things, so the children have, they've got an activity like play dough or something, but they've got a hundred different things they can use with it. It's more letting them have the choice rather than putting an activity out, there's lots of shelves with, different things and they can go to that and choose [. . .]* (Joanna)

Children in this room brought many of their ideas for play from home. According to the room leader,

> *a lot of our play in the room is dramatic play and a lot of it is actually um home type play and that's why we have the room setup the way we do. With the home corner, table chairs, the stove, dolls cradles, blankets because this is what the children are so interested in, playing. They're playing out things that they see happening at home.* (Joanna)

A good example of their use of the home corner for dramatic play was undertaken by Marie,

> Marie plays with a toy that she has brought from home. She gives it cuddles and kisses. She moves to the home corner and gets a chair. She moves the chair and sits her toy on top. She places the chair right in front of the camera. She then gets a plastic cup and pretends to pour something in it. She places the cup on her toy's mouth and waits for it to drink. She looks at the camera and smiles.

One-on-one adult–child interactions were not observed inside or outside the room. Interactions with small groups were frequently seen inside the room. Evidently, following their idea – explained above – of encouraging and extending specific activities, early childhood professionals were seen sitting down with small groups of children and talking to them.

Adult-directed activities occurred at least twice per day when the room leader would have an assembly time with all the children present in the room. These happened before and after meal times and were described in the section entitled "daily routine".

Children in the 3–4 Room: Outside Play

Similar to the early childhood professionals in the other rooms, adults in the 3–4 room were rarely observed interacting with children. In this room, adult–child interactions were only seen when children asked an adult for help to do something or approached an adult to ask questions.

Differently from the previous rooms, children in this age group did not use many objects when playing outside. The only objects they were seen using were (a) a kitchen set and dining room placed near the sand pit, (b) shovels in the sandpit, (c) two swings and (d) tricycles. Parallel to what was said when describing their inside play, these children used these objects for far more than exploration and manipulation. Kitchen sets were used for preparing meals and eating; shovels were used as tools for filling the pots and kettles; swings encouraged conversations about who should push who and how they could use swings in different ways; and tricycles were used accompanied by sound effects (as if they were pretending to ride a motorbike or car).

Children were mainly seen undertaking physical play (e.g. running, chasing each other, jumping, etc.) or involved in imaginary play situations. One interesting imaginary play episode was undertaken by Ellen:

> Ellen is walking on the wooden bridge. She is singing while walking. All of a sudden she starts hopping. She places her hand on "someone's body" and says "hop, bunny, hop". She continues saying "hop, hop" and talks about her friend the bunny. She smiles and looks quite happy. She does this a few times until she is interrupted by Christine. Ellen stops.

Role play was also seen on various occasions. Children pretended to be animals, family members, babies and even doctors.

In general, most of the prior examples revealed how children brought ideas from home – and from previous experiences – into their play at the Centre. Another amusing example of how a child might play with her dad at home was played out by Ellen and Christine:

> Ellen and Christine are walking around the garden. Christine starts running and Ellen chases her. Christine starts running in circles on a wooden structure that surrounds a tree. Ellen starts saying "I love you daddy, I love you!" and continues chasing her. Christine laughs and runs faster. Ellen laughs and continues pretending that she is chasing daddy.

Children in this age-group spent a lot more time with peers than in previously described groups. They seemed to use their language and social skills to communicate with each other. Problem solving and stronger concepts of both responsibility and respect for each other were apparent. It is no surprise then that the words like communication and social skills were frequently mentioned by the early childhood professionals in this room. It is also no surprise that cooperative play was heard more often than solitary or parallel play. However, it is important to mention that the early childhood professional who participated in the study from this room, did not use these labels for play (solo, parallel and cooperative) as much as the staff from the 1–2 and 2–3 room. She preferred using labels like creative play, social play, dramatic, role or pretend play, constructive play and physical play. When asked about her ideas on cooperative play, she explained:

> *Each child will go through different stages but, from my experience um, they say that certain play will start happening at certain ages or stages of development but I've actually seen, babies, who are playing cooperatively they're interacting, will be doing the same thing they're mirroring each others, actions and they're laughing together. So that to me is more and that's a stage so that's more a associative or cooperative play but they say babies don't do that, but that happens later on um when they get to you know the three to five age group. [...] I also see kinder age children who are mostly engaged, still just in solitary play too. That's just their preference and that's um, their characters that they acquire to children who become very engrossed in what they're doing and perhaps they want others, to share in their play. So it's it's, the categories are there, because it makes it easier for us to say this is the stage of play but it's varying for each child. It's the categories are very general but, every child is very individual.* (Joanna)

In sum, there were evident differences between children's play in the three rooms studied. It seems clear that some of the differences were related with the children's age. However, we can also identify clear links between the materials available to children, the early childhood professionals' approaches to play and pedagogy, and the children's experiences in the outside world, to both the themes and types of social interactions that the children engaged in.

How the Teachers Talked About Play

The teachers who participated in this study used a range of terms to describe the play in their centres. For instance, they referred to: pretend play, creative play, fantasy play, role play, social play, constructive play, cooperative play, solitary play, onlooker play and dramatic play. When viewing the video recordings of the focus child in their centre, the teachers tended to analyse the activities of the children in relation to these categories of play. For example:

> *(Child in a swing) I would say mostly imaginative play. Possibly a bit of role-play as well, she might have been mimicking someone pushing the swing but mostly solo play. She was playing her own way, aware of the others around her but mostly on her own. The second one (Bike riding with Ja) is a bit more of parallel play. She was chatting and interacting with Ja but she was just more playing and allowing him to follow her around* (Aimee).

Although not stated, many of the categories of play used by the teachers can be directly linked to the theories of Parten and Piaget. All the teachers indicated that they had gained these insights in relation to analysing play from their previous education undertaken at TAFE institutes. For example,

> *I went to TAFE, during my studies... we were taught there was solitary play, um which it tended to be younger, the younger children ...because they play on their own, they do interact with other children but they tend not to, you know, build together or they're quite young so that seems to be the younger, and then they, as they get older they advance to parallel play which is, say two children, both playing in the home corner, but just next to each other. They're both stirring in a pot or they're both um sitting building with blocks but they're not actually, playing together they're not building together they're not talking*

together, they're just next to each other but, they've got to that stage where, that's okay, they don't need, cause when they're younger they just want to run away from them and they want their own space. So parallel play is where, they've advanced to being next to each other being able to play side by side, and then the cooperative play, as they get older again, they're able to, sit down and do a box together or cook in the home corner and hand someone a plate and you know and pretend they're in bed or and things like that things that take cooperation or, sometimes sharing things like that tends to be, um a few children interacting together, in what whatever they're doing. So, yeah got I got that one from TAFE that was what we were taught (I-hm-hm) yep (Michelle).

The teachers had a great capacity of easily and quickly identifying how children were playing in their centres, using these categories to discuss play. However, teachers also found the categories limiting at times, and developed their own categories for labelling the activities of the children. For example, Michelle found that many of her children liked to repeat the things they were saying or doing.

Um, experiment it was a I made that up. That was a thought that came into my head at the time. Um, and the repit repetition that was just, the word I chose to describe, yep yeah both of them I just chose and the dramatic play is something that we we learnt at TAFE as well, a way to categorise, different sorts of play (Michelle).

Similarly, teachers also found that they blurred categories together at times, as a child moved from one type of play into the next and back. Children would be playing by themselves, but would also be relating to a child at a distance, through known and established play patterns. For example, one child was separated from her play partner, when she moved to another room (due to her age). When she was in the outdoor area, she would move around the boundary of the fence, seemingly playing by herself. However, she would periodically look over the fence and make contact with her play partner. This would occur through gestures, eye contact, passing leaves through the fence, or simply calling out sounds that were known to her and her play partner. These expansive play sessions were difficult to categorize by the teachers using traditional labels.

Some of the activities of the infants and toddlers were much harder to discuss in relation to play. For instance, many of the toddlers climbed onto the construction table (which had a lip on it to hold in the pieces and toddlers), and systematically dropped the Lego pieces behind the table.

Um, (pause) um that's, I don't know that's kind of difficult to say because, (pause) I don't know it's, (pause) I I really couldn't label it I wouldn't know how to label it because it's just, (pause) I don't know it's strange, just throwing blocks I, yeah wouldn't quite know how to label it (Michelle).

Contrary to Parten's theory of play, where she suggested that children under the age of three engage in solitary or parallel play, the teachers spoke at length about predominance of fantasy play in their centres. For example,

Joanna: *Each child will go through different stages but, from my experience um, they say that certain play will start happening at certain ages or stages of development but I've actually seen, babies, who are playing cooperatively they're interacting, will be doing the same thing they're mirroring each others, actions and they're laughing together. So that to me is more and that's a stage so that's more a associative or cooperative play but they say*

babies don't do that, but that happens later on um when they get to you know the three to
five age group.
Interviewer: *Yes but through experience you've seen it happening before?*
Joanna: *It can happen earlier and I also see kinder age children who are mostly engaged,*
still just in solitary play too. That's just their preference and that's um, their characters that
they acquire to children who become very engrossed in what they're doing and perhaps they
want others, to share in their play. So it's it's, the categories are there, because it makes it
easier for us to say this is the stage of play but it's varying for each child. It's it's the
categories are very general but, every child is very individual.

Although the teachers clearly understood that Parten's theory of play was age based, and on the whole they supported this perspective, they did cite many examples of fantasy play and cooperative play. This is consistent with earlier research undertaken by Fleer (cited in Dockett & Fleer, 1999) who also found many instances in her sample set of children aged 2–3 years, engaging in elaborate group fantasy play (with and without objects to support them). It is also consistent with work by Howes and colleagues who found that Parten's categories were limiting in the views of children's social development that they allowed (for a review, see Howes & Tonyan, 1999).

Collectively, the teachers drew upon scientific knowledge about play that they had acquired through their early childhood education. In this particular sample, all the teachers had TAFE qualifications, and the standard curriculum for TAFE courses for some time now in Australia has been to introduce Parten's theory of play to students in order to support them with understanding the nature of play in early childhood education. Similarly, most TAFE courses have modules in child development which feature Piaget's stages of development (among others), and in many cases students are introduced to the Piaget's writings on play. The findings of this study demonstrate that the teachers drew upon their scientific knowledge to observe, analyse and talk about the activities of infants and toddlers in their centres.

What the Teachers Valued

In analysing the videotapes of their focus child in their centre, the teachers expressed particular beliefs and perspectives that are dominant in Australian early childhood education (Fleer & Richardson, 2004a). In particular, teachers discussed common assumptions about observing and programming for young children. For instance, all of the teachers discussed identifying and following the children's interests. For example,

I take everything from their interests, hmmm, whether it be something that they've been
talking about at home, something that they bring into the centre if they have seen trucks
working at the street or something, hmmm, we take it from there. We see the tractors a lot
so quite often we'll have the trucks and stuff out to play with (Aimee).

The teachers also spoke about the importance of not interfering in children's play, describing their role in facilitating and extending children's play. They supported the concept of "self learning" (Joanna), as this example illustrates:

Um I'd still say it's very much, um using, the environment, um to facilitate self education, by setting the environment up in such a way that the children are, engaged, with the environment and engaged with each other according to their interests and according to their interpretations of how they want to use the materials they've got. So I'm just really the facilitator, I'm, having to do a good job of, of observing what, their interests are, and then facilitating the play based on that and that's something that changes, all the time but some things remain constant like the interest in family play, the interest in role play um, there's a constant interest in in animals. [...] I'm, sort of, setting things up so that they're learning. It's self learning but there's some core learning too. Um there's a core curriculum where I think children need to learn about, um, for instance nature (Joanna).

In this example, it is also possible to see the importance of organizing the environment to match the children's developmental level. This orientation to learning is a characteristic of Piaget's theory, and is consistent with the education that these teachers had before graduating as early childhood professionals. The focus on providing a range of appropriate materials, which match developmental levels, is dominant in many early childhood centres in Australia. However, alternative perspectives are also evident and being supported (e.g. see Anning et al., 2004; Fleer, 2005, 2006).

Teachers also valued programming that was based on close observations of the children, particularly in relation to the interests they displayed. This approach to planning in common in Australia, and supported by many Government documents and staff responsible for leadership (see Fleer & Richardson, 2004a, b, c). This orientation to planning has fostered the proliferation of the programme content which features child-oriented themes and materials and play practices well known to children, as illustrated below:

I think of it as very spontaneous, coming from the children, like I said earlier, I take my program planning from observations on the children, what they are interested in, to challenge with some things as well, and take everything from the children, ... I would say that about play. It is really hard when you try to put into words because you just do it and you don't often think about definitions (Aimee).

Sitting behind the play-based programmes operating in the centres was also a commitment to valuing the general routines in the centre as places for supporting learning. The teachers spoke about the importance of routines operating in the centre. Although play was important for supporting learning, they also felt that there were many structured times and routines that equally supported learning and should not be lost when thinking about the experiences of infants and toddlers.

... I'm seeing that they're learning through things other than just play, they're learning through routine, um they're learning through structured activities like reading a story, um but play is more self guided, um a story is something that, it's set it's there, it's not something that they're making up as they go along. Um routine times like sitting down and having afternoon tea or morning tea, um alright they're learning social skills they're learning to talk to tell people what they'd like they're learning to make choices but, play is something that's more self guided (Joanna).

This teacher saw play as being a kind of self-guided practice, which contrasts with the nature of routines and structured activities, such as story time or small group time. Teachers also noted play activities that supported learning that they valued, such as self-reliance, independence, and individual learning.

> (self reliance)...*for her to be able to just, go around and play on her own and just talk to herself amuse herself without, needing that adult, to constantly be going 'oh yeah' you know 'good job' and, that constantly needing that adult to talk to* (Michelle).
> (rather than saying) ...*alright we're going to do this, we're going to do that' just standing back, watching, the way they play and the way they're interacting and if they need exten-sional help then, you go and and um you extend on their play* (Joanna).
> (independence)...*it is important to be able to, be okay with playing on your own, to be okay with that to not, need, an adult stimulation, all the time constantly they need to be able to amuse, themselves, and, yeah I just I think that that independence* (Michelle).

Interestingly though, one teacher also spoke about the importance of fitting into the group.

> ...*although she's an individual she's still a part of the group and she's learning to ask for what she wants* (Joanna).

Staff noted that because they had video recordings of the toddlers to view, they had noticed a significant amount of group interaction not normally visible. For instance, one staff member commented on the amount of talk and interaction there was be-tween toddlers. Because staff are usually focussed on the group as a whole, the video tapes (taken from a focus child's perspective), gave staff insights into playing and interacting in the centre, they had not previously had access to before.

Connections Between Home and Centre

Whilst teachers reported planning for children's play and learning based on chil-dren's interests, the staff relied mostly on what they observed in the centre. Many structural issues (e.g. long hours, limited child-free planning time, low salaries, small centre budgets for resources and consumables, such as photographs) pre-vent close communications between home and centre contexts, despite statements about the importance of family involvement prevalent in Australia (Hughes & MacNaughton, 2000). For example,

> *We try to communicate as much as possible with them (parents). Sometimes you don't phys-ically have the time to chat with them because you are trying to supervise children. There's only so much you can get to know about* (Aimee).

Close observations of the children provided the best means for connecting with the children's play experiences, or gaining better understandings of the children's lives, so as to better understand the play activities of the children.

The age of the children also provided a further challenge for staff focussing on children's interests, as noted by one staff member:

> *And home yeah definitely, definitely because you know they, they come in and tell us every-thing cause obviously the children aren't quite up to talking, not yeah, although the children do come in and, and, do like Imogen will sing songs 'Hey di ho', one of the songs she sings at home we don't sing here, but she comes in, and holds my hands and tries to sing the song with me. So that's something that I've picked up obviously she's got that from home or, or*

from somewhere outside the centre so that then gives me the? to go and ask mum 'oh what's this about'. So even if the parents don't come to us? sometimes the children will do things that will make us think oh, maybe something, you know they've learnt that at home so then we can ask the parents and they can extend on, what the children have started (Michelle).

Due to limited resources in many centres, information flow tends to move from the families to the staff.

Yeah... It's hard. Because we don't see them in the home, we only know what the parents tell us, the information they tell us. They might tell us if they played with other children, family visits, that sort of thing (Aimee).

Although staff supported close family–centre links, they had no formal structures in place to facilitate a dialogical relationship with families. Staff had to mostly guess or make assumptions about the children's play activities at home. They had no way of easily confirming or obtaining elaborated information about, the particular play activities of the children exhibited in the home.

The Findings of this Study Within the Context of Other Empirical Australian Studies

We had very limited Australian research to draw upon in interpreting our findings. Only two studies, both doctoral theses, generated empirical evidence about the play of children of 2–3 years old. One of those studies examined the effects of play with children of the same age or of a different age by video recording play in structured observation sessions (i.e. selected dyads were removed from their ongoing centre activity for a videotaping session) and will not be reviewed here because the play observed and conclusions drawn bear little relation to our current research that examined play in naturalistic settings of home and centre (Kowalski, 2000). The other study, a doctoral thesis conducted by Strinovich (2002), examined peer interaction in unstructured situations. Although the focus of the thesis was on examining differences in behaviour across mixed-age and same-age classrooms and comparing 2- and 3-year-old children, we can draw some parallels with our own research. Strinovich identified "functional play", "symbolic play" and conversation as the main activities of both 2- and 3-year olds when playing with same-age peers.

One study, described by Piscitelli (1992) examined the play of children slightly older than those in our research, but was conducted in a manner similar to our work. As described by Piscitelli, a practitioner working in the Australian Capital Territory, Barbara Creaser, described three styles of play – dramatists, explorers and spectators – but suggested that children tended to show elements of each style of play rather than fit neatly into categories of play. This teacher's view of play based on her practitioner research parallels nicely with many of the views articulated by early childhood professionals in our research that children tended to quickly shift between categories of play and seldom fit neatly into the categories that they had available to them to describe play. Certainly, the terms for these three styles of play from Creaser's work fit with many of the play episodes described above and so are not solely the play of preschool-age children. Piscitelli lists dramatists play as involving pretend, imagination, divergent thinking, drama and creation. Pretend, imaginative, and dramatic play were all terms used by teachers, particularly in describing the play of children in the 2–3 and 3–4 rooms. Similarly, investigation and building, two of the descriptors for Creaser's explorers' play were also commonly used by teachers in our study.

Another study examining the play of preschool-age children, from 49 to 64 months, classified children's play using a time-sampled observational scheme (Wyver & Spence, 1995). The authors of this study videotaped and then classified children's play in 60-s intervals according to type of play ("nonplay", exploration, physical, constructive, object-dependent pretend, sociodramatic pretend and thematic pretend). The most frequent types of play they observed, physical, constructive, object-dependent pretend (i.e. pretend play that revolves around the features of the objects included in the game, like "eating from toy crockery", p. 44) and sociodramatic pretend (i.e. acting out situations from "everyday life", like "pretending to be parents") were among the kinds of play we observed as well.

We also found little empirical evidence gathered in Australia regarding either parents' or teachers' views of play. One study examined Indigenous parents' views of play and found that the participants reported strongly valuing play, with almost 70% of respondents reporting that they believed play was "totally important", with the remaining parents reporting that they believed play was "very important" or "important" (Windisch, Jenvey, & Drysdale, 2003).

However, many papers made reference to the importance of play for early childhood professionals in Australia (Mallan, 1998; Windisch et al., 2003; Cooper & Sutton, 1999; Piscitelli, 1992). Another author, Helen Hedges (2000), writing from New Zealand to professionals and researchers in an Australian journal, described what she saw as the traditional view of play dominant in early childhood and suggested some possible alternatives. Hedges (2000) described what she called a "traditional, Piagetian" play-based view of learning in early childhood as "learning through play" and argued that teachers develop an alternative view of play as "teaching through play" that involves a greater role for teachers based on concepts of scaffolding, guided participation (expert guiding novice, with novice actively involved), and co-construction (together creating new knowledge).

Taken together, then, our research fits with existing Australian research in important ways, but extends that research by including naturalistic observation of children's play, by better capturing the changing and dynamic nature of young children's play and by examining teachers' views of young children's play.

Conclusion

Teachers' Views About Play

In this study we analysed the play in relation to Rogoff's three foci of analysis and found that many personal, interpersonal and institutional or cultural dimensions were being foregrounded in the teachers' views about play in the Australian centre.

Personal Focus of Analysis

In brief, our analysis of our interviews with teachers suggest that these teachers were using the scientific knowledge commonly taught in teachers' accreditation programmes to observe, analyse and talk about the children's activities. We could trace many of their ideas back to the terminology and theories of Parten and Piaget. The limitations of these theoretical perspectives have been widely discussed in the research literature about children's play (e.g. Howes, 1987; Howes & Matheson, 1992). It was interesting to note that these teachers articulated their frustration with these same limitations at times blurring categories or at times creating new ones in order to describe children's play.

Interpersonal Focus of Analysis

Adults in all rooms emphasized the importance of providing freedom of choice and not directing children's play, although the extent to which this articulated belief and adults' behaviour is not entirely clear: some adult-direction was observed in each room. There appeared to be consistency in the articulated discourse surrounding adults' roles, but possible inconsistency in enacted behaviour. This seems to reflect a common pattern at least among early childhood professionals in Victoria, Australia (Rivalland, 2005). For example, adults seemed to be more the focal point and were likely to be involved in one-on-one interactions with the younger children than with the older children, particularly indoors. This apparent shift in the adults' roles relative to the children seems to correspond to the adults' perceptions that older children were more likely to be involved in sustained peer interaction.

Institutional or Cultural Focus of Analysis

Our analyses of the teachers' responses also suggest that these teachers valued a core set of early childhood practices similar to those identified in previous research with Australian/Victorian teachers: identifying and following children's interests, not interfering in children's play, organizing the environment to match the children's developmental level, programming based on close observations of the children, particularly their interests, using routine times and activities to support children's ability to practice and consolidate what they are learning.

In addition, one goal of this research was to examine the connections between play at home and in the centre as a basis for understanding how children's everyday and scientific concept formation might be best supported in play. Interestingly, despite the fairly consistent discourse among the teachers emphasizing the importance of sharing information between the home and centre, the teachers articulated significant barriers in doing so. As a result, they were often left to guess or make assumptions about children's home lives. The most common recognition of the ways in which home life was "brought in" to the centre were in identifying themes of pretend play most likely observed at home as children do not participate in those activities at the centre (e.g. home routines like cooking or caring for babies).

Observations of Children's Activity and Play

In sum, this research suggests some conclusions regarding the ways in which the children's daily activities and general routines were organized, patterns of children's activity, and adults roles in that activity.

Chaiklin (2006) has defined practice as "a collective, historically-developed, societally-organised, usually institutionalised, tradition of acting that aims to produce objects that seek to satisfy societally-generated needs". There were many aspects of a recognizable cultural form of early childhood practice that we see as representing common ways of organizing care in Australia and beyond. Across all age groups, children experienced a balance of time for choosing among a variety of activities available to them and regular, routine group activities like meal times, reading activities, and nap times. Similarly, adults alternated between taking the role of facilitator during most of their time, including facilitating shifts to group, routine activities to which many of the children were quite accustomed, to taking more of the role of director or guide in occasional adult-directed activity.

In addition, there were some variations across the three rooms observed that reflect a sample of the ways in which individuals and groups adapt this cultural form based on particular circumstances. For example, adults in the 1–2 room tended to play a focal role in the youngest children's play, but this is also the room in which the teachers did not really comment on the materials available to children or the activities organized for children. Similarly, it was also in the rooms for the younger children (both 1–2 and 2–3) that we observed more one-on-one interactions with adults. By contrast, in the room including children 3–4 years old, adults tended to engage with small groups of children and were seldom seen interacting one-on-one and one teacher commented on the importance of having a variety of materials available to children to facilitate their play.

We noticed some patterns in the children's activity. Some of these trends, particularly when read in relation to developmental literature about play, seem likely to reflect common developmental patterns observed in early childhood settings. Across all three rooms, children were observed regularly bringing experiences from home into their play in the centre. These tended to take the form of enacted scripts (e.g. "mixing" ingredients as in a kitchen at home) for children in the 1–2 and 2–3 rooms, but were more elaborated and included more language in the 3–4 room. Such a pattern fits with previous research examining developmental trends in young children's pretend play (e.g. Howes & Matheson, 1992). Similarly, we saw differences in children's play with objects across the three rooms. Objects were more prevalent, more central in children's play in the 1–2 and 2–3 rooms than they were in the 3–4 room. We did observe some imaginative play with objects in all the rooms, however, children seemed to be less constricted by the characteristics of the objects in the rooms including more older children: children in the 1–2 room were observed most often in manipulative play with objects, whereas children in the 2–3 room were observed in more imaginary role play using features of objects and children in the 3–4 room used objects in more creative and complex ways, including more elaborate construction and pretend play involving more complex, extended language with peers. In addition, the children in the 3–4 room seemed less bound in their pretend play to the features of the object, engaging in more pretend play without objects. Again, these patterns in both use of objects and the emergence of more language and less object-defined play fit with existing developmental literature examining children's play (Howes & Stewart, 1987).

Other trends observed seem likely related to the ways in which the different rooms were organized and differences in how adults were interacting with children in the different rooms, but it is difficult to disentangle whether these also reflect changes in children's capacities or commonly held assumptions about those changing capabilities, as evidenced in teachers' articulated views about the children's activities.

Overall Conclusions

As described in the Introduction, Australia is currently witnessing changes in the discourses surrounding early childhood education (Edwards, 2003a, 2003b; Fleer & Robbins, 2003; Fleer, 1992, 2002). Practitioners and academics alike are reconsidering previously accepted ways of doing things through programme development and writing. However, accreditation processes and other 'regulating discourses' continue to limit the kinds of conversations to be had around play (Ailwood, 2003). One thing that these results highlight for us is the fact that not everyone participates in those conversations.

As Ailwood (2003) writes, "[a] whole language has been created for describing the play of young children... Such a language enables the rationalizing of play – rendering play workable, knowable, and practical" (p. 295). Our results suggest that these teachers are quite fluent at speaking the language of play prevalent in early childhood, but that they also struggle with the limitations of and sometimes resist that language as well. The current professional climate includes few supports, particularly institutionalized supports, for ongoing professional conversations over time or for such reconsideration. Professionals working in childcare centres, spend up to 8 hours day^{-1} with children, and if in a richly resourced centre may have up to 2 hours week^{-1} to write up observations, develop their programmes, or liaise with other professionals (inside or outside the centre).

Recent political and policy writings have argued for more "joined up" policies wherein people working with children would work in interdisciplinary teams. Such trends would likely open up disciplinary languages to many more voices and discourses, but it is not clear what conditions will be necessary to ensure that languages do not simply become more entrenched. Similarly, examining structural barriers between home and centre discourses about children's activities and play in order to bring discourse about home-centre communication closer to reality could open up other new and exciting ways of informing early childhood practice.

Acknowledgments funding from the Faculty of Education, Monash University, provided some support for this project, with the remainder of the costs being provided by funds generated by Marilyn Fleer's consultancy activities. Carol Linney transcribed the video and audio-tapes that were generated by this project.

References

Ailwood, J. (2003). Governing early childhood education through play. *Contemporary Issues in Early Childhood, 4*, 286–299.

Anning, A., Cullen, J., & Fleer, M. (2004). (Eds.), *Early childhood education: Society and culture* (226 pages). London: Sage Publications.

Australian Government. (2003). Responses to *Towards a National Agenda for Early Childhood* Commonwealth Task Force on Child Development, Health and Wellbeing, ACT.

Blaise, M. (2005). *Playing it straight! Uncovering gender discourses in the early childhood classroom.* New York: Routledge Press, UK.

Bredekamp, S. (1987). *Developmentally appropriate practice in early childhood education programs. Serving children from Birth through Age 8.* Washington, DC: National Association for the Education of Young Children.

Bredekamp, S., & Copple, C. (1997). *Developmentally appropriate practice in early childhood education programs* (Rev. ed). Washington, DC: National Association for the Education of Young Children.

Chaiklin, S. (2006). Practice-developing research: Introduction to a future science. Manuscript under review.

Clyde, M. (1995). Concluding the debate: Mind games – what DAP means to me. In M. Fleer (Ed.), *DAPcentrism: Challenging developmentally appropriate practices.* ACT: Australian Early Childhood Association.

Cooper, R., & Sutton, K. (1999). The effects of child abuse on preschool children's play. *Australian Journal of Early Childhood, 24,* 10–14.

Cross, T. (1995). The early childhood curriculum debate. In M. Fleer (Ed.), *DAPcentrism: Challenging developmentally appropriate practices.* ACT: Australian Early Childhood Association.

Dahlberg, G., Moss, P., & Pence, A. (1999). *Beyond quality in early childhood education and care. Postmodern Perspectives.* London, Great Britain: Falmer Press.

Daniels, H. (2001). *Vygotsky and pedagogy.* London, UK: Routledge.

Dockett, S., & Fleer, M. (1999). *Pedagogy and play in early childhood education: Bending the rules.* Sydney: Harcourt Brace.

Edwards, S. (2003a). New directions: charting the paths for the role of sociocultural theory in early childhood education and curriculum. *Contemporary Issues in Early Childhood, 4*(3), 251–266.

Edwards, S. (2003b). "The curriculum is...:" Early childhood educators' conceptions of curriculum and developmentally appropriate practice. A comparative case study across two Victorian early childhood educational settings. Unpublished PhD thesis, Monash University. Melbourne.

Fleer, M. (1992). From Piaget to Vygotsky: Moving into a new era of early childhood education. In B. Lambert (Ed.), *The Changing Face of Early Childhood* (pp. 134–149). ACT: Australian Early Childhood Association.

Fleer, M. (1996). Theories of 'play': Are they ethnocentric or inclusive? *Australian Journal of Early Childhood, 21*(4), 12–18.

Fleer, M. (2000). *An early childhood research agenda: Voices from the field.* The Commonwealth Department of Education, Training and Youth Affairs: Canberra: McMillan Printing Group.

Fleer, M. (2002). Sociocultural theory: Rebuilding the theoretical foundations of early childhood education. *Delta, Policy and Practice in Education, 54*(1), 105–120.

Fleer, M. (2005). Essay Review: Studying teachers in early childhood settings. In O. N. Sarach, & B. Spodek (Eds.), *Information Age Publishing, Connecticut, USA. International Journal of Teaching and Teacher Education, 21,* 333–341.

Fleer, M. (2006). A sociocultural perspective on early childhood education: Rethinking, reconceptualizing and reinventing, In M. Fleer, S. Edwards, M. Hammer, A. Kennedy, A. Ridgway, J. Robbins & L. Surman (Eds.), *Early childhood learning communities: Sociocultural research in practice* (pp. 3–14). NSW, Australia: Pearson Education.

Fleer, M. & Kennedy, A. (2000). Quality assurance: Whose quality and whose assurance? *New Zealand Research in Early Childhood Education, 3,* 6–12.

Fleer, M., & Richardson, C. (2004a). *Observing and planning in early childhood settings: Using a sociocultural approach* (60 pages). Canberra, ACT: Early Childhood, Australia.

Fleer, M., & Richardson, C. (2004b). Moving from a constructivist-developmental framework for planning to a sociocultural approach: Foregrounding the tension between individual and community, *Journal of Australian Research in Early Childhood Education, 10*(2), *11*(2), 70–87.

Fleer, M., & Richardson, C. (2004c). Collective mediated assessment, in A. Anning, J. Cullen, & M. Fleer (Eds.), *Early childhood education: society and culture* (pp. 119–136). London: Sage Publications.

Fleer, M., & Robbins, J. (2003). 'Yeah that's what they teach you at uni, it's just rubbish': The participatory appropriation of new cultural tools as early childhood student teachers move from a developmental to a sociocultural framework for observing and planning. Paper presented at the Australian Research in Early Childhood Education conference, 23rd–24th of January 2003, Monash University, Melbourne, Victoria.

Fleer, M., & Williams-Kennedy, D. (2002). *Building bridges: Literacy development for young Indigenous children.* ACT: Australian Early Childhood Association.

Göncü, A. (1999). (Ed.), *Children's engagement in the world. Sociocultural Perspectives.* Cambridge, United Kingdom: Cambridge University Press.

Göncü, A., Mistry, J., & Mosier, C. (2000). Cultural variations in the play of toddlers. *International Journal of Behavioral Development, 24*(3), 321–329.

Hedges, H. (2000). Teaching in early childhood: Time to merge constructivist views so learning through play equal teaching through play. *Australian Journal of Early Childhood, 25,* 16–21.

Howes, C. (1987). Peer Interaction of Young Children, *Monographs of the Society for Research in Child Development* (Vol. 53). Philadelphia: Psychology Press.

Howes, C., & Tonyan, H. A. (1999). Peer relations. In L. Balter, & C. Tamis-LeMonda (Eds.), *Child psychology: A handbook of contemporary issues* (pp. 143–157). Philadelphia: Psychology Press.

Howes, C., & Matheson, C. C. (1992). Sequences in the development of competent play with peers: Social and social pretend play. *Developmental Psychology, 28,* 961–974.

Howes, C., & Stewart, P. (1987). Child's play with adults, toys, and peers: An examination of family and child-care influences. *Developmental Psychology, 23,* 423–430.

Hughes, P., & MacNaughton, G. (2000). Consensus, dissensus or community: The politics of parent involvement in early childhood education. *Contemporary Issues in Early Childhood, 2*(1), 83–93.

Kowalski, H. S. (2000). Toddlers' emerging symbolic play: the influence of peers in the day- care context. Unpublished doctoral thesis: University of Wollongong, NSW.

Lubeck, S. (1998). Is developmentally appropriate practice for everyone? *Childhood Education, 74*(5), 283–298.

MacNaughton, G. (1995). A post-structuralist analysis of learning in early childhood settings, In M. Fleer (Ed.), *DAPcentrism: Challenging Developmentally Appropriate Practices.* ACT: Australian Early Childhood Association.

Mallan, K. (1998). 'The Yeti's on the other side': The narrative nature of children's play. *Australian Journal of Early Childhood, 23,* 16–21.

Millikan, J. (2003). *Reflections: Reggio Emilia principles within Australian contexts.* Castle Hill, N.S.W.: Pademelon Press.

Piscitelli, B. (1992). Reflections on play: Why is it necessary? *Australian Journal of Early Childhood, 17,* 24–31.

Press, F., & Hayes, A. (2000). OECD Thematic Review of Early Childhood Education and Care policy. Australian Background Report. Department of Education, Training and Youth Affairs: AGPS.

Rivalland, C. M. P. (2005). *Beliefs and perceptions in childcare: Listening to the professionals.* Unpublished Honours theses, Monash University, Melbourne.

Rogoff, B. (1990). *Apprenticeship in thinking: Cognitive development in social context.* New York: Random House.

Rogoff, B. (1998). Cognition as a collaborative process, In W. Damon, (Chief Editor) D. Kuhn & R. S. Siegler, (Vol. Eds.), *Cognition, Perceptions and Language.* Handbook of Child Psychology (5th ed., pp. 679–744). New York: John Wiley & Sons, Inc.

Rogoff, B. (2003). *The cultural nature of human development,* New York, USA: Oxford University Press.

Senate Employment, Education and Training Committee. (1996). *Childhood matters: The report of the inquiry into early childhood education.* Commonwealth of Australia, Canberra.

Siraj-Blatchford, I., & Clarke, P. (2000). *Supporting identity, diversity and language in the early years.* Maidenhead: Open University Press

Strinovich, E. (2002). Two- and three-year-old children's peer orientation, styles of play, and social competence in same-age and mixed-age day care. Unpublished doctoral dissertation: Flinders University of South Australia.

Tobin, J. J., Wu, D. Y. H., & Davidson, D. (1989). *Preschool in Three Cultures: Japan, China and United States.* USA: Yale University Press.

Vygotsky, L. S. (1987). Thinking and speech. In L. S. Vygotsky, *The collected works of L.S. Vygotsky, Vol. 1, Problems of general psychology.* (pp. 39–285). R. W. Rieber & A. S. Carton (Eds.); N. Minick (Trans.) New York: Plenum Press.

Windisch, L. E., Jenvey, V. B. & Drysdale, M. (2003). Indigenous parents' ratings of the importance of play, Indigenous games and language and early childhood education. *Australian Journal of Early Childhood, 28,* 50–56.

Woodhead, M. (1998). (Eds.), *Cultural worlds of early childhood.* London, United Kingdom: Routledge.

Wyver, S. R. & Spence, S. H. (1995). Cognitive and social play of Australian preschoolers. *Australian Journal of Early Childhood, 20,* 42–45.

Chapter 4
Play and Learning in Chile

Verónica Aedo, Leonor Cerda, Patricia Dintrans, Mirna Pizarro, Silvia Redón
and Verónica Romo

The Socio-Political Context

During the 1990s, Ivan Núñez (Núñez Prieto, 1997), an important worker at the
Ministry of Education, claimed that Latin America had suffered in the last few
decades of the twentieth century due to the relevant changes in its political, economic and social policies just prior to the twenty-first century. According to Nuñez,
we *must* distinguish the cultural background of the society. In the last few decades,
our country has suffered dramatic changes in all areas: we have changed in such a
way because of globalization that has turned a kind and domestic country into an
ambitious nation open to the world, with the aim of overcoming underdevelopment
as soon as possible. Meanwhile, the theme of identity, of the ways of relating to each
other, no longer seems to be ours. Globalization has brought to us different ways of
relating and ways of being (Casassus, J., 2001), and many people, especially the
young, have begun to imitate those foreign ways. In fact, many people seem to feel
strangers in a world that looks each day more violent and more selfish. It is true that
our country lives, since the return of democracy in 1990, in a very quiet environment, and most Chilean people recognize progress and have the perception that the
country is economically better; however, at the same time, they do not believe that
we are happier than before the dictatorship period.

In many Latin American countries, education was totally shaken up by dictatorship during the 1970s and 1980s. This led to a reduced standard of teacher training.
In Chile, for instance, university-level teacher training ceased. It was with the returning of democracy in the 1990s that governments began to restore higher levels of
training and actively supported participation in early childhood education for young
children. With the Educational Reform initiated by the democratic governments,
the country defined its main principle in education as Respect for Human Dignity,
a principle that is embodied in the transversal objectives of Chilean Educational
Reform.

V. Aedo
Teacher in the Pontificia Universidad Católica de Chile, Vice-president of OMEP Chile
e-mail: vaedog@puc.cl

I. Pramling-Samuelsson, M. Fleer (eds.), *Play and Learning in Early Childhood*   81
Settings, DOI 10.1007/978-1-4020-8498-0_4,
© Springer Science+Business Media B.V. 2009

Today, preschool education is organized in Chile by a national program called Bases Curriculares de la Educación Preescolar (Curricular Basis for Early Childhood Education), a framework that was created under the banner of the educational reform. This is a curricular framework that all centers must use for constructing their own Center Curricular Project. This curricular framework covers children from 0 to 6 years old, and it sets out the general learning standards that are expected to be reached by children in two main periods: from 0 to 3 and from 3 to 6 years of age. Each professional of the preschool level must take this framework as the main basis of his/her project and must cover learning for all in a consistent manner.

The curricular framework tries to take into account all the social and cultural needs of children of the twenty-first century in Chile. It was constructed with the participation of many people who were actively involved at the preschool level, and it gives consideration to the relationships between preschool education and primary education with full respect to the diversity of children.

Public educational centers that take care and give education to infants between 0 and 6 years of age are the Junta Nacional de Jardines Infantiles (JUNJI) (National Early Childhood Education Board), Fundación Integra (Integra Foundation) and schools that depend on the Ministry of Education. There are also other kindergartens and schools that belong to the private educational sector. The adults who work with these children are professionals who have studied at university, and other technicians who have graduated from professional institutes recognized by the state.

In 2001, preschool education (for 4–6-year olds) in Chile reached 41% of the population.[1] Recent initiatives have attempted to redress the imbalance between preschool participation for the rich (more than 50%) and the poor (12%). In 2005, this situation improved dramatically, with preschool education reaching more than 80% of 4–6-year olds. However, the situation remains less favorable for younger children. The most stimulating learning environment must be created for all children in the country, with special attention to those in disadvantaged situations. These challenges also involve the training of professionals for the preschool level; they must be the best teachers, because they are working with human beings beginning a life on earth.

It is now possible to say that Chile has got wonderful opportunities that offer great hope for the future – a good curricular framework, a clear understanding by some politicians of the significance of education for young children, a future compulsory accreditation system for all teachers' training programs. Sergio Bitar, Minister of Education in Chile in 2005, sets it out as follows: "it is possible to give our children an education that can push them up to be participative citizens in a democratic society, whose aim is to fight for the welfare of everybody in the country." "It is absolutely urgent," says Bitar, "that we must find an equilibrium point so as to give our people an education for making each of them be a reasonable consumer, and also a responsible citizen."

---

[1] It was still a very low rate when compared with Mexico (69%) or Spain (90%).

While such improvements are encouraging, the current climate of globalization presents a potential threat to the maintenance of quality in early childhood education in Chile. This is manifested in issues such as indiscriminate consumption, materialism, inequity of provision, devaluing of diversity, excessive standardizing of educational goals, and an associated loss of Chilean identity (Berstein, 1997). As Chileans, it is our duty to keep a critical eye on early childhood education initiatives to ensure that the goals and values that guide the Chilean Educational Reform are upheld. The investigation of play provides an opportunity to maintain this critical eye by looking into the education of very young children, who represent the future of Chile.

Learning and Play in Chile

The aesthetic element seems to be present whenever there is a playful situation. It is a very relevant one in understanding what is going on with play in Chile, mainly because, as in many cultures, play and artistic expressions are integrated. Aesthetics is also significant because of the potentiality of the aesthetic for working ethics aspects of life, a very relevant point in Chilean and Latin American countries. Vidart,[2] from an anthropological point of view, affirms that playing activity has been present in all human cultures from the very beginning of the existence of human kind. And, he says, it is highly probable that playing was born together with art and as a means for creating appropriate social behaviors.

In Chile, play is considered in the context of game playing or "the game." According to Huizinga (1971), Chilean children mainly play two kinds of games. The first – the socio-dramatic game – involves the child pretending to be someone or something else that may even not exist; or something or someone that is another thing or person. For example, this stone is a little car or we are pirates or that spot on the wall is a plane. This kind of game is very common in infancy, and the relationship between learning, playing, and art is emphasized. The second type of play that Huizinga highlights is called the "free game" in which the child's imagination takes flight with the sole purpose of giving pleasure. The child discovers different objects in the clouds, or just enjoys the forms that mean nothing, with colors or sounds. This kind of game seems to be sustained by those who derive their enthusiasm from every different thing in life, in a similar way to many artists, creators or appreciators. It is possible to state that in these kinds of games, the aesthetic element is very strong, and also that much is learned about the inner and external world, the bases of empathy and ethical behavior.

The curricula state explicitly that play must be one of the main methodologies for reaching learning in young children. The same applies to the expressive aspects, which are clearly emphasized with Expected Learning and activities for this area.

---

[2] Vidart, D (1995) "El juego y la condición humana" Ediciones Banda Oriental-Uruguay.

The intensity that is present in all aesthetic experience (Dewey, 1980) as well as in playing activity and learning experiences is a very important common characteristic that is clearly stated in Chilean curricula. This intensity has to do with integral participation: with sensations, feelings, thoughts and actions. This is called "sensibility," but has also to do with the time that is allowed to us for living the experience. One may think that this aspect (time) is the main enemy of our real experiences, of our playing and aesthetic experiences in Chile today. This is because we seem to be preoccupied with economic success. Núñez (1997) says that in Chile, we tend to look too easily for explicit indicators of educational success, giving priority to the tangible aspects of formal learning, such as knowing how to read, how to add up, and how to solve a problem. All these abilities are observable and therefore easily evaluated. But the real educational task, that is assigning meaning to activity, requires time and space. Unfortunately, neither time nor space is a priority in contemporary Chilean society.

Introduction to the Empirical Study

Table 4.1 Outlines the participants in this study, and associated contextual details:

Table 4.1 Participants

Institution	Socio-economic level	Children involved	Age range of children involved	ECE setting details
Centre 1 (urban)	Low	Ailyn (female) Sebastian (male)	2 years 4 months	Private funding, high-scope curriculum
Coast 1 (rural)	Middle	Martina (female)	2 years 3 months	Private funding, classical integral curriculum
Coast 2 (urban)	Low	Lucas (male)	2 years 4 months	Public funding, classical integral curriculum
Centre 2 (urban)	Low	Vicente (male) and Danae (female)	1 year and 9 months	Public funding, classical integral curriculum
Centre 3 (urban)	Low	Diego and Rodrigo (both males)	4 months and 11 months	Public funding, classical integral curriculum
South 1 (rural)	Middle	Yerón (male)	2 years 7 months	Public funding, classical integral curriculum
South 2 (urban)	Low	Sebastián	9 months	Public funding, classical integral curriculum

Findings: The Nature of Play in Chile

The most frequent playful activity in the group of children younger than 1 year consisted of manipulating toys and elements. It was also possible to perceive games or motivation with rhythmic, linguistic or psychomotor games, for example, to initiate an activity with a little song.

Other activities that can be assumed as instances of a frequent game in children between 1 and 2 years was the game with blocks of sponge or other large objects that they manipulated and displaced; this kind of activity was done with much enthusiasm.

The most typical game of the boys and girls older than 2 years is related to the area of the home, like playing to be moms and dads, to cook in the kitchen, role play in which they imitate actions of the adults of the classroom, among others:

> The child leaves the doll on the table, and he looks for the teapot, he serves it in a cup, he goes to where the teacher is sitting but he does not say anything to her; the child remains next to her; the teacher does not react either. Then, a girl with a doll comes into the space and she says to the teacher 'Doll fall down' ... the little boy returns to the kitchen table, takes the metallic pot, goes to the girl with the doll, and gives it to the doll (this time the teacher says something to stimulate the action).

The children are individually playing at the beginning until more partners join them to form a collective game. In some cases, it is possible to see a "leader", usually someone who is older or who has more developed oral language skills. To develop the game mentioned (house game or role playing), the children use the material of an area of the house (kitchen, washing machine, chairs and table, articles from the kitchen, disguises, among others).

Similarly, the families interviewed described the favorite games of the children as those that involved some sort of representation of roles: "He likes playing in dad's truck, arranging baskets with dad. He likes playing with wooden pieces and says that he is doing small houses." In addition, families state that children of these ages were also enthusiastic in playing harder games (gross motor play) such as kicking balls, lifting objects, running and climbing.

Pleasure in Playing: The Rhythmic Games

The game gave pleasure to the boys and girls observed. The more pleasant the game seemed to be the more time they would dedicate to it and, as a result, new forms of game would be discovered:

> Sebastián (2 years 4 months) approaches the exit door. Then he returns to the plush box, a technician takes him out and sits him on the floor together with other children... Sebastián stands up again and takes a comb from a table and uses it as a phone and then he combs himself. Then, he dances to the rhythm of a song that is playing on the radio, and that says something about the legs. Sebastián has then a short rest on a big soft block and leans up slowly until he falls down to the floor. He laughs.

To motivate the children's game the teacher often presented rhythmic activities (such as a musical story) and offered materials that accompanied repetitive action. The teacher's actions generally produced a reaction by the child who would make some sound or gesture in response. The goal is "to provide the use of creativity, to fulfill their fantasy," said a teacher. Another teacher went on to describe such play:

> The youngest ones, between 0 and 1 year, are generally at the stage of exploring their bodies. They very much like the games with mirrors. The children are sat in front of the mirror. Sebastián crawled to the mirror and started looking at himself, touching himself in the mirror; there are other children who give themselves kisses in the mirror, then Sebastián approaches them and starts making sounds to them, playing with them.

The games most often observed in children of these ages (0–2 years old) are undoubtedly the exploration, the manipulation, the rhythmic games: motor or linguistic or reproducing rhythmic engines: "the children start investigating in the room another type of game, for example, they start looking for some toys, they strike them to hear how they sound, they start working to the halfway line," a teacher affirms, referring to children aged from 1 to 2 years. The members of the families had the same opinion:

> "I have seen Danae, from the beginning, observing the people; first the children and later the adults and then she stays near an adult. I can see that she has a good time with the games that he/she proposes to her... she plays at galloping horses very much, jumps, rolls, and gives twirls, everything that has to do with her psychomotor development. This is the most frequent game I see my daughter play." The game, it seems, has a fundamental role in children. As one of the mothers said, "it is like the work that an adult does."

The oldest children in the study (2–3 years) demonstrated the pleasure they gained from such game playing. One teacher explained:

> They are capable of concentrating for a very long period on solitary games where they can imitate different actions, like ironing a cloth, manipulating some objects. In the same way they can play with another child stating their own rules and organizing their game, for example, a game with a ball that must be thrown from one point to another. It is clear that it provides them with the use of the creation of a game that they have invented.

The families also recognized the significance of rhythm, the music, and associated corporal and verbal games as sources of pleasure for boys and girls. One mother articulated her response to the footage as follows:

> To play music, with the rattle that she has, she likes that I sing to her. If when I sing to her I start doing her movements she likes it very much. To play at tickling her or to speak to her in funny ways, she also likes that... We play children's songs and the little girls dance. It is something they love very much. (Similar to Kamii, 1985)

Communication in Games: Imitative Socio-dramatic Games, Role Playing

Role playing games happened with high frequency in most of the groups of children from 2- to 3-year olds that were observed. This kind of game happened both in spontaneous and guided games. Children were observed representing diverse familiar roles or others in their play, especially in their engagement with the doll house. It was possible to observe Yerón, for example, realizing actions like repairing the gadgetry of the house, taking care and feeding the children among other actions. His teacher explained:

> The children in the sector of the doll house play different roles doing diverse actions. Yerón irons on the table. Félix comes into the house with a toy gorilla. He says that they are going to celebrate the gorilla's birthday. When Yerón sees Félix with the gorilla she says to him that the gorilla is sick.

It was possible to observe the children establishing monologues about the actions that they were representing, facing conflicts (Arbuthnot, J., 1975) in making decisions about something, and all this allowed them to enjoy an interesting playful activity that made them really learn:

> While Yerón was offering a piece of cake to the teacher, Félix came into the doll house's sector with the gorilla and he says that it is ready for medicine. Carolina, another girl, says "it is cured." The teacher asks "What was wrong with him?" and Yerón affirms that he gave him a remedy. "I saw him and then I gave him medicine" and says to Félix: "I'll give you the car, but not more." Félix receives the car and goes away.

Some of the teachers observed were able to clearly articulate the relevance of the game in children's learning, particularly in relation to social and communication skills:

> The game is an essential way in the learning of children of preschool level. Studies have demonstrated that the game stimulates psychological functioning in children including creative thought, solution of problems, skills to relieve tensions and anxieties, skills to acquire new understandings, skills to use and develop language.

Or as another teacher states:

> During the game the children are capable of sharing, starting conversations with other children without major difficulties, sometimes without spoken language but using signs and idioms.

Cultural Reflexes in Games

Children were observed imitating behavior or events by representing scenarios and characters that were related to fictitious personages (TV) in their play. A teacher told us that:

> due to television, movies, games and toys that are provided to him, he plays some imitative games that are not always suitable for him. There are a lot of children that can watch aggressive cartoons and commercials on television where we could see images of children which society, our Chilean society, expects from the children: consumerism.

It is openly recognized that the aggressiveness of the games in children has to do with what they watch on TV:

> their games were only of aggressiveness and entire copies of television characters, even the language that they had was ad hoc to the television.

A director of one of the centers also recognized:

> Their games were based on aggressive behaviors watched on TV, like kicking, punching, spitting.

There were differences in the games of boys and girls. One teacher suggested that this was due to the construction of gender identity in a culture as strongly male chauvinist as the Chilean one:

> We see in our society that there is still a distinction of roles ... we give emphasis to the characteristics of genre, we separate the boys and the girls ... what each one has to play; generally the gifts for a boy are always cars, and for the girls are dolls ... although here in the kindergarten they are not aware of this distinction ... but still in the society a big emphasis is given to these distinctions, a connotation to create a man's prototype, a prototype of a very strong man and a weak woman. We see this still much marked in our society.

Interestingly, the teachers who gave emphasis to the relevance of local culture in the development of games, especially directed ones, were those who worked in the provinces. As one teacher pointed out:

> Looking at the local culture we are going to include a big number of games, such as the free games, the traditional, cultural games of our country, of our zone. . . . It is an endless source of activities and of achievements for the children ... taking this into account we need to achieve significant learning, we cannot leave the culture they come from as an unimportant source of resources.

Exploration and Games: A Form of Invention

Several of the adults of the groups observed, both professional and family members, told us that it is the exploratory game or the exploratory activity which allows the boys and girls to initiate their playful activities:

> "From the moment Danae enters the classroom, I have seen her observing the people in there, first the children and later the adults and then she approaches an adult," a girl's relative told us.

Or

> They play games of exploration ... they walk around, looking for something that could be of interest to them until they find something like a ball ... things that attract their attention.

One of the professionals interviewed stated that she drew her inspiration from observing the young child at play:

> exploring is what attracts my attention the most. For example, I saw him (pointing to a little boy) busy exploring a motorboat, and when the child began to be interested in it, he was first creeping and then he started crawling ... and I think about how they perceive everything, without stopping in anything.

This kind of exploration activity is also present in the videos:

> The children of 1 to 2 years old have toys spread out in the space, they look for the toys without really playing a game with them but rather looking at them, and then walking again

around the room exploring what there is there. They seem to enjoy it" ... "Vicente plays with a bowl with water that has a ball, sponge and other objects inside it; the adult talks with the child and indicates to him the name of the objects that he manipulates" ... "Danae and Constanza put figures on the magnetic panel and took back the figures into their hands, put them on the panel again while exploring the effects of the magnetism of the objects." Aggression and collaboration in games.

In the videos and with respect to the interviews, it was possible to appreciate aggression in the games of some of the children observed, primarily in the groups of older children and in those who live in cities with a big population: "He plays with his cousins with balls, hide and seek, but they end up fighting and he always ends up by crying," as a mother told us. Or, as it is perceived in a video: "Aylin is in the courtyard and throws something to a child who is inside the sand pool."

> In another case, children of the same ages (2–3 years), could be observed in a hostile action: He is wrapped in a carpet on the floor and he is raising his legs, then gets up and together with Nicolás he began to push another child until they throw him to the floor and then they try to wrap him up and remain doing so even though the little boy was weeping and asking them to stop ...

Another case:

> A boy (Lucas) is playing in the kitchen when Antonia approaches saying his name (boy's name); he doesn't answer and Antonia hits him twice and runs away; when Lucas looks at Antonia she is not there.

On the other hand, it is also possible to perceive moments of cooperation and empathy between the boys and girls especially with the youngest ones or those who live in less congested cities:

> Yerón wanted to bathe the baby and Fernanda takes the bath tub for him and says to him "do not bathe this baby because he is very clean." Yerón asks Fernanda to play the role of a dad and she says to him "yes. . .and he works here?" and she gives him a piece of perforated wood.

Family members sometimes observed friendlier relations in the educational center than at home:

> "The only difference is that he fights too much at home ... I think that he is always upset" ... "There is a good relation among the children. . . kinder, of more companionship, there is a big friendship" ... "when I saw the video there were no fights among the children, everyone has their space, their autonomy, they share a space, this space is common, but everyone has their place and there were no evident fights, anything" ... "when the children were singing they were all shouting but then they began to listen to each other and that surprised me because this is not easy."

So in toddler groups in Chile, we can observe and hear about hostile behavior as well as friendship among children.

Families and Children's Games: Time, Work and Tiredness

Several of the relatives interviewed (most of them the mothers) told us that they did not have time to play with their sons and daughters; they explained that this was because they saw their children for short periods of time as when the children arrived home they fell asleep:

> We have little time to devote ourselves to the children . . . we come very tired from our work and children also come tired.

The professional recognized this difficulty and told us that:

> The most important challenge and, undoubtedly, our motivation for working with relatives, is to help them to look for moments to play with their children even though briefly; it could be, a teacher told us, at any moment, while they are changing diapers, while they are giving them a bath, while they are dressing them, etc., . . .but it is true that their lives are very stressful.

The mothers and relatives nevertheless recognize the relevance of the game and some of them recognize the educational meaning that it can have, associating it with the development of certain skills:

> "I believe that the kindness of the teachers is fundamental; taking part in the games there is an evident kindness, the affection that is present, they and the child generate a chemistry". . . "and that helps in their development . . . playing tenderly" . . ."the adults can face the children while they play and direct the game so that it is truly beneficial for them." Or, as another mother told us, "The impression that I have is that she (her daughter) appreciates all the activities of the kindergarten and I believe that this is because there is a great combination of game and learning."

And some of the parents look for the moments to play with their sons and daughters:

> she plays the whole day with the dolls, she prepares the meal for them and uses the pans and the silverware and says that they feed the babies. She throws the dolls in her car . . . I look at her and accompany her when I can . . .
>
> Vicente has a box where he keeps all his toys, there he chooses and piles them up, he likes very much playing with cars and makes noises while he plays. He is delighted while he plays and especially when the adults approve what he is doing with a clapping of hands, a kiss . . .. He plays with me with toys, with the phone, I teach him the numbers on the phone . . . When I bathe him I also play with him.

Surprises Provoked by Children's Games

It is interesting to see how some families were surprised because of what they were observing in the video. For example, a mother said:

> I was surprised with Danae. . . she was piling up the buckets, I have never seen her doing that in the house, also it was much quieter while she was playing. And she shares with other children and I was very used to see her playing alone and I realize that here in the school she shares and plays with others . . . We are impressed when seeing the children sharing, singing and doing different activities that we have never seen them do before.

Some of the professionals told us they feel that the video does not show the best moments of their classes. The teachers were informed that in the educational project we were interested in capturing the major playful activities but that it is not possible to observe all play events during the filming:

Freedom is hardly reflected in what the children could do with the materials that we offer them. It is important that there is no distinction of roles, genre; they instinctively play with the cars, with the motorbikes, with the vehicles, the cups and plates, prepare imaginary meals with the clay, with sand, etc.

A mother finally shows her surprise when confronted with the reaction of her daughter:

But as I say to you now she feels like playing with a stick, which is rather absurd, she has a horse but she likes playing riding the stick and this is her horse … I suppose this is what they have done in the kindergarten.

The Pedagogical Meaning of Children's Games

Without exception, the professionals in charge of the observed groups showed their conviction about the relevance of the game as an instance of learning:

… all the games involve learning in the kindergarten, in the house, … they are always related with learning.

Or:

The game in the child is as important as feeding is… the more possibilities a child has to play, the more significant learning will be there for him/her.

In several of the observed centers, the professionals arranged the space in such a way that the exploration of materials promoted play and, sometimes, they deliberately established situations (house, store) to stimulate children's explorations and games. The observed actions and the response of the children seemed to lead to an educational experience in all the settings observed. The repetition of exploration seemed to be very pleasant for the children. Such solitary exploration was perceived by teachers as an example of autonomy and spontaneity. One teacher clearly told us:

As a teacher in the classroom, while planning, I seek to offer the children an environment of learning, arranging the space, the furniture, the materials, in order to explore, to invent and to learn about their world, considering five ingredients of active learning like the manipulation, election, language of the child, materials and support of the adult which allows them to interact in direct experiences with persons, objects, ideas or events.

In many cases, teachers recognized the significance of a playful attitude in children. One teacher said:

It is perceived that the game and the playful attitude are a kind of habitual attitude and a daily experience on the part of children; those children were neither influenced by the observer nor by the recording. Even in those moments, children showed a playful attitude that was quite clear in some spontaneous dialogues… they even incorporated the person who recorded them into the playful relationship.

Many of the members of the children's family who were interviewed, recognized the value of the game and the strong relation to the development of their sons and daughters:

> When I ask myself why the children play in the house or in the kindergarten ... well, what I know is that ... it is to develop them, to motivate them and in general for their own development.

Observing the videos, the idea that the teachers expressed is corroborated in the footage that showed playing and learning happening simultaneously:

> The room was arranged for playing: boxes with different kinds of objects were present for children in different places... they take out objects from the boxes and strike them so that they sound. Sebastián hides behind the cradles making sounds with a rattle and laughs when he is discovered by some other children.

Or, in the case of some younger children:

> The room was clearly arranged for playing... Vicente and Martina stay with the adult opposite the magnetic panel, the adult shows them a box where it was possible to find the figures for the magnetic panel; Martina and Vicente take some figures from the box and then they observe them; Martina takes them to her mouth and Vicente begins to leave them next to the box. Another boy, Oscar came into the game and the adult says to him "Oscarito you want to take this one" the child observes the adult and looks at another side, then it shows the box that Vicente had, the adult adds "This is the duck cua cua," and offers it to the child; he observes her and then takes it and gives it back to the adult. The adult puts the figure of the duck on the magnetic panel and the child takes the figure again and puts it next to the box that Vicente was playing with. Vicente gathers the figures and begins to put them on the panel.

A number of teachers told us that playing allows development and learning:

> Even the language, mathematics... during the game and the experimentation, can have the first temporary and spatial relations, and also they can feel the characteristics and the properties of the objects: form, size, color.

However, even when it was possible to observe this kind of game, playing was sometimes considered useful only for certain areas of learning. One teacher said:

> The emphasis occurs in the emotional part, the affective development of children.

Or, as another teacher told us, a free game allows fundamentally:

> the contact with others and the exploration, but it has to go accompanied by materials selected under some pedagogical criteria, and also with a coherent distribution of spaces and an internal regulation that facilitates the freedom and respect both for the playmates and for the materials.

On the other hand, some of the teachers and family members stated that there were some activities, particularly routines, which could not be considered playful. Such consideration, they said, would detract from the pedagogical goal of the activity. One teacher explained:

> The recognition of their space for keeping their hygienic stuff, the hanging of clothes in the corresponding clothes rack and the appropriate way of having breakfast in cups or bottles cannot be a moment of playing ... Another instance of personal interaction is at the time of the hygienic habits like, for example, brushing their teeth, where the teacher must be a model for the children and she cannot teach them a serious thing in a playful way... that is not the correct way.

The concept of game or playing as a distraction or motivation appeared to contradict the constructivist perspective of learning which teachers said formed the basis of their practice. Taking a constructivist approach meant that the teacher had to view the child as a performer of his own learning, by offering activities for stimulating divergent or convergent thoughts in accordance with the needs of every child and respecting his/her individuality. In contrast, the former approach reinforced the idea of the game as a recreational activity that has no relevance in the development or learning of children. Curiously, such games took place in settings where there was a major presence of playful activity which revealed that there are also contradictions between the theoretical perspectives, where the pedagogical practice and the educational action are based.

A clear conception of game or playing did not exist for many of the members of the work teams, neither was there a clear definition of the child's activity as a playful experience without being confused with actions nor repetitive activities that they constantly realize. On the other hand, there was a conception of the game as an activity of recreation and not as a significant support to appropriate learning in children.

In the opinion of one of these interviewed teachers, the concept of game was described as a guided activity in which the child has the opportunity to interact with diverse objects and materials. What was observed is coherent with the information delivered by the teacher. That is, the educational project that is performed by the children during the year is the same as the play directed games like dancing, singing or throwing balls, etc.

It is interesting to emphasize that when the professionals specifically mentioned the characteristics of learning, they did not do so in the context of play or aesthetics:

> The decisions I take as a classroom teacher are to offer children a learning environment, arranging the space, the furniture, the materials, so as to allow them to explore, to invent and to learn.

Recognition by Families of What is Done at Kindergarten

The families generally recognize that the work of professionals in the kindergarten is very good.

> I think he is very well developed here... and they do everything through games, but not any game... because here many things are taught him. I believe that not all games provide good learning... it is necessary to plan them... with direction so the children can be guided in the activities...

Or, what another mother states is:

> In relation to the games I find it very interesting because at home I do not always find things that he likes. To see Vicente assembling things, piling up, playing with puzzles, and all that... well, I think it is a good thing, and the difference that I see is that Vicente here in the school has the space to play, to do the things. At home I have many dangers, here there

is nothing dangerous, I saw in the video all what I would like Vicente could play at home. Often I try to imitate what you do here. Well, Vicente sings at home constantly, not so much as Salvador, but Vicente sings, and I believe then that he must sing here all the time.

It is interesting to note how mothers, such as the former one, recognize as valuable what is done at school, but do not recognize the pedagogical intention of the playful activities; maybe because this pedagogical intention is not always clear to the teachers either.

Conclusions

We do believe that we now have a little more knowledge of what is happening at preschool with our children from 0 to 3 years old. We are able to conclude from this study that dramatic – or role – playing games are common among children of the oldest group (2–3); construction and rhythmic play among children aged 1–2 years; while in the youngest age group play comprises mainly of linguistic and rhythmic games in the company of adults.

We found that games often mirrored the culture that surrounds these children and that they are exposed to TV in their daily lives. Occasions of aggressive play were more often observed in older children who lived in large cities. Gender differentiation was apparent in many forms of play. While parents clearly valued games and the associated role they saw in the teacher who facilitated them, their own social and economic circumstances did not permit them to interact with their children in this way themselves. The time for playing with their children was minimal.

Most of the teachers observed played with their children; however, in many of the observations, teachers were not in the classroom, and at these times we observed the children in the presence of the technicians, which meant that the more appropriate role of an adult as a facilitator could not be seen. It seems from what some teachers said or acted that they did not always have a clear understanding of the pedagogical objective and meaning of playing nor of some games.

This study found that there was no clarity or agreement across teachers about the concept of game, although there was some consensus that playing was beneficial for social or affective learning. It might be supposed, because of the training of teachers in Chile, that the professionals would have clarity with regard to the reasons that underlie the guided games proposed for their children and also the reasons that guide them in their intervention in the spontaneous games of children. However, this level of awareness is not always clear. This was also found in some other studies in Chile (Sarmiento, 2004). Perhaps the reason for this poor understanding by some of the teachers has to do with the impoverishment of teachers' training in Chile.

In drawing upon cultural-historical theory, the study sought to analyze play in relation to Rogoff's three foci of analysis. In particular, it was noted in this study that the findings could be grouped in relation to personal, interpersonal and institutional or cultural dimensions, as noted in the summary table below:

Focus of analysis	Summary
Personal focus of analysis	Teachers' personal knowledge of the play they expect for particular age groups, such as 0- to 2-year infants playing with their bodies, and role play for 2- to 3-year olds. Teachers' knowledge about what inspires children being gained through close observations of children at play. Teacher knowledge and use of Parten's theory of play for analyzing children's play.
Interpersonal focus of analysis	The importance of singing and dancing for communication between children and between infants and adults.
Institutional or cultural focus of analysis	The role of TV in children's play (e.g., aggressive cartoons), gender differences established in routines (e.g., sorting children into boys and girls). Selection of play materials is linked to curriculum areas. Constructivist learning.

What is clear is that we must continue looking for descriptions, answers to different pedagogical questions and educational proposals that can be researched. In this way we can improve the teachers' training and in turn influence education, not just the care of our little ones. Through this we can realize the kind of Chilean society we seek for the future.

References

Arbuthnot, J. (1975). Modification of moral judgement through role play. In *Developmental Psychology N° 11.*

Berstein, Basi (1997). Escuela Mercado y Nuevas Identidades Pedagógicas. Cide. Chile. Documentos N° 13.

Casassus, J. (2001). (El autor es especialista principal de UNESCO. Este texto es de su exclusiva responsabilidad y no compromete a la Organización): "Cambios paradigmáticos en educación." Chile, UNESCO.

Dewey, John (1980). *Art as Experience.* USA: Perigee Books.

Huizinga, J. (1971). *Homo Ludens.* Edit. Universitaria de Sao Paulo, Brazil.

Vidart, D. (1995). "El juego y la condición humana" Ediciones Banda Oriental-Uruguay, 1995.

Kamii, C., De Vries. (1985). Juegos colectivos en la primera enseñanza. Madrid. Parte 1, capítulo I, II, III, IV, XI.

Lowenfeld, V. (1976). *Desarrollo de la capacidad creadora.* Edit. Losada, Bs. Aires.

Núñez Prieto, I. (1997). Publicado en Cristián Cox y otros, "160 años de educación pública. Historia del Ministerio de Educación," Santiago, MINEDUC, pp. 58–100

Rogoff, B. (1990). *Apprenticeship in Thinking. Cognitive Development in Social Context.* Oxford: Oxford University Press.

Sarmiento, R. et al. (2004). "Cambio en las prácticas pedagógicas" Universidad Central, MINEDUC, Chile; documento de sistematización de trabajo de asesoría.

Chapter 5
"Eduplay": Beliefs and Practices Related to Play and Learning in Chinese Kindergartens

Nirmala Rao and Hui Li

Introduction

This chapter, like others in this volume, considers the role and meaning of play in early childhood settings. It is concerned with the following questions: (i) What is the status of play in national early childhood curriculum guidelines and to what extent are these followed in early childhood programs?; (ii) How do early childhood teachers arrange the day to support children's play and learning?; (iii) How do children play?; (iv) How do teachers support children's meaning making in play? and (v) What is the meaning of play and learning for children ranging in age from birth to 3 years, according to their teachers and parents? Information about play and learning in China was garnered through analyses of videotaped observations of how four toddlers spent 1 day in different early childhood settings and through interviews with their teachers and parents. In interpreting the interview and observational data, we considered the relationship between curriculum guidelines about play and what was observed, but particular attention was given to the relationship between play and learning. This was because we assumed that the beliefs and practices of parents and teachers would reveal cultural beliefs about play and learning and that children's play would be influenced by the physical and social environments arranged by adults for their charges.

We begin with an overview of the context of early childhood education in Mainland China. Next, we address notions of play in kindergarten curriculum guidelines that have been issued by the state. We then turn to our empirical study and outline its methodology and discuss the main findings. Finally, we present the term "eduplay" as one that aptly reflects the relationship between play and learning evident in our findings.

N. Rao
The University of Hong Kong, Hong Kong, China
e-mail: nirmalarao.is@gmail.com

I. Pramling-Samuelsson, M. Fleer (eds.), *Play and Learning in Early Childhood Settings*, DOI 10.1007/978-1-4020-8498-0_5,
© Springer Science+Business Media B.V. 2009

The Context of Early Childhood Education

At the outset, it is necessary to operationally define the term "early childhood education" in the context of this chapter as there are numerous terms used in the literature to describe services that are aimed at meeting the needs of young children. The difference in the usage of terms arises from the age group that is covered and the content of the services. There are three main types of early childhood centers in China: *nurseries*, which provide care for children from birth to 3 years; *kindergartens*, which provide care and education to children between 3 and 6 or 7 years; and *preprimary classes*, which cater to the needs of children from 5 to 6 or 7 years. These classes are typically attached to rural primary schools. Nurseries come under the jurisdiction of the Department of Public Health, while kindergartens and preprimary classes are regulated by the Department of Education. However, as nurseries have begun to focus on education as well as care, the Department of Education has taken the responsibility of overseeing their "education" curriculum (Wong & Pang, 2002).

Preschool Educational Institutions
While the term "early childhood education" is used to refer to services for children from birth to 6 or 7 years, official documents refer to kindergartens and preprimary classes as *preschool educational institutions* (GOC, 2000). School entry age varies across regions and is either 6 or 7 years. It should be pointed out that in China, official figures about access and enrolment are only provided for children above 3 years who are enrolled in different types of kindergartens or in preprimary classes in rural primary schools. Kindergartens are managed by the government, private individuals, or local communities. Local Education Departments typically run "model" programmes. As in other countries, the state issues regulations for kindergartens.

Coverage and Provision
The following population statistics are based on statistics provided by the United Nations Population Division (Population Division, UN, 2004). In 2005, China's population exceeded an estimated 1.3 billion, and there were 84 million children (44 million boys and 40 million girls) below 4 years of age and about 95 million children (50 million boys and 45 million girls) ranging in age from 5 to 14 years. The number of preschool children in China far exceeds the total population of many countries, and given the size of the population and the diversity of needs of children living in different regions, making provisions for services and ensuring their quality is a challenging endeavor.

Over the past decade, the crude birth rate in China has declined[1] (Population Division, UN, 2004). This has meant that the number of kindergartens (and consequently enrolment levels) has declined since 1997 when there were 192,000 kindergartens (GOC, 2000). Yet, the gross enrolment ratio (GER) for preschool

---

[1] From 18.3 in 1990–1995 to 13.6 in 2000–2005.

educational institutions increased markedly from 29.9% in 1991 to 47% in 1996 (GOC, 2000). In 2003, there were 116,390 kindergartens and 973,000 kindergarten heads and teachers (National Bureau of Statistics of China, 2005).

It should be noted that there are very wide disparities in GER between rural and urban areas (36.1% vs 83.4%) and that enrolment figures only include children above 3 years. By 2002, preschool education was almost universal in cities, and preschool services were rapidly developing in rural areas (MOE, 2003).

Teacher Qualifications

In 2000, there were about 946,448 kindergarten heads and teachers. In terms of their highest educational qualification, 12% were graduates of 2-year or 4-year colleges, 45% were graduates of normal schools,[2] 27% were graduates of vocational schools, and 17% and 10% were senior secondary school and junior secondary school graduates, respectively (Wong & Pang, 2002). The academic and professional qualifications of kindergarten teachers have increased in recent years, with teachers in major cities having higher qualifications than those in rural areas. Furthermore, a recent study of teachers' qualifications in South-west China found that teachers in government-linked (public) kindergartens had attained higher educational and professional qualifications than those employed by private enterprises (Du, 2005).

Family Size

The one-child policy has affected early childhood development and education in China. The majority of urban preschool children do not have siblings, and as a result, parents give ample attention to the care and education of their only child. However, there have also been concerns that the single child is overindulged, self-centerd and lazy, and experiences what is called the 4-2-1 syndrome (four grandparents and two parents focusing their attention on one child). Early childhood educators have to take into account children's family experiences when planning educational activities. For example, more effort may be exerted in providing opportunities for play with peers in kindergartens than for solitary, constructive play, which can be supported in the home.

Play in the Early Childhood Curriculum

Early childhood education has gone through three major waves of curriculum reform in the past century (Zhu and Wang, 2005). The first wave occurred between 1920 and 1930 when a Japanese version of kindergarten education was imported

---

[2] A normal school or university is one which offers teacher-training programs. The term normal school is derived from the French term, *Ecole Normale*. Normal schools were the first ones to establish teaching standards or *norms* which were to be emulated by other educational institutions. The term "Normal University" is still used in English translation of the Chinese term for teacher training institutions (Pinyin: shīfàn dàxué). In China, Teachers Colleges have lower entrance requirements than normal universities.

into China. As a result, child-centerd philosophies and practices were evident in kindergartens. The second major reform occurred in the 1950s after China became a socialist state. The Soviet model of early childhood education was adopted, and the child-centerd approach was replaced by a more teacher-directed, subject-based approach. The third wave of curriculum reform began with the open-door policy in the 1980s and is on-going (Zhu and Wang, 2005). The importance of play in the early childhood curriculum has been reiterated in relevant policy documents since the 1980s.

The State Education Commission issued the very influential *Regulations on Kindergarten Education Practice* in 1989. This was a watershed for early childhood education as the concepts of developmental appropriateness and individual needs were deemed key principles in preschool education. Wong & Pang (2002, p. 63) state that "play became an important means of promoting holistic development. Appropriate guidelines were to be given to children while respecting their choice in play. Teachers should create a warm psychological environment in which children can learn. Integrated learning should replace subject-segregated teaching and it should permeate throughout the daily activities." The document was circulated throughout the country, and the reform was widely implemented. However, some of these reform ideas were based on Western, democratic, and scientific ideals, which are not totally congruent with Chinese cultural traditions. This led to some difficulties in implementation. Furthermore, teachers were not given enough practical suggestions on how to implement the new regulations (Li & Li, 2001; Zhu, 2005; Zhu and Wang, 2005). This led to the issuance of more detailed guidelines, in *Guidelines for Kindergarten Education Practice*, in 2001 (State Educational Commission, 2001).

The kindergarten educational reforms have led to changes in views about children and learning. As Liu and Feng (2005, p. 94) assert, "the 'revolution' which occurred in kindergartens is no longer one of curricular reform but an ideas revolution, through which phrases such as 'respecting children', 'active learning', 'teaching for individual learning needs', 'play-based teaching and learning', 'teaching and learning through daily life in kindergartens' emerged and are now often heard in kindergartens." In a similar vein, Zhu and Wang (2005) argue that the varied curriculum approaches followed in China today are reflective of the openness and diversity now evident in the country. Despite changes, early childhood curriculum in China has retained some distinctively Chinese characteristics and reflects Chinese beliefs and values. For example, various official documents emphasize the cultivation of good habits, self-discipline, emotional control, and moral development (Wong & Pang, 2002). Indeed, early childhood education in China has been characterized as a hybrid of traditional Chinese, Western, and communist cultures (Wang & Spodek, 2000).

Cross-cultural Equivalence of Meanings
Two Chinese words can be considered equivalent to the English word, "play." They are "wan" (play) and "youxi" (play with rules or games). "Wan" is the equivalent

of free-choice play, whereas the term "youxi" denotes the existence of rules which should be followed.

Children's Perceptions of Play

Liu (1995) examined young children's perspectives on play and the type of play prevalent in kindergartens in China in the 1990s. She found that large group lessons were the most common indoor activity in kindergartens and that there was little time assigned for indoor free play. When asked to choose their favorite activity among group lessons, "wan" and "youxi," 98% of the 5- to 6-year-old children reported that their favorite activity was the group lesson because this enabled them to gain knowledge and skills, whereas "wan" was simply free play. Liu (1995) asserts that children's choices reflect cultural values transmitted by teachers. For example, teachers emphasize learning in groups and speak highly of the value of group lesson for garnering knowledge and skills. Further, teachers allocated comparatively little time for indoor free play and seldom paid attention to children when they were engaged in free play. Children's responses may reflect their own beliefs or a social desirability bias.

Liu, Pan, & Sun (2005) conducted another study in 2004 to examine the influence of the *Regulations on Kindergarten Education Practice* (1989) on children's perceptions of play. As mentioned earlier, the *Regulations* accorded importance to play in the early childhood curriculum and teachers were expected to make play the basic activity in kindergartens and emphasize "learning through play" over "learning through group lessons." Liu et al. (2005) interviewed 150 children, ranging in age from 5 to 6 years, enrolled in 15 kindergartens in Beijing. Among other questions, children were asked whether they preferred "play or group lessons," 57% of the children responded that they preferred play, compared to 98% in 1995. About 29% of the children said they preferred free play to group lessons, while 14% of the children said they liked both play and group lessons and did not indicate a preference for either activity.

Liu and her colleagues found that group lessons were the main activity in kindergartens in 1995 and 2004 (Liu, 1995; Liu et al., 2005). However, there were interest and activity corners in all 15 kindergartens and children spent an average of 49 min engaging in free play in an interest corner and 20.8% of children regarded activities in an interest/activity corner as play. Liu believes that the educational reforms have led to positive changes in educational practice in the early years as more time is allocated to free play and there is a corresponding decrease in time spent in group lessons.

It is clear that early childhood education policy including contemporary curriculum documents promote child-centerd early education and emphasize play as the major means of learning. However, to what extent is play evident in early childhood centres? What are teachers' and parents' perceptions of play? How is play used for meaning making by children? These questions are considered in the following sections.

Method

Location

The case studies are drawn from Shenzhen, a city in Southern China, which is adjacent to Hong Kong. Shenzhen has a population of about 10 million and is among the most developed and prosperous cities in China. The city has six districts, of which four form part of a Special Economic Zone. The case studies are drawn from Futian district, which is the center for administration and commerce in the Special Economic Zone (Shenzhen Government, 2005).

Participants

To obtain a range of kindergartens, the principals of four kindergartens (two public and two private) with a prekindergarten class were invited to participate in the study. All agreed. The public kindergartens are operated by the local education authority. One of them has won numerous awards and is considered a model programme. Similarly, one of the private kindergartens is a highly regarded, award-winning programme, while the other is considered average by early childhood professionals in the area. We chose to include one boy and one girl from each type of kindergarten. Hence, we randomly selected one child of a predetermined gender from the prekindergarten class in each of the four kindergartens. Information about the selected children, their kindergartens, teachers, and parents is provided in Table 5.1.

The kindergartens varied in physical size and in the number of enrolled children. The class size of the target children ranged from 14 to 29 children, and most of the prekindergarten classes had two teachers and one assistant. All teachers had professional qualifications in education but their academic qualifications varied, and the interviewed teachers were either graduates of normal schools (a 3-year preservice teacher-training course after junior secondary school graduation), teacher-training colleges (3-year in-service or preservice professional-training course after senior secondary school), or normal universities (4-year degree in education). The mothers of the target children were very well educated and all of them had completed tertiary education. Hence, our population was not representative of kindergartens in China, but of those in major cities in China.

Procedure

Observations of the four children were conducted in April 2005. All of the children attended full-day programmes and were videotaped from the start to the end of a typical day. The child was the focus of the observation, and particular attention was given to observing the child at activity times (as opposed to nap times).

After the observations were conducted, a few video clips of the target child "at play" were selected. The child's teachers and mother were interviewed in individual

Table 5.1 Background information about target children

Child's name/age/gender	Type of kindergarten (date established)	No. of children in kindergarten (size of kindergarten)	No. of staff in kindergarten	"Quality of kindergarten"** teacher qualifications	No. of children/staff in child's class	Mothers'/interviewed teachers' educational levels**
Dou Dou/30 months/Female	Public (1992)	374 (189 boys and 185 girls) (4,000 m²)	29 teachers/26 support staff	"Excellent quality" all teachers are college graduates or degree holders	29 (10 boys and 19 girls)/3	College graduate/college graduate
Yu Qiang/30 months/Male	Public (1997)	270 (138 boys and 132 girls) (3,572 m²)	18 teachers/22 support staff	"Average quality" majority are college graduates	26 (20 boys and 6 girls)/3	University degree/college graduate
Zi Zhen/36 months/Female	Private (1994)	295 (177 boys and 118 girls) (3,298 m²)	26 teachers/28 support staff	"High quality" all teachers are college graduates	25 (12 boys and 13 girls)/3	University degrees/university degree
Ye Hao/28 months/Male	Private (2001)	99 (62 boys and 37 girls) (900 m²)	8 teachers/9 support staff	"Average quality" most are graduates of normal schools	14 (11 boys and 3 girls)/3	University degree/normal school graduate

* Rated by educational authorities or based on views of early childhood experts in Shenzhen/China.

** University graduates have completed a 4-year degree in education from a Normal University. College graduates have completed a 3-year in-service or preservice professional-training course after senior secondary school. Normal and vocational school graduates have completed a 3-year preservice teacher-training course after junior secondary school graduation.

Table 5.2 Analytical framework

Focus of analysis	Summary
Personal focus of analysis	Teachers' knowledge of Vygotsky's theory, particularly the insights gained from understanding the concept "scaffolding"
Interpersonal focus of analysis	The role of adults in children's play, as: leading play, supporting play, providing free play opportunities, or interacting to maximise direct teaching
Institutional or cultural focus of analysis	Teacher beliefs about the importance of play as a pedagogical approach for learning was framed from an instructional perspective

sessions and shown these clips at the beginning of the session. The interviews, which were videotaped, took place on the same day as the observation. They were conducted by an experienced early childhood professional. All respondents were probed on their beliefs about play and learning in early childhood. In addition, the child's teacher was asked about her professional training and experience and about her role in children's play in kindergartens. The mothers were asked about their educational background, employment history, and about who took responsibility for the child when he or she was not in the kindergarten.

Data Management

Each child was videotaped for about 8 hours, which generated a considerable amount of data. The videotapes were viewed by the two authors, and clips were transcribed and translated into English by an experienced teacher who is currently completing a Ph.D. in Education. Based on the transcripts and videotapes, the authors independently generated categories related to play and learning. These were discussed and a list of categories that were appropriate to characterize the observation and interview data were agreed up on.

In drawing upon cultural – historical theory, the study sought to analyse the play in relation to Rogoff's three foci of analysis. In particular, the analysis featured an examination of teachers' personal knowledge about play, their interpersonal enactments of play, and the institutional or cultural factors which directed how play was organized or conceptualized by professionals, as noted in the summary in Table 5.2.

Results and Discussion

The main objective of this study was to consider the role and meaning of play in kindergartens in Mainland China. In the following section, information garnered through our observation and interviews is presented and analyzed under the following headings: The physical context for learning; The structuring of the day; Children's play; and Parents' and Teachers' views on the meaning of play and learning.

The Physical Context for Learning

Notwithstanding their age and gender, children's play is affected by circumstances, including the physical environment, the material available (toys and books), peers, the psychological atmosphere, and the degree of structure in the day. The four kindergartens were very pleasant. They were all brightly lit, well-ventilated and had a variety of materials for play. The classrooms were arranged with learning corners and desks were in small groups. According to western standards these classrooms would be considered "developmentally appropriate" (Bredekamp & Copple, 1997).

The Structuring of the Day

How did teachers arrange the day? In some Asian countries, free play is used as a reward for children who complete their assigned tasks or worksheets rather than treated as a learning activity in itself. This was certainly not the case in the kindergartens we observed, where "learning by playing" seemed to be very important in curriculum design.

The degree of structuring during the day has a very important influence on the time and space in which children engage in free play. The four kindergartens all opened at about 7:30 a.m. and closed at 5:30 p.m. The timetable for one of the kindergartens is shown in Table 5.3. Similar schedules existed in the other three kindergartens. As the table shows, many activities and transition points punctuate the day.

Notwithstanding the fact that children are "playing" as they participate in other activities, the degree of structure may indeed limit the extent that a child can pursue a free-choice activity or interest. However, children did pursue an area of interest in

Table 5.3 A typical day in the kindergarten for Dou Dou

Time period	Activities
7.30–8.00 a.m.	Greeting and free play
8.00–8.30 a.m.	Breakfast
8.30–8.45 a.m.	Free play, reading, and chatting
8.45–9.30 a.m.	Learning corner activities
9.30–9.45 a.m.	Tea break
9.45–10.10 a.m.	Theme activities
10.10–11.10 a.m.	Outdoor activities
11.10–11.30 a.m.	Story time
11.30–12.00 a.m.	Lunch
12.00–12.10 p.m.	After-lunch walk
12.10–2.30 p.m.	Nap
2.30–3.30 p.m.	Clean up, outdoor activities, and snack
3.30–4.30 p.m.	Subject activities (language/music/math/arts)
4.30–5.00 p.m.	Free play and packing up
5.00–5.30 p.m.	Farewell routine

successive activities. For example, Yu Qiang was quite taken by superheroes such as Ultraman, a popular Japanese cartoon hero. He engaged in imaginative play involving superheroes during free play and pursued his interest in drawing activities and in outdoor sand play.

> *(The whole class was divided into two groups. One group was doing mathematics activities and the others were given the choice of playing in any of the interest corners in the classroom. The teacher and a few children including Yu Qiang are in a corridor outside the classroom.)*
>
> *Teacher*: Yu Qiang, what do you want to play?
> *Yu Qiang*: I want to play with a gun.
> *Teacher*: Then go to the Construction corner and play on your own.
> *Yu Qiang*: Later on, I can play with the gun! (*speaking to the Observer*)
>
> *(Yu Qiang runs to the Block Area, where he sits at the table. Within two minutes, he constructs a gun with plastic cogs.)*
>
> *Yu Qiang*: What a beautiful gun! (*talking to himself*)
>
> *(Yu Qiang begins to enjoy playing with his gun. He points the gun in different directions with no clear target. He also makes gunshot sounds.)*
>
> *(After a while, Yu Qiang goes back to the table, and takes off one cog from the gun thus decreasing the length of the body. He then constructs a similar structure with some other cogs so that he has two "guns" and holds one in each hand. In the meantime two other boys also come to the construction corner and Yu Qiang and one of the boys engage in parallel play for some of the time.)*
>
> *Yu Qiang*: I have two guns. (*Turns around and shows them to the researcher*)
> *Teacher*: Who are you shooting at?
> *Yu Qiang*: Baddies.
> *The teacher leaves. Yu Qiang and another boy continue to play with their weapons.*
> *The teacher returns.*
> *Teacher*: Who are you shooting at?
> *Yu Qiang/classmate*: Shooting the "Baddies."
> *Teacher*: Then let us draw the "baddies."
>
> *(Yu Qiang Clip 0207)*
>
> *The teacher sticks another piece of paper on the wall for the children to draw Baddies whom they would like to shoot. One boy draws a Monster.*

Yu Qiang: I want to draw Ultraman.
Teacher: Do you want to shoot Ultraman?
Yu Qiang: NO. I will draw him next to the "Baddie."
Teacher: OK.

(Yu Qiang draws something in the corner of the paper.)

Teacher: Good. When you shoot the Monster, be careful not to hurt Ultraman. You begin to do your work, later on please tell me how many Monsters or Baddies you have destroyed.

(Yu Qiang Clip 0209)

These clips suggest several things of note about Yu Qiang's play and the context which supports it. First, despite the highly structured day in the kindergarten, Yu Qiang is able to pursue his interest in Ultraman and the teacher allows him to do so. Superhero play is common in preschools in the Western world and is common in more developed Asian cities. Our observations of kindergartens in cities in China show that this is true. Japanese cartoons are particularly popular in China.

There has been a debate in the literature as to whether superhero play should be allowed in preschools. On one hand, teachers are concerned about classroom safety, the messages children learn when this type of play is permitted in preschools, and the fact that children tend to consistently engage in superhero play, which precludes engagement in other types of play that may be more beneficial to child development. On the other hand, teachers report that superhero war play is so appealing to young children that it is hard to prevent children from participating in such play (Levin, 2003).

Yu Qiang's teacher did not prohibit "gun play" but sent him to a quieter area of the classroom where there were few children when he stated he wanted to play with guns. The teacher also suggested that Yu Qiang draw "baddies" when he had been engaged in shooting for about 15 min so as to redirect his attention to what could be considered a more positive activity. The theme of good versus evil was also evident in Yu Qiang's play. This theme is common in the play of children all over the world and Yu Qiang's teacher reinforced the idea of good versus evil in her interactions with him.

How Do Children "Play"?

To answer this question, we developed a typology of children's activities during the school day based on our classroom observations and previous studies of play in kindergartens in China (Liu et al., 2005). Four categories, which involved play but varied in terms of the level of teacher-imposed regulation, were developed. The categories, in order of decreasing structure, are:

(a) Teacher *leads* and participates in games, activity, or play: This includes teacher planned, initiated, or arranged activities that may be part of the current teaching theme;

(b) Teacher *supports* games, activity, or play: Teacher provides structure and supports activities that are initiated by children;

(c) Child engages in games or activities *chosen by the teacher*: Child, either independently or with peers, engages in tasks and activities chosen by the teacher; and

(d) Child engages in *free play*: This is genuinely free-choice play, and children engage in solitary, parallel, or cooperative play.

Teachers are active participants in children's activities/play in (a) and (b), but are observers (and do sometimes intervene) in (c) and (d). Another category, direct

Table 5.4 Types of activities observed in the four kindergartens

Types of activity	Description	Examples
Teacher **leads and participates** in games, activity or play	This includes teacher planned, initiated, or arranged activities that may be part of the current teaching theme.	• The teachers and children are playing a game that involves singing, holding hands, and standing in circle. The latter increases or decreases in size depending on the words in the song, "Blowing, blowing a small/big bubble."
Teacher **supports** games, activity, or play	Teacher provides structure and supports activities that are initiated by children.	• The children decide to act out the story of "The Rabbit and the Wolf." The teacher helps them with their planning, reframes their ideas, and supports their choice of activity.
Child engages in games or activities, **arranged by the teacher**	Child, either independently or with peers, engages in tasks and activities chosen by the teacher.	• The teacher has arranged a game where children take turns to throw an object at a target. This physical activity is not related to the teaching theme.
Free play	This is genuinely free choice play, and children engage in solitary, parallel, or cooperative play.	• A child plays with plastic toys and puppets.
Direct teaching	The teacher engages in either small or large group instruction.	• The teacher reviews the English names of animals with which the children are familiar. She then mimics the actions of an animal and asks them to name the animal. After they do so, she teaches the children the English name for the animal.

instruction, which did not involve play, was also used to code the observational data. Table 5.4 gives examples of the various categories.

The time that each of the four target children spent in each of the four different types of activity is depicted in Table 5.5 and Fig. 5.1. Children engaged in these four different activities for about 1.5 hours during the day. There were, of course, individual differences, but children spent the most time in teacher-led activities. Children spent an average of about 62 min in activities developed or supported by the teacher, compared to about 21 min in genuinely free-play activities. Given the children's age and Chinese beliefs about play and learning (Liu et al., 2005), this is not surprising.

As shown in Fig. 5.1, play-based learning was the major activity in the kindergartens, and the children spent 65.5% of their total activity time (excluding mealtimes and naps) in learning by playing. The award-winning public kindergartens allocated about 70% of the total activity time to play-based learning activities, while the "average" quality private kindergarten only allocated about 49% of total activity time for this. This may be because public kindergartens are expected to fully and effectively implement government guidelines. However, there were appropriate materials in the private kindergartens and the teachers in these settings had a lower level of professional qualification. Therefore, the private kindergartens allocated more time to formal instruction, which requires fewer play-related resources, and this left less time for play-based learning.

It should be pointed out that some private kindergartens have highly qualified staff, ample educational resources, and adhere to government recommendations. However, not all parents can afford the fees charged by these "high" quality kindergartens, and preschools may not be able to afford the salaries for highly qualified

Table 5.5 Time spent in different types of activities by target children

	Dou Dou	Yu Qiang	Zi Zhen	Ye Hao	Average
Teacher leads and participates in activity*	41'29" (28.6%)	47'25" (33%)	34'04" (30.6%)	24'21" (23.9%)	36'32" (29.0%)
Teacher supports activity*	27'13" (18.7%)	18'14" (12.6%)	19'29" (17.5%)	0 (0%)	16'13" (12.2%)
Teacher chooses "free play" activity*	20' (13.8%)	13'06" (9%)	6'28" (5.8%)	0 (0%)	9'53" (7.15%)
Free play*	23'34" (16.2%)	22'53" (16%)	12'49" (11.7%)	25'04" (24.5%)	21'05" (17.1%)
Direct teaching	(22.5%)	(29.4%)	(34.4%)	(51.6%)	(34.5%)
Total activity time**	145'	144'	111'	102'	125'30"

* A form of play-based learning.
** Does not include meal or nap times.

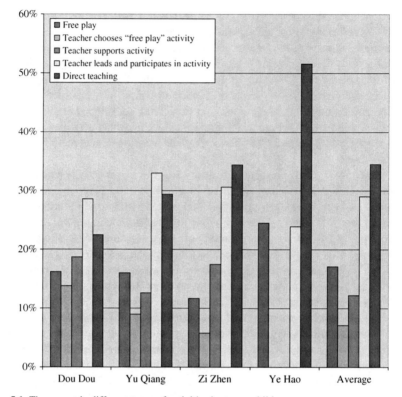

Fig. 5.1 Time spent in different types of activities by target children

teachers command. Progressive guidelines require high-quality teachers and adequate resources, and unfortunately many private preschools do not have these.

During the course of the day, as shown in Fig. 5.1, Dou Dou, Yu Qiang, Zi Zhen and Ye Hao spent about 24, 23, 12, and 25 min, respectively, engaged in genuinely free-choice play. What was the subject of their attention during this period? What did teachers do?

How Do Teachers Support Children's Meaning Making in Free Play?

As mentioned earlier, children engage in "learning by playing" throughout the school day. However, we are particularly interested in what children did during free play and what their teachers did when the children were at play.

The children engaged in pretend play when they had a free choice of activities. Certain themes were evident in this type of play. For example, like children in other parts of the world, these children engaged in superhero play (for example, Yu Qiang) and played "mummies and daddies" using puppets (Dou Dou and Zi Zhen).

The target children pursued their interests through the course of the day when they had free-choice activities and teachers allowed them to do so. For example, Dou Dou played with "rabbits" made of plastic cogs for much of the morning and Yu Qiang continued his "superhero" play. He constructed a gun to shoot the "baddies," drew the "baddies" and made Ultraman-like movements when dancing in music class. Another example comes from Zi Zhen's class. The story of "The Rabbits and the Wolf" was discussed, and then performed during circle time. During free play, Zi Zhen then drew rabbits.

The teachers repeatedly intervened in the free play of the children to reinforce basic concepts and learning experiences. The following excerpts illustrate this assertion.

> *Teacher: T*: What is the colour of your little rabbit? What colour is this?
> *Dou Dou A*: Blue. There are three colours.
> *Teacher: T*: Oh, there are three colours. What are they?
> *Dou Dou A*: Blue, white, and green.
> *Teacher: T*: Good (*Thumb-up*.)

(Dou Dou Clip 0104)

> *Teacher: T*: What colour is the bird?
> *Zi Zhen C*: It is blue.

(*Zi Zhen Clip 0039*)

> (*The boys inform the teacher how many targets they have shot down with their guns.*)

> *Teacher*: How many?
> *Yu Qiang*: Puts five fingers up using his left hand
> *Teacher*: One, two, three, four, five. Oh, I see. You shot five Monsters.
>   How about you?
> *C*1: Four. (*but shows 5 fingers*)
> *Teacher*: This is four. (*Reshaping the boy's fingers by putting one down*)
> *Yu Qiang*: I shot two.
> *Teacher*: Two is like this. (*teacher shows Yu Qiang how to denote the number 2 with his fingers*)

(*Yu Qiang Clip 0209*)

Teachers often scaffolded the children's learning and helped them to make meaning of their experiences. Early childhood teacher preparation in China today embraces Vygotsky's ideas and encourages teachers to scaffold children's learning. An example comes from the interaction of one teacher with Dou Dou during free play. Dou Dou was making a picture of rabbits with pieces of paper and the teacher led her to think about different aspects of the rabbit through the use of questions.

The teachers not only helped the children to understand their experiences, but their practices reflected fundamental cultural beliefs about the role of early childhood education in children's development. For example, there was an emphasis on hygiene and the formation of good habits. Consistent with the findings of Liu and Elicker (2005) and Liu et al. (2005), we found that the teachers did focus on transmitting knowledge and skills, although this was often done in play-like situations. Liu and Elicker (2005) observed teacher–child interactions in Chinese kindergartens. They found that teachers initiated 69.1% of the interactions, while the rest were initiated by children. Of the interactions initiated by teachers, the most common involved maintaining discipline (28%) and directing (37%). The latter was coded when teachers instructed, guided, or coached the children to help them acquire new knowledge or skills, including how to play with a new toy.

What is the Meaning of Play and Learning According to the Teachers and Parents?

All the teachers and parents were asked about the role of early childhood education and the relationship between play and learning. The extent of similarities in their responses is remarkable. All the respondents alluded to the close relationship between play and learning and that play was a vehicle of learning. Many of them also equated play with early childhood education. Excerpts from the interviews are given below.

Dou Dou

"Early childhood education is very important, and habit and routine training is critical. Play is part of early childhood education; it is a *means of training routine and discipline*...Play can facilitate children's development. Play is when children have *fun* with toys. A child *learns through play*, the child's learning is quite different from an adult's learning." (Dou Dou's teacher)

"Play is to *have fun* with toys... (Play and learning) *are very close to each other*. For example, Montessori work in the classroom is by nature a kind of play." (Dou Dou's mother)

Yu Qiang

"*Play is a means for children learning* in preschool; for example, Montessori work is a kind of learning. *Early childhood education is very important* to child development. Play facilitates child development, and scaffolds the child's learning. Learning in play is very natural." (Yu Qiang's teacher)

"Play can enhance children's IQs, so I have bought many construction toys ...and he can develop his intelligence from playing with these construction toys. Play is *linked with learning*. Play is the first kind of learning from birth. Children's play is a *kind of early childhood education*." (Yu Qiang's mother)

Zi Zhen

"Play is the major content of children's daily life; the majority of their time is occupied by playing. Play is the most *natural, happy and favourite activity* for young children. Children like playing. *They explore this world, gain experience, and understand concepts through playing.* Play is the most important activity in preschool years. Every activity should be *play-oriented in early childhood.*" (Zi Zhen's teacher)

"Early childhood education is very important. . ., can change the structure of your brain. . . . Play is the *means of early childhood education.* You cannot force a child to learn, so you need to pleasant the learning to make it like a play. *Play is the means of learning.*" (Zi Zhen's mother)

Ye Hao

"Play is a kind of teacher-organized activity involving children with some roles. . .There is a kind of *reciprocal relationship between play and learning.* . .Play can make children more active and behave better." (Ye Hao's teacher)

"Children of his age *should learn through playing.* Play means making sentences, kicking balls and group activities." (Ye Hao's mother)

Why are all these responses so remarkably similar? Are teachers' practices consistent with their stated beliefs? The reasons for the consistency between teachers' beliefs are straightforward. All these teachers had professional training, in which they would have learned about the importance of play. Furthermore, in cities like Shenzhen, there are ample opportunities for continued professional development, and these teachers would have taken advantage of them. Two of the kindergartens are highly regarded and one is a model programme. Hence, the teachers were likely to know how to implement the *Regulations on Kindergarten Education Practice* fairly well. However, the responses of the four mothers were very similar to those of the early childhood professionals, possibly because they were very educated and well informed. None of the target children had siblings, and educated parents of single children tend to exert much effort in finding out about early development because they want their child to succeed in life.

Conclusions

This chapter set out to answer questions related to play and learning in early childhood settings in China. Documentary analyses and case studies suggest that adults believe that the relationship between play and learning in the early years is very close. We believe that the term *"eduplay"* connotes what is expected by the government, teachers, and parents in early childhood settings and is an appropriate term to conceptualise teacher practices in Chinese preschools.

Beliefs About Play and Learning

The most influential early childhood curriculum mandate in the past two decades, *The Regulations on Kindergarten Education Practice,* put forward new principles for kindergarten education. Among these was the notion that play is a fundamental activity that should be integrated into all other activities in preschools (State

Educational Commission, 1989). However, it has been difficult for practitioners to fully adopt the ideas advocated in the *Regulations* due to inconsistencies between philosophies outlined in the regulations and powerful and deep-rooted cultural beliefs about learning (Wang & Mao, 1996; Zhu and Wang, 2005). For example, the *Regulations* emphasized play over formal instruction and recommended that a harmonious democratic relationship between the teacher and the child be established (Liu et al., 2005). This is not consistent with the traditional idea of obeying the teacher without arguing, and Confucian view that learning is beneficial to human development but play is not. Furthermore, the *Regulations* suggested that teachers move from being transmitters of knowledge to facilitators of learning and creativity. However, in the past, the teacher was characterized as a fountain of knowledge who force-fed Peking ducks.[3] Nonetheless, our observations suggest that play-based learning was prevalent in the kindergartens and accounted for over 65% of the activity, in comparison to direct teaching, which occurred 34.5% of the activity time. It appears that traditional cultural beliefs about learning in China have taken a back seat to what is considered as good educational practice (Rao, Cheng, & Narain, 2003).

The kindergarten teachers and parents who we interviewed believed that the relationship between play and learning was very close and regarded play as the main vehicle for learning. The emphasis was on "playing to learn." These beliefs reflect the influence of curriculum reforms on early childhood, teacher education, and the mass media, but are also a function of the age of the children for whom teachers have responsibility.

In line with curriculum guidelines, teachers and parents recognize the educational value of play. Indeed, the focus is on *early education* and the instructional value of various "playful" activities. Only two of the interviewees (Dou Dou's mother and Zi Zhen's teacher) spoke of play as a leisure activity, or spoke of the value of play in its own right. In general, play was considered the means to educate a young child.

The relationship between play and learning was very close for both teachers and parents. Because of this and the focus on the educational value of play, we feel that the term "eduplay" captures the beliefs of teachers and parents about what should happen and indeed occurs in Chinese early childhood settings.

Teacher Practices

The children participated in play-like activities throughout the day. However, much of that time was spent engaging in activities that were arranged by the teacher, who was often an active participant. There was less time allocated to genuinely free play where the children could pursue their own interests. The highly structured day is partly due to children's age, but also a reflection of Chinese cultural beliefs about the

---

[3] This refers to forcing food into the mouth of the duck by holding its throat.

early years being a time for training young children (Liu et al., 2005; Rao, McHale, & Pearson, 2003).

The teachers intervened in free play to help the children master some basic preacademic concepts such as size and shape, number and colour, etc. We believe that it was appropriate for them to do so. In some countries, early childhood teacher preparation programmes appear to present only a constructivist "children will learn for themselves" perspective, resulting in the concept of "developmentally appropriate practice" being interpreted by the teachers as unstructured play and minimal adult intervention. Li (2005) has suggested that early childhood educators in China keep an appropriate balance between education and play in implementing the reform proposals. Our observations suggest that the curriculum is underpinned by a developmentalist philosophy, and appropriate teaching approaches are used to facilitate young children's acquisition of basic skills.

Pramling-Samuelsson (this volume) considers play and learning as being two sides of the same coin in early education. Our findings suggest that the relation between education and play is also very close in China. While traditional Confucian values emphasize academic achievement and learning, curriculum regulations have empowered kindergartens to make play the basis of early childhood education. However, as mentioned earlier, this ideology is not consistent with traditional Chinese beliefs about education. Several decades on, our observations suggest that direct teaching is evident and genuinely free play accounts for only about 17% of activity time in kindergarten. Eduplay, a form of play-based education with "Chinese characteristics," appears to be prevalent in Chinese preschools, and it is in the context of eduplay that teachers help children to make meaning out of their experiences.

Acknowledgements Thanks go to Wu Yunxia and Pei Miao for their help with the data collection and analyses. Correspondence concerning this chapter should be addressed to Nirmala Rao, Faculty of Education, The University of Hong Kong, Hong Kong, China. E-mail may be sent to nrao@hku.hk

References

Bredekamp, S., & Copple, C. (Eds.). (1997). *Developmentally appropriate practice in early childhood programs* (Rev. ed.). Washington, DC: National Association for the Education of Young Children.

Bureau of Statistics of Shenzhen. (2005). *Census 2004.* Retrieved on October 28, 2005 from http://www.sztj.com/pub/sztjpublic/

Du, L. L. (2005). The investigation and research on preschool teachers' quality. *Journal of Zunyi Normal College, 7*(2), 47–49.

GOC, Government of the People's Republic of China. (2000). *Education for all: the year 2000 assessment final country report of China.* Beijing: Government of the People's Republic of China.

Levin, D. E. (2003). Beyond banning war and superhero play: Meeting children's needs in violent times. *Young Children, 58*(3), 46–51.

Li, H. (2005). Developing school-based curriculum in Hong Kong *Kindergartens: Insights, challenges and solutions.* Hong Kong: The Hong Kong Institute of Education.

Li, H., & Li, P. M. (2001). A Dialogue on the ways of reforming early childhood education in China. *Early Childhood Education*, No. 7, 8, 9 (serial paper).

Liu, J., & Elicker, J. (2005). Teacher-child interaction in Chinese kindergartens: An observational analysis. *International Journal of Early Years Education, 13*(2), 129–143.

Liu, Y. (1995). *Research on young children's perceptions of play: questions and reflections*. In the 5th academic conference of the chinese association of early childhood education (in Chinese). Beijing: Beijing Normal University Press.

Liu, Y. (2004). *The multi-perspectives of cultural, psychological, and pedagogical research on children's play*. Beijing: Beijing Normal University Press.

Liu, Y., & Feng, X. (2005). Kindergarten educational reform during the past two decades in Mainland China: Achievements and problems. *International Journal of Early Years Education, 13*(2), 93–99.

Liu, Y., Pan, Y. J., & Sun, H. F. (2005). Comparative research on young children's perceptions of play: An approach to observing the effects of kindergarten educational reform. *International Journal of Early Years Education, 13*(2), 101–112.

MOE, Ministry of Education of the People's Republic of China (2003). *Basic education in China*. Retrieved on October 28, 2005 http://www.moe.edu.cn/english/basic_b.htm

National Bureau of Statistics of China. (2005). *Census 2004*. Retrieved on October 28, 2005 from http://www.stats.gov.cn/

Population Division, UN, Population Division of the Department of Economic and Social Affairs of the United Nations Secretariat. (2004). *World population prospects: The 2004 revision* and *world urbanization prospects: The 2003 revision*. Retrieved October 28 2005 from http://esa.un.org/unpp

Pramling-Samuelsson, I. (2008). Play and learning in Swedish early childhood education. In I. Pramling-Samuelsson & M. Fleer (Eds.), *Play and learning in early childhood settings: International perspectives* (Chapter 7, this volume). Springer.

Rao, N., Cheng, K. M., & Narain, K. (2003). Primary schooling in China and India: Understanding how sociocontextual factors moderate the role of the State. *International Review of Education, 49*, 151–174.

Rao, N., McHale, J. P., & Pearson, E. (2003). Links between socialization goals and child-rearing practices in Chinese and Indian mothers. *Infant and Child Development, 12*, 475–492.

Shenzhen Government Online. (2005). *Administrative division*. Retrieved on October 30, 2005 from http://english.sz.gov.cn/

State Educational Commission. (1989). *Regulations on kindergarten education practice*. Beijing: Government of the People's Republic of China.

State Educational Commission. (2001). *Guidelines for kindergarten education practice*. Beijing: Government of the People's Republic of China.

Wang, J., & Mao, S. (1996). Culture and the kindergarten curriculum in the People's Republic of China. *Early Child Development and Care, 123*, 143–156.

Wang, X. C., & Spodek, B. (2000). *Early childhood education in China: A hybrid of traditional, communist, and western culture*. Paper presented at the meeting of the annual meeting of the National Association of Young Children, Atlanta, GA.

Wong, M., & Pang, L. (2002). Early childhood education in China: Issues and development. In L. K. S. Chan & E. Mellor (Eds.), *International developments in early childhood services* (pp. 53–69). New York: Peter Lang.

Zhu, J. (2005). Reflection on two decades of reform in early childhood curriculum in Mainland China. *Hong Kong Journal of Early Childhood, 3*(2), 5–8.

Zhu, J., & Wang, C. (2005). Contemporary early childhood education research in China. In B. Spodek & O. N. Saracho (Eds.), *International perspectives on research in early childhood education* (pp. 55–77). Greenwich, CT, US: Information Age Publishers.

Chapter 6
The Meaning of Play and Learning for 0–3-Year-Old Children in Japan

Mari Mori, Akiko Nezu, Chikage Samizo, Tomomi Naito, and Mamiko Ishizuka

Introduction

The purpose of this chapter is to illustrate the views about children's play and learning of the teacher–caregivers and the parents of five children from five day care centers in Japan. The study was conducted in a qualitative way. That is, five children (a day) at five day care centers were videotaped and analyzed. Then, interviews with five children's teacher–caregivers and parents were recorded. The researchers analyzed and interpreted the data. Through the processes of analysis, themes and issues emerged and were categorized. The main findings of our study on the significance of play and learning were that (1) play is important for children's lives, (2) play and learning for 0–3-year olds should not be considered separately, and (3) the cultural and societal contexts of society were closely related to the view that play for children is important. These findings would help readers understand why society and child care settings place importance on children's play for supporting growth and development. In addition, the findings can be a departure point for exchanging ideas and measures elaborating thinking on children's rights internationally.

Background of the Study

Current Issues of Japanese Society-Related Young Children

Shoshika (decreasing number of children) is still underway.

(Asahi Shinbun, 2006)

Japan consists of many islands, which include 4,000 small islands (Seki, 2005). Japan's population is approximately 120 million. Japan has been considered a homogeneous society; however, the number of non-Japanese residents has been increasing. The statistics indicate that the registered population of foreign nationalities

M. Mori
Department of Human Sciences, Toyo Eiwa University, Yokohama, Japan
e-mail: mamo@toyoeiwa.ac.jp

I. Pramling-Samuelsson, M. Fleer (eds.), *Play and Learning in Early Childhood Settings*, DOI 10.1007/978-1-4020-8498-0_6,
© Springer Science+Business Media B.V. 2009

is about 1.31 million, which is about 1.03% of the total population in Japan. The population of foreign nationalities has increased to 14.9% between 1995 and 2003 (The Ministry of Internal Affairs and Communication, 2005); the number includes children from 0 to 3 years as well. Therefore, it is expected that re-examining the contents of educational programs and the capabilities/sensibilities of staff is critical for early childhood education/care settings now. Thus the *Hoikusho* (day care center) and the *Yochien* (preschool/kindergarten) must evolve in order to meet the needs and interests of every child.

One of the serious societal issues in Japan is the decreasing number of Japanese born children. This concept is termed *shoshika* (Asahi shinbun, 2006; Mainichi Shinbun, 2006; Yomiuri Shinbun, 2006). The Ministry of Health, Welfare, and Labor announced the fertility rate in 2005 as 1.26, having been 1.29 in 2000. The rate in 2005 was low when compared to countries such as Sweden (1.75), France (1.90), and the United States (2.05) (Shakai Jitsuroku Data, 2007). The rate in Japan was expected to bring a serious problem politically due to the declining human resource base, economically due to the declining number of tax payers and increasing pension payments for elderly persons, and social-cultural changes due to losing traditions and decreasing morale for life.

In fact, the government has striven to deal with this issue. The government has developed family support plans (e.g., Angel Plan in 1995, New Angel Plan in 1999, and further new measures in 2004) to cope with the low number of children and to help nurture and support families to raise their children. The major contents of the "Next Generation Nurturing Support Measures" in 2004 (Shinnippon Hoki Publishing, 2005) are:

(1) expansion of capacity for small children at day care centers;
(2) establishment of better job conditions for working parents with children;
(3) spreading the philosophy of gender equality;
(4) establishment of a maternal child health and medical system;
(5) preparation of the educational environment for supporting children in the community;
(6) realization of educational environments in which all children can grow without stress;
(7) reduction of educational expense; and
(8) developing housing accommodation for young families.

One of the serious factors behind the low birthrate in Japan was considered to be the difficulty for families to have and raise their children — the limited number of child care centers for 0–3 year olds especially in urban areas, and the difficulty of taking a long period of maternity leave with payment. These factors prevented families from having children (OMEP, 2001; OMEP, 2003). Many media reports indicate that working mothers-to-be hesitated to have babies, because they would have difficulty finding a place offering education and care for their children. They were anxious about finding a place which would take care of their babies when their period of maternity leave ended. Many studies on child rearing have found that many young parents feel anxiety about having and raising their children both psychologically and economically (Nezu, 2004). The need for reforming early childhood care and education has become an urgent matter for society. In particular, program content for the 0–3 year olds is seen as a major issue for the field of early childhood education and care in Japan.

Brief Description of Early Childhood Care and Education in Japan

History and Structure

The practice of early childhood care and education is provided for by two major facilities, "*Yochien*" (preschool/kindergarten) and "*Hoikusho*" (day nursery/child care center) as indicated in Table 6.1. The first *Yochien* (preschool/kindergarten) was established in Japan in 1876, affiliated with the Tokyo Women's Normal School (now, named Ochanomizu Women's University), and it has been claimed as an educational institution (Oda & Mori, 2006). On the other hand, *Hoikusho* was established in 1890 by individuals in order to protect and to provide a place for young children while their parents' work, and since then it has been considered a social-welfare institution.

The total number of "*Nintei Kodomoen*" is 105 throughout the nation as of August, 2007 and is still in the process of development. Therefore the study did not include the characteristics of "*Nintei Kodomoen.*" In addition, the participants of five children were videotaped at various types of day care centers, and not at *Yochien*; so the researchers in this study decided not to refer to the content of *Yochien* curriculum guidelines.

Day Care Curriculum Guidelines in Terms of Play and Learning

Since this study focused on the play and learning of 0–3 year olds, we examined the curriculum guidelines of *Hoikusho*, day care centers, known as "*Hoikusho Hoiku-Shishin.*" In the curriculum guidelines, the importance of play and learning through an environment is emphasized in the same manner as the curriculum guidelines for *Yochien*, issued by the Ministry of Education. Moreover, the "*Hoikusho Hoiku-Shishin*" pays special attention to fostering a sense of humanity through a combination of care and education, since children spend longer hours at *Hoikusho* for supplementing education and care to that provided at home (OMEP, 2000). The major objectives and emphasis on development for under 3 year olds are indicated in Table 6.2.

In terms of play and learning for children at day care centers, the guidelines stress that knowledge, skills and attitudes for forming one's character are gained through play and real life experiences. The guidelines indicate that communication skills, self-reliance, self-expression, and knowledge about the surrounding world would be attained by indoors/outdoors, individual/group free play time. Thus, play is perceived as an important activity for children. In addition, the process of learning

Table 6.1 Characteristics of *Hoikusho* and *Yochien* (The Ministry of Education, Culture, Sports, Science and Technology, 2001; Shinnippon Hoki Publishing, 2005)

	HOIKUSHO (day care center)	YOCHIEN (kindergarten/preschool)
Basic notion	Welfare facility	School
Jurisdiction	The Ministry of Health, Welfare, and Labor	The Ministry of Education, Science, Sports, and Culture
Law	Child Welfare Law, in Chapter 39	School Educational Law, in Chapter 77
Body of establishment	Governmental accredited, municipally authorized, independent, unauthorized, play group, family support center	National, Municipally Certified, Independent, Unauthorized
Curriculum guidelines	*Hoikusho Hoikushishin* (Guidelines for Day Nursery Practice)	*Yochien Kyoiku Yoryo* (National Curriculum Standards for Kindergarten Education)
Contents of practice	Basic Development from 0- to 6-year olds	Five areas of development Health/human
	Five Areas for 3–5 year olds as indicated in Kindergarten Curriculum Standards	Relationship/language/environment/ expression
Hours a day	8 hours a day in principle	4 hours a day in principle over 39 weeks throughout a school year
Child–teacher ratio	Under 12 months 3:1, 1–2-year olds 6:1	35:1 in principle
	3-year olds 20:1, 4–5-year olds 30:1	
Children	From 6-week old infants and children needing nursery care to enter elementary school	From 3-year olds to enter elementary school
Staff/teacher certification	Day nursery license	MA degree certificate, BA degree certificate, 2–3 years degree certificate
No. of sites	22,570 (as of April, 2005)	13,949 (as of April, 2005)

Table 6.2 Objectives and development of under 3-year olds in "*Hoikusho Hoiku-Shishin* (Day Care Guidelines)" (OMEP, 2000)

Under 6 months	Health/safety
Under 15 months	Weaning/walking/early verbal development
Under 2-year olds	Physical development/verbal development/interest in peers
2-year olds	Rapid growth in bodily function/mimicking/development of early expression
3-year olds	Mastering of basic living habits/adapting to group life

is not expressed directly, rather it is embedded in play and living experiences at the day care center.

With these issues, examining the content of the program for 0–3-year olds by teacher–caregivers and children's parents is critical for developing an understanding the guidelines and practice at day care centers. The need for developing the content of the programs to enhance children's growth and development in a healthy way, physically and psychologically, is an important and urgent matter. Thus, this study aimed to explore and capture the views of teacher–caregivers and of parents on children's play and learning. Although the study is very limited in many ways – number of observed children, duration of observation, places of observation, and so on – it does give an idea of how the practices are carried out in some Japanese early childhood programs by practitioners; and it gives their and the parents' views on play and learning.

Procedure of the Study

Consensus of the Researchers

Prior to the study, we, the five researchers developed a consensus for conducting the research as shown below:

- We perceive the study not as a final product, but as a departure point for developing a research forum focusing on the play and learning of young children.
- We try to describe play, as a key to children's learning and development, in an empirical way.
- We conduct this study in order to clarify the rights of children and contribute to the work of OMEP.
- We believe and perceive learning as being embedded in the play of children.
- Although the study cannot and should not generalize as a representative study of Japanese children and day care centers, it illustrates the significance of play and learning in the eyes of the teacher–caregivers and the parents, and can help international readers to understand the views of Japanese scholars on play and learning.
- The study would help early childhood professionals to rethink how to play their role.

Limitations of the Japanese Study

We identified two major limitations: generalization and subjective perceptions. As indicated in Table 6.1, there are 22,570 day care centers in Japan as of 2005 (The Ministry of Health, Welfare, and Labor, 2006). Therefore, the five children and five sites of this study could not generalize about the significance of the play and learning of young children as a whole. However, we feel that this small study would help readers understand how the significance of play and learning is perceived by the participants. In addition, the directors of the five sites have close relationships with members of the OMEP Japan Committee. This means that attitudes toward the study were positive from the beginning, which might have influenced the participants' responses. That is, they would have positive attitudes toward play as a variable for learning for young children. Furthermore, the specific conditions on the days of videotaping, such as the health condition of the focus children and other children and the weather, were not controlled, and may have influenced the relationship between children's play and learning.

In terms of the possibly subjective perceptions of the researchers, two day care centers were affiliated with colleges where three of the five researchers work; therefore, the degree of subjectivity was higher than with the other three centers. In addition, selection of the interviewed teachers was done by the directors of the sites. The interviewed teachers might have experienced some pressure from the directors. We could not conclude the findings as being representative of the voices of all the teacher–caregivers in Japan.

Duration of the Processes of the Study

In the fall of 2004, the five researchers discussed and determined the basic criteria for selecting the sites of the study. The five researchers selected a place for observations and interviews. The five researchers would visit all five sites or would conduct interviews at the different sites. Rather, one or two of them would be responsible for observations and interviews. Then, five researchers received permission for the study from the directors of the day care centers focused upon.

From December 2004 to May 2005, observations of the children being studied were carried out through videotaping and written field notes were taken by the researchers. The videotapes of each child were edited down to 30 minutes and these tapes were used to conduct interviews with the teacher–caregivers and parents of the children. After the interviews, the five researchers gathered and analyzed the data in the fall of 2005.

Overview of Five Cases

Characteristics of Children, Parents, Teacher–Caregivers, and Day Care Centers

In order to protect the privacy of the participants, all names of individuals and centers are pseudonymous. In terms of describing the characteristics for site and child selection for inclusion in the study, we identified the following common characteristics. For the children, we included characteristics common to all five children such as age and gender of the children and their parents/makeup of the families any other specific characteristics. In terms of interviewing parents, job status/age and gender/any other specific characteristics were included. In terms of interviewing the teacher–caregivers we considered their educational background/professional experience as teacher–caregiver/any other specific characteristics. In terms of day care centers, we included location and environment/body of management/philosophy of program/number of children/strength of program/relationship with families.

1. "Kei" (male, 2 years 5 months) at Akasa day care center in Tottori

Kei was a 29-month-old boy, an only child from a two-parent family. He began to attend Akasa day care center 5 days a week at 14 months of age. His mother also attended the day care center when she was a child. Both the mother (36 years old) and the father (36 years old) have full-time jobs and live with Kei's grandmother.

Two teacher–caregivers of Kei's classroom attended a 2-year college to acquire teacher–caregiver licenses. Mrs. Ohma has 29 years and Mrs. Okuma has 9 years of experience as teacher–caregiver.

Akasa day care center, in which Kei attends, is located in Tottori, the country side of Japan, facing Japan Sea (Fig. 6.1). The center is a licensed independent day care center; and it cares for about 100 children ranging from 6-week babies to 6-year-old children. The philosophy of the program is to enrich the life of individual children through free play and an inside/outside environment. They also emphasize the importance of learning through projects that encourage children's families, and people in the community to become engaged in.

2. "Shin" (male, 1 year 1 month) at Kawa day center in Tokyo

Shin was a 13-month-old boy, from a two-parent family, and has a sister who is 5 years old. Both mother (34 years old) and father (34 years old) have a full-time job and live with Shin's grandparents. Shin's sister also attended Kawa day care center, therefore the parents had developed a trust and close relationship with the teacher–caregivers before Shin entered the center. Ms. Aoi, a classroom teacher–caregiver of Shi's, attended a 2-year college course to acquire her teacher–caregiver license and has 20 years of teaching experience.

Kawa day care center, which Shin attends, is located in a suburban area of Tokyo, and most parents commute to their workplace, the center of Tokyo, which takes roughly one to one-and-half hours. The center is a licensed independent day care center, with a total of 110 infants, toddlers, and preschoolers. The philosophy of the program is to nurture the growth and development of the individuals. The program espouses the belief that parents' participation enriches the center's practice. The center is located in a suburban area, and has various kinds of trees and flowers in its playground.

3. "Moe" (female, 2 years 11 months) at Tamtam day care program in Kanagawa

Moe was a 35-month-old girl, an only child from a two-parent family. Moe's mother (38 years old) is a full-time mother and housewife and did not have a regular job when the study was conducted. Moe's father was 40 years old, who engaged in a white collar job.

Fig. 6.1 Children at Akasa Day Care Center, Tottori, Japan

Ms. Kanno, a teacher–caregiver of Moe, is a graduate of O national women's university. Ms. Kanno was in her late 30s, having 5 years of teaching experience at kindergarten/preschool.

Tamtam day care program is located in a campus of Kama Women's College, a 4-year private institution which issues a teacher–caregiver license, kindergarten teacher license, and elementary teacher certificates. Tamtam day care program is located in Kamakura, a historical place near Tokyo, and a residential area. Therefore, the director is a faculty member of the college, and the staff are highly qualified professionals hired by the college. Since Tamtam day care program was established to support and nurture mothers to raise their children without feeling anxiety, the program is a part-time half-day program which opens for children between 2 and 3 years old and their parents. The philosophy of the program is to support parents, especially mothers, to experience the joy of child-rearing.

4. "Yuki" (female, 1 year 7 months) at Saka day care center in Chiba

Yuki was a 19-month-old girl, an only child from a two-parent family. Both mother (late 20s) and father (early 30s) have a full-time job. Yuki's mother has lived overseas prior to giving birth to Yuki. Since Yuki's grandparents and relatives live nearby her residence, they help to look after Yuki.

Ms. Nozawa, a teacher–caregiver of Yuki's class, and the interviewee of the study, attended a 2-year college course to acquire a teacher–caregiver license. Ms. Nozawa had 20 years of practical experience.

Saka day care center, which Yuki attends, is located in Chiba, a neighboring prefecture of Tokyo, thus most parents are commuters to their place of work, the center of Tokyo, taking at least one hour by train. The center is a licensed independent full-time day care center, which opens from 7.30 a.m. to 7.00 p.m. 6 days a week, and cares for a total of about 50 infants, toddlers, and preschoolers. The center perceives every child as a gift of God, and it provides rich free play time to nurture the development of children. The program also believes that children learn through experiences related to nature. The program holds an after school program for elementary children, and a play center program which provides a place for young children and their parents to play together.

5. "Sachi" (female, 1 year 9 months) at Popo child and family support center in Tokyo

Sachi is a 21-month-old girl, an only child of a two-parent family. Sachi's mother (in her 30s) was a full-time housewife/mother when the interview was conducted. Sachi's father (in his 30s) works at a corporation located in Tokyo.

Ms. Noda, a respondent of the interview, graduated after 2 years at college to receive a teacher–caregiver license. Prior to work at Popo, she worked at a different day care center. She has more than 10 years of teaching and caring experience.

Popo family support center is located in a building belonging to a private junior college, in an urban area of Tokyo. Therefore, the director of the program is a faculty member of the college, and the staff is somehow related to the college. Since Popo support center was established to support and nurture mothers to raise their children without a feeling of anxiety, the program is a part-time half-day program which opens for any child between 1 and 3 years old. Parents and children can stay at the center during its opening hours, from 10.00 a.m. to 4.00 p.m.. The philosophy of the program is to provide a place for children and their families to play and interact with other children and families. In addition, the staff provides mothers with practical support and training for child rearing during its opening hours. The maximum capacity per day is 50 families.

Findings of the Study

Parents' Views on Children's Play and Learning

A focused interview session took place at each site with one or two researchers after showing the 15-minutes edited videotape to the teacher–caregivers and the parents. The researchers recorded and took notes while interviewing. Each session took about 1 hour and 30 minutes. The researchers then transcribed the tapes and analyzed the data during five researcher meetings.

Focused Questions for the Interviews

The following are the questions for interviews with parents:

(A) Tell us about the child's play at home.
(B) What do you think of play in the child care setting?
(C) What do you think of play for children?
(D) What do you think of learning for children?
(E) What do you think of the role of the day care center in terms of play and learning for children?
(F) Are there any other comments?

Views of Parents on Play

The parents responded immediately by describing how and what their children play at home.

- "He likes to play puzzles and with cars by himself these days. He never gets bored of doing these things." (1. Kei)
- "Mostly she plays by herself. She likes a pretend play, such as pretending to be Minnie Mouse." (3. Moe)
- "He plays with blocks. Nowadays he throws blocks and other things, which is different from my daughter when she was his age." (2. Shin)
- "I (mother) try to play with my daughter for two hours a day at least. We take a walk, play with Japanese traditional playing cards, and arts and crafts. She likes to play using her fingers and fine motor skills." (3. Moe)

The parents mostly talked about their children's individual play at home. They also talked about inside house play. Only Moe's mother consciously talked about how she herself played as a play partner for her daughter. In this study, two mothers did not hold full-time jobs. So three mothers did not see how their children play during a day.

When the parents talked about their views about play in child care settings, they largely focused on playing with other children.

- "It is valuable for my son to play with other children, older and younger children." (1. Kei and 4. Yuki)

- "He likes to play in the sand-box. I do appreciate that Hoikuen is allowed to do dynamic play which is difficult for him to experience at home." (1. Kei)
- "He likes to play outside, such as riding a bicycle and playing with sand and mud with his friends." (1. Kei)
- "I can see the different ways my daughter plays at the program. She talks to others actively, which I have rarely seen at home." (3. Moe)
- "Playing with other children is challenging for my daughter since she has little experience of interacting with other children." (5. Sachi)

The parents valued play in child care settings because it helps their children to interact with other children. The parents strongly agree with the importance of play in child care settings because it provides many opportunities for children to choose what to play with, to interact with other children, and to develop communication skills. In addition, they valued outside play at child care settings for fostering physical strength.

Views on Learning

All five researchers experienced difficulties in getting responses from the parents to describe the meanings of "learning." Most parents carefully chose certain words to express their thoughts on "learning."

- "I think a child's life itself is learning." (3. Moe)
- "Wow, it is difficult to express . . . Broaden a capacity of concentration? Deepen a capacity of memory?" (1. Kei)
- "I have never thought of the word 'learning' consciously. Learning may not be explained by the word itself. Rather, through interaction with people and things, the word 'learning' could be feasible." (4. Yuki)
- "I want my child to learn to trust others, and to become trusted by others." (1. Kei)
- "I want my child not to be afraid of people. In other words, I want my child to learn to find interest in communicating with others." (4. Yuki)
- "Being impressed by anything, finding things interesting, and exploring something would be learning which is included in play itself." (3. Moe)
- "I do not think it is important for young children to attend after school programs, such as English, reading and counting classes." (5. Sachi)

From the interviews, it was found that "learning" does not stand by itself. In other words, the learning of children from 0–3 years cannot be explained without discussing living experiences. All parents talked about children's learning as the hope, belief and values that would be appropriate for the lives of children. In addition, they expressed the view that learning is embedded in play. Therefore, they put significance on play as having a critical role for children's learning and development. Interestingly, some parents expressed the view that children's learning could not be separated from playing with others. They saw that the development of human relationships could be an important part of learning for the children's age. Furthermore, one parent showed her anxiety about learning and the early study of reading, writing, and counting as extra curricula activities.

Emergent Themes for Views on Play and Learning

From the interviews, several themes emerged as follows:

- Play is important and necessary for every child's life.
- Play is the critical component for children to develop communication skills and exploring the world.
- Play helps children to encounter people in various activities.
- Learning is embedded in play. Thus, children's play and learning should not be separated.
- Child care settings play an important role for children in expanding their human relationship circle and development of trust in others.
- Outdoor play is important in Japanese day care settings.

Although all parents expressed the importance of play for young children, they showed difficulty in identifying the meaning of learning independently. They did not view children's play and learning separately. This led to the need for further consideration of the methodology of the study, and definition of words in this particular study.

Teacher–Caregivers' Views on Children's Play and Learning

Focused interview sessions and data analysis were conducted in the same way as the interviews with parents.

Focused Questions for the Interviews

The following are the questions for the teacher–caregivers:

(1) Tell us about the child's play in the child care setting.
(2) What do you think of play in the child care setting?
(3) What do you think of play for children?
(4) What do you think of learning for children?
(5) What do you think of the role of play and learning for children at day care?
(6) Do you have any other comments?

Views of Teacher–Caregivers on Play

The teacher–caregivers talked about their views on playing having connections with the everyday life of children in the study. Especially, they all agreed that the role of play in the day care setting is to provide children with a chance to interact with others to find fun and happiness. Some teachers talked about the relationship between children's play and moral development.

- "Playing at the day care center is an important tool enabling children to interact with others." "The children can understand what is right and not right through play." (4. Yuki's TC: teacher–caregiver)

- "Playing at this center, 'Popo,' has allowed children to play freely by themselves, and to develop human relationships." (5. Sachi's TC)
- "The child in the video observes how other children play while she is playing." (3. Moe's TC)
- "The child in the video loves to play in the sand-box. He never gets bored of staying there even for 40–50 minutes." (2. Shin's TC).
- "The child in the video wants to copy other children. He would like to have the same toys and do same thing, and to be taken care of by the teacher–caregiver the same way she takes care of other children." (2. Shin's TC)
- "He (the child in the video) loves to play with blocks." (1. Kei's TC)
- "He loves pretending play and imaginative play, for example, he sees a carton box as a dump car and so on. He repeated the play many times." (1. Kei's TC)
- "He likes to play outside." (1. Kei's TC)
- "Children experience fun through play." (1. Kei, 3. Moe, 4. Yuki, and 5. Sachi's TC)

Interestingly, all teacher–caregivers talked about the importance of play in a concrete manner, that is, playing is not an abstract matter, rather, it constitutes the children's lives.

Views on Learning

All five teacher–caregivers took time to respond when asked the meaning of learning for 0–3-year olds. When they talked about children's play, they showed very positive attitudes towards responding. Some teacher–caregivers mixed up the meaning of learning and teaching. They did not distinguish learning from play.

- "I have not become conscious about children's learning while being with children." (4. Yuki's TC)
- "I do not teach the children special subjects as the children are very young." (4. Yuki's TC)
- "I think children learn through their daily lives at a day care setting." (4. Yuki's TC)
- "Every child has already acquired learning skills through their experience." (5. Sachi's TC)
- "Children have abilities to adapt to living under any conditions. I believe that is the best for living and learning skills." (5. Sachi's TC)
- "Playing with others is learning how to live with others which is very different from what the child does at home. The child is learning how to live in society." (3. Moe's TC)
- "Children's learning starts from coping with what others do." (1. Kei's TC)
- "Learning is seeing." (1. Kei's TC)

The teacher–caregivers tried to find words to explain children's learning in day care settings. They mainly talked about learning as taking place in every part of living at day care. They found it difficult to explain how learning takes place within children's play and how play can connect the areas of children's development in multiple ways. This is related to the teacher–caregivers' professional identity: That is, the teacher–caregiver is viewed as a nurturing person supporting children's growth and development, rather than as a teaching person.

Views on the Role of the Teacher–Caregiver

When the teacher–caregivers were asked about the significance of children's play and learning, all of them unconsciously talked about their roles as teacher–caregiver in terms of children's play and learning. It was very interesting to see that the interviewees strongly identified as professionals.

- "My role as a teacher is to provide many opportunities for children to get to know each other. For example, when I find a child who does interesting things, I let others be aware of it." (4. Yuki's TC)
- "I hope that children would understand the importance of keeping an order and taking turns at the center which is also the rule for society." (4. Yuki's TC)
- "I hope children will share the joy of play with other children." (4. Yuki's TC)
- "Through play, children would be aware of how to be responsible persons in society." (4. Yuki's TC)
- "I tried to talk to children gently since children would pick up the way of talking from us." (1. Kei's TC)
- "I am aware of the flavor of each season. For example, I try to set up water play during summer." (2. Shin's TC)
- "Sometimes, I would play with clay consciously in front of the children so that they could develop their interests in clay." (2. Shin's TC)

None of the teacher–caregivers expressed her/his role as one of enhancing children's academic learning. They saw themselves as a model for children to explore the world, rather than as being an instructor to teach children what to do. They perceived their roles as one of providing an environment for children to play and learn.

Emergent Themes for Views on Play and Learning

All the teacher–caregivers in the study insisted that play is a necessary experience within children's lives both in home and in child care settings. They perceived that children develop and learn through play. However, the teacher–caregivers also showed difficulty with defining the meanings of learning. Some teacher–caregivers confused the meaning of learning and the 3Rs (reading, writing, arithmetic). They saw learning as embedded in playing. However, they faced difficulties explaining what and how learning is embedded in playing. The interviews created the need for further study in terms of teacher–caregivers' views on children's learning in play beyond the present study.

From the interviews, several themes emerged as follows:

- Play is important and necessary for every child's life.
- Play is a critical component for children to develop communication skills and explore the world.
- Play is fun.
- Play allows children to encounter people from various situations.
- Learning is embedded in play. That is, children's play and learning should not be separated.
- Learning takes place through observations.
- Children learn complicated relationships with people which form the foundations for moral development.
- Child care settings play an important role for children to expand their human relationship circle and to develop trust in others.

Discussions from the Findings

As we conclude the study, three major points emerge through the interviews, which merit further discussion.

Play is Essential for the Lives of Children Both at Home and in Child Care Settings

Both parents and teacher–caregivers in the study strongly support the need for children to play freely at home and in child care settings. The respondents describe children's play both from what they had seen in the videotapes as well as from their everyday lives. The parents were very satisfied with the practices within the day care settings that guaranteed opportunities for children's free play. This fulfils what "The Guidelines of Practice at Day Care Centers" have stressed as important.

Role of Play for Young Children is Mainly to Develop their Social Relationships that Reflect the Social and Cultural Context of Japan

Both parents and teacher–caregivers in the study talked about the role of play as enhancing children's ability to interact with others. In other words, the respondents were highly focused on children's development of human relationships, compared to other areas of development, such as cognitive development, physical development, emotional development, and esthetic development.

In particular, the parents talked about the difference of play between home and child care. They said that their children's play at home was mainly characterized by individual play. However, while watching the videotapes, they were caught by the scenes of how their children were playing with others. This could be related to the researchers' ways of making the selection. In other words, we should be aware of any possible bias on the part of researchers. The parents mainly talked about the importance of developing communication skills for interacting with others. They perceived that these activities would contribute to their children becoming responsible people in society in the future. In addition, the responses would reflect the current situation of Japanese society. As we talked about "*Shoshika* (the declining fertility rate, and the decreasing number of children)" in the first section of this article, both parents and teacher–caregivers were aware that most children rarely interact with others at home. Therefore, child care settings are the place for providing many opportunities to meet with people from different backgrounds, characteristics, and age levels. Playing with siblings or children in their neighborhood had been replaced with peer play in the day care centres and/or Kindergartens, as the main forum for play. This finding suggests that research is needed into the role that day care settings in Japan have for supporting play.

Play and Learning are not Separated

The responses of the interviewees clearly depicted that both parents and teacher–caregivers were at a loss to define and articulate the meaning of learning for children. They said that play itself is an important thing for lifelong learning, which is inevitable as children grow and develop. However, they were not aware of how play and learning were connected. Interestingly, the researchers did not find any big differences in the views on children's learning between the parents and the teachers. The teacher–caregivers did not talk about the relationship between play and learning from the perspectives of developmental theories and/or educational theories. Rather both groups of participants in the study thought that the word learning is closely related to early education, such as reading, writing, and math activities. They did not distinguish between intellectual learning and academic learning in general.

Issues for Further Study

After having done the interviews and analysis of the study, we, all five researchers, found a number of issues which require further discussion and research. The issues raised are as follows:

Design of the Study

In terms of the design of the study, we have found several points to be clarified in future research.

Generalization

We do not have enough samples to claim that the findings of the study are representative of the views of parents and teacher–caregivers in Japan. The participants and child care settings in the study were selected intentionally because they were known to the researchers or the OMEP Japan committee. They were not chosen randomly. In addition, when we undertook this comparative international study, we needed a detailed and thorough background knowledge of the centers in order to select participants in relation to the methodology of the study.

Period of Time for Observation

It is not enough to present a videotape to the interviewees as a typical day of children in some child care settings. In particular, the play and learning of children from the age of 0 to 3 years old may be more easily influenced by the weather, physical and mental conditions, people, surrounded by a video camera, and so on. Although some researchers in the study were familiar with the sites, some children were not familiar with being videotaped. We need to examine how and what to observe, and to depict children's play and learning in different ways.

Relationship Between Practice and Theory

The findings revealed that the participants in the study did not clearly explain the relationship between play and learning. The word "learning" was a problem for Japanese to define and describe since the word "learning" is usually related to academic learning in general. There is a need to examine how the word "learning" is defined, and interpreted in practical situations. The challenge is to develop a theory of learning through play, in logical ways, with concrete supporting data.

Final Comments

Thoughts on the Role of OMEP for the Field of Early Childhood Care and Education

Overall, we need to re-examine the role of OMEP for the field of early childhood care and education that could make children and their families happy throughout the world.

Since we, the five researchers, are members of the OMEP JAPAN Committee, our pledge is to protect and guarantee the rights of children. We see ourselves as advocates for children's rights. Reflecting this basic principle, we need to strive to contribute to raising the awareness of people of the importance of play for young children throughout the world.

We see the findings and the problems in the study as a departure point for designing and conducting research in the future. We would like to continue to have rich dialogue with parents, teacher–caregivers, and administrators, not only domestically, but also internationally.

Acknowledgements We thank Dr. Stephen Soresi, associate professor at Toyo Eiwa University, Yokohama, Japan for reading and making comments on our manuscript.

References

Nezu, A. (2004) Gendaiteiki kadai [Issues of modern era in Japan]. In K. Ogawa (Ed.), *Yochien jisshuu* [Practicum at Yochien Preschool/Kindergarten]. Tokyo: Jusonbo.

Oda, Y, & Mori, M. (2006). Current challenges of kindergarten (Yochien) education in Japan: Toward balancing children's autonomy and teachers' intention. *Childhood Education, 82*(6), 369–373.

OMEP. (2000). The Japanese National Committee of OMEP 1998. *Fact sheets of early care and education in Asia and the Pacific* (Vol. 1, pp. 17–26).

OMEP. (2001). Family service support systems in Japan. *Fact sheets on early childhood care and education in Japan* (No. 6). Japan: The Japanese National Committee of OMEP.

OMEP. (2003). *Fact sheets on early childhood care and education in Japan* (No. 7). Japan: The Japanese National Committee of OMEP.

Seki, H. (2005). *Social study home page of elementary school attached to Hiroshima University.* [On-line] http://www2.ocn.ne.jp/hiroseki/index.html

Shakai Jitsuroku Data. (2007). *Goukei tokushu shusseiritsu no suii.* [Changes of Fertility Rate]. [On-line] http://www2.ttcn.ne.jp

Shinnippon Hoki Publishing. (2005). *Graphs and charts on Japan's child welfare services, 2005.* Tokyo: Shinnippon Hoki Publishing Inc.

Shoshika [Lowering number of children]. (2006, June 2). *Asahi Shinbun* [Asahi Daily Newspaper], p. 1.

Shusseiritu 1.25 [Fertility Rate is 1.25]. (2006, June 2). *Mainichi Shinbun* [Mainichi Daily Newspaper], p. 1.

The Ministry of Education, Culture, Sports, Science and Technology. (2001). *National curriculum standards for kindergartens.*

The Ministry of Internal Affairs and Communication. (2005). "Population census." Statistics Bureau, The Ministry of Internal Affairs and Communication.

The Ministry of Health, Welfare, and Labor. (2006). *Report of social welfare administration.* [On-line] http://www.hws-kyokai.or.jp/html-table/table10-f.htm

Yomiuri Shinbun. (2006, June, 2). *Lowerest rate in the past.* [Yomiuri Daily Newspaper], [On-line].

Chapter 7
Play and Learning in Swedish Early Childhood Education

Ingrid Pramling-Samuelsson and Sonja Sheridan

The Socio-political Context in Sweden

Sweden is a growing nation with a diverse population of 9 million inhabitants. Contemporary Swedish society is made up of people from many different continents and ethnic backgrounds. Every fifth child has at least one parent of non-Swedish origin. In the largest cities, about one third of the population are immigrants.

For most of the last 60 years, Sweden has been governed by a Social Democratic government, which has taken responsibility for the next generation by introducing reforms such as child allowance, maternity leave, and access to preschool for all children. An Act of Parliament in 2003 gave each child the right to participate in preschool activities from the age of four, even if their parents were out of work or on maternity leave. The Maximum Fee Reform gives parents the right to have the child in preschool for a maximum fee (not more than 3% of the family's total income, the remaining costs are financed by the state and the municipality), and a "ceiling" was set for the cost of first, second and third child, etc., per month. The aim of this reform is equality between children and between communities. An extended parental leave policy makes it possible for all children to spend their first year of life at home with their families. Parental leave is to be shared between the parents and gives them almost full salary compensation for 450 days (Skolverket, 2003a, b).

The various reforms of the past few decades have prepared the way for integrating preschool into the Swedish educational system and producing a national curriculum for children ranging in age from 1 to 5 years (Ministry of Education and Science in Sweden, 1998a). In Sweden, early childhood education has never been just a question of child-minding. Even for the youngest children, there have always been pedagogical intentions, and these have been strengthened by the preschool curriculum, especially as the national curriculum for preschool is linked to the curriculum for compulsory school (Ministry of Education and Science in Sweden, 1998b). The aims are that the curricula should express a common view

---

I. Pramling-Samuelsson
Göteborg University, Department of Education, Göteborg, Sweden
e-mail: Ingrid.Pramling@ped.gu.se

I. Pramling-Samuelsson, M. Fleer (eds.), *Play and Learning in Early Childhood Settings*, DOI 10.1007/978-1-4020-8498-0_7,
© Springer Science+Business Media B.V. 2009

of knowledge, development and learning in the direction of the overall goals, in order to enhance quality throughout the education system.

Preschool starts from age 1, and most children are in preschool from their early years. Preschool is usually open from 6.30 a.m. to 6 p.m. The average time of participation is 30 hours per week per child. The children are organized into toddler groups (1–3 years) and sibling groups (1–5 years). The size of the group varies, but on average toddler groups comprise 14 children and 3 teachers, while sibling groups comprise 18 children and 3 teachers. All teachers are qualified, about half of them having a university degree (3.5 years), and half having trained as nursery nurses for 2 years at upper secondary/senior high school (see Pramling-Samuelsson & Sheridan, 2004, for a more detailed discussion of Sweden's social political context).

Introduction to the Empirical Study

Five children were observed for a whole day in five different preschools: Axel (boy, 3.2 years), Elin (girl, 3.1 years), Oskar (boy, 2.9 years), Linda (girl, 2.7 years) and Hans (boy, 2.3 years). Three children were in a sibling group (1–5 years) and two in toddler group (1–3 years). The number of children in the groups varied from 13 to 16. During the observations, 8–16 children were present. In each child group, the staff comprised three teachers (two preschool teachers and one nursery nurse).

The preschools were randomly selected and were situated in different socio-economic areas, both in big cities and in small municipalities. The quality of the participating preschools was estimated to be average (see Harms & Clifford, 1980).

During the period of data collection, children stayed in the preschool between 5 and 8 hours a day. Observations of children were recorded, and there are approximately 2 hours of video recordings of each child. Field notes were taken by the observer throughout the day. Further, one of each child's preschool teachers and both parents were interviewed. The observations took place during late autumn and just before Christmas, which has influenced both planned activities in the participating preschools and the children's play.

Parents' Views of Play and Learning

Parents believe that their children get on well in preschool and are happy to stay there; None of them is sad when the parents leave them. The parents' attitudes towards preschool are very positive. At the same time, parents appear to have little knowledge of ongoing activities in preschool and their own child's whereabouts. The way some parents and preschool teachers picture children in preschool seems to differ. The parents may describe their child as active, leaders of games, talkative and creative. The same child is portrayed by the teacher as shy, quiet, enjoying solitary play, or in conflict with other children.

The parents describe preschool as an active and stimulating environment for the child when compared to home, where there is more peace and quiet. They assume that educationally exciting activities led by engaged and professional teachers take place in the preschool. Parents believe that children do and learn different things in preschool from what they do at home because the staff are educated and are there for the children all day. "They manage to do so many things in a short time in preschool, things that you do not manage to get the time to do at home," one parent said. Furthermore, all parents mention that social relations and peer interaction are the foremost contributions of preschool. They also think that preschool helps to make children independent. Many parents give examples of how their children manage things at preschool which they do not manage at home.

The parents imply that their children are different at home and in preschool. They think that children express two partly different identities (Vanderbroeck, 1999). At home, there are more conflicts and the children may whine in order to get their own way, while in preschool, they adapt more easily to the interests of others and to common rules. They attribute this to the fact that the relationship between parents and children differs from that between preschool teachers and children. According to one parent, "The staff in preschool have a more neutral approach towards the children and do not enter into emotional conflicts as easily as parents do at home. So the children also learn 'good manners' in preschool."

Some parents also comment that children are exposed to a larger variation of social values in preschool than at home. The children are engaged in learning to re-spect others, to take turns, to set boundaries, to communicate, and they play in ways that stimulate their fantasy and creativity. All parents feel that children are making a lot of progress in their language development in preschool. Many parents state that their child's verbal communication has improved in an obvious way since they started preschool, as children are forced to make themselves understood by the staff and children. All five child participants have siblings and all parents feel that having a sibling has a crucial impact on children's play as well as learning. The children just "follow" their older siblings, and those who have younger siblings often play pretend "mum–child" games. In the case of children with newborn siblings, parents reported that innovative features emerged in the target child's play.

For most parents, play and learning constitute a diffuse whole in preschool. Some parents state that it is natural for children to play, and that play is part of childhood, while learning involves the child exerting an effort. Despite this, they say that chil-dren learn while playing and that children play what they have experienced. They also emphasize that children in play observe other children and grown-ups and learn from them.

Preschool Teachers' Views of Play and Learning

Teachers emphasize the importance of knowing about the two worlds of the child, the preschool and the home. However, they reveal that they have no knowledge of what the child does at home. On the other hand, they seem to have great knowledge of each child's play and preferences in preschool. Something that preschool teachers often emphasize as a positive aspect of children is that they can play, fantasize and get involved in something for a long time. In contrast, they find it problematic when one child runs around, ruining things for other children. Children should be happy, confident and be able to keep themselves busy. They point out that children's social development is fundamental to all kinds of learning. Therefore, they focus on children's learning to share toys, to take turns, to give and take, to control their temper, to play both by themselves and together with other children. The teachers also emphasize the importance of language and communication, and many preschool activities revolve around communicating, singing and reading books.

Teachers consider themselves as facilitators of children's play and learning, the ones who observe and give support when needed. They emphasize the value of being present in the world of the child and the importance of being a "fellow researcher" together with children. They often state that it is all about making children feel involved in activities. One teacher, Sonja, states

> There has been a change in the role of the teacher from when I started working in preschool. Perhaps you have different eyes now, sort of...what they are able to do. For example, getting dressed, you help them (children) to start... they find their own solutions, in another way perhaps. If someone is going to put on..., well, you ask: "What do you have to do to get your mittens on?" And, perhaps they have found out that they can use a chair or something. The view has probably changed in the last few years.

What this teacher expresses is that nowadays you listen to the children and make them feel involved in the everyday routines in preschool. For instance, children have to rinse their plates after lunch, dress and undress or help to feed and tend the chickens (they have chickens at one preschool) by themselves. All of the teachers express confidence in the children in a variety of ways and are aware of each child's competence.

The teachers' main foci and awareness are on children's play, while the concept of learning is vaguer. Even if the teachers say that children learn all the time, they mainly relate their learning to play. They believe that children are unaware of their own learning in play and perceive this unconscious learning process as positive. They emphasize that children in play mainly develop their social competence, and that their play reflects their everyday experiences. The teachers know what the children are doing when they play, but do not participate in their play unless the children need some kind of support to continue to play. According to the teachers, children need time and space for play. The prerequisites are peace and quiet, physical space, flexible room arrangements and a variety of challenging materials.

The teachers differ in their views of the relation between play and learning. The different perspectives we could distinguish are that

1. play and learning are the same thing;
2. children make up games from what they have learnt;
3. in play, children prepare for adulthood; and
4. play and learning are integrated.

The last perspective, the integration of play and learning, is advocated in the curriculum for preschool (Ministry of Education and Science in Sweden, 1998).

Another teacher, Ann stated

> Well, that's the difficult part, all the time, I think. It's easier to see learning in the play...
> but to see the play in the learning, that's something you think about all the time because it's
> more... since... the learning... that is something that most often comes from us as adults,
> and then it's more difficult to see, or to bring out children's own... then it can easily become
> something else than what you had in mind... how difficult it is to put one's thoughts into
> words!

> Interviewer: Yes, but it's just fine, just go ahead, I think it's very interesting.

> Ann: And that's good also, but at the same time we're supposed to focus on something,
> such as, think about this: "What do spiders do?" And then they might start to do something
> else and... well, they start to take over, with their play. And there has to be interplay, in a
> good sense. To integrate the play in the learning..., well, then I have to be very sensitive
> and open for... for their interest, for the interest and make sure that they're with me in the
> learning. And that I try to involve more play too, integrate their own play in the... and my
> play as well (laugh) or my own connections with play in what I'm trying to teach them.
> And then, in some way, it becomes... then one plus one do not make two, but five in some
> strange way, I think. You then bring in the intuition, the excitement and the imagination...

In the interview, Ann explains that play is about "give-and-take", interaction and communication, but not least – a shared focus. The intentions are that both children and adults contribute to how something develops, allowing the children create an understanding of their world. This demands reciprocity, being able to encounter the unexpected and unpredictable. It is interesting to note that even Ann, who has such a reflective view of play and learning, relates play mainly to children's activities and learning to aspects of adult guidance. The analyses of the data also demonstrate that very few teachers interacted with the children in such a way that learning and play were integrated. Perhaps a teacher must possess what Anna Craft (2003) calls *possibility thinking*, and see that "as if" and creativity are conceptions which are just as important in play as in learning (Pramling-Samuelsson & Asplund-Carlsson, 2003). When play and learning are integrated, both children and adults contribute to the creation of meaning (Johansson & Pramling-Samuelsson, 2006).

The Child's World and Experience in Preschool

What are the themes that appear in observations? What do these say about young children's experiences in the Swedish preschool? For a young child, preschool seems to be a world that is shared with other children. Grown-ups are always present but in the background. There are many child-initiated activities (different forms of play) and few teacher-initiated and/or planned activities, such as painting, baking, etc. A recurrent schedule frames the day in preschool. Its structure is built on meals, rest, assembly, and indoor and outdoor activities. In Sweden, independent of the weather, the children play outdoors at least once a day.

The only times during the day when *all the children are gathered* are at *mealtimes* (the children sit with a teacher around a number of tables) and at *assembly,* at which they always sing and make movements to the songs. Furthermore, they talk about who is missing that day, and why he or she is not there. At one preschool, they have dolls representing each child, and the child or the children who are ill are put to bed.

The *material* the children play with most frequently, without gender differences being obvious, is Lego and other blocks of different sizes, animals and other small figures, balls, books, cars, and dolls. Indoor activities are block-building, doll corner, painting, cutting and drawing. Outdoor activities involve playing in a sand box, running around and riding bikes. One game that is very specific to Swedish culture is when two children take two large plastic spades each and walk around using them as "walking-sticks", an activity which has become very popular for outdoor exercise among adults in Sweden.

Pretend Play

All children engage in different kinds of role play – individually, in interaction with other children, and together with adults. Let us look at some examples.

> Oskar is sitting at a table playing a labyrinth game. Suddenly Oskar moves his hand to his ear and says: "Hello!", as if he is talking on the phone. The teacher answers: "Hello!" pretending that she also has a phone.
>
> Hans sits at the table rolling out ginger-bread dough. He makes a ball of the dough and shows it to the teacher and says: "Look". He continues, squeezing together another ball and shows the teacher. She asks him what it is, and Hans says: "A duck". He makes several and the teacher says that he is good at making ducks.
>
> Linda walks around in the playroom, bends down and picks up a plastic ice-cream cone and holds it out to the other children and to a teacher who is sitting on the floor. She smiles, walks on, pretends to lick the ice-cream and holds it out to another girl, letting her lick the ice-cream too.

In all the three observations above, we can see how children take the initiative in pretend play, and how they also invite adults to take part. The adults seem to be sensitive to the invitations and acknowledge the children's initiatives. However, none of the teachers extends or challenges the play initiated by the child.

We shall also look at a pretend play in which two children or more play by themselves. The adult just passes by the room they are playing in.

> Axel and Emma pretend that they are cooking food. Suddenly Axel finds some carpentry tools and starts to pretend that he is drilling and hammering. He also hammers on the pretend food. He picks up a pizza slice and puts it in his mouth, laughs and pushes away all the pizza slices. Both he and other children laugh. Another child pushes away the pizza and Axel tells him that it is his pizza. He takes a spatula, walks around, looking at the shelves. He puts down the spatula and takes a white plastic ring, putting it in his mouth, just like Elin. Once again, he takes the spatula in one hand and the pizza cutter in the other. He rolls the cutter back and forth on top of the table. It looks as if he is taking up something with the spatula. Walks away and fetches a plastic bowel. Bends down, looking for something. Takes a pretend knife and runs out on the floor. He stands with his legs wide apart and says: "Paw". He kicks a large Lego block and the teacher comes by. She asks: "What are you playing?" Axel answers: "We are cooking." He goes back into the "dolls corner".

In this play situation, Axel hovers between hammering and shooting, on the one hand, and cooking, on the other. But when the teacher comes by and asks what they are doing, he knows exactly what to say, that is, what is acceptable in preschool. Shooting and banging is not! Cooking and making coffee are pretend plays which often occur, and which the children know is appreciated by the adults. Often they invite the adults to taste what they have prepared. This also seems to be a pretend play in which adults can easily feel involved (Tullgren, 2004).

In the next example, we follow Elin and her friend Johanna, who are cooking food, eating and drinking coffee together in the doll corner:

> "Yes, coffee", says Elin and pours some coffee. "I have no coffee", says one of the boys who has sat himself down at the table again. The other boy comes with a saucepan and all four are sitting at the table eating. "She wants her gruel", says Elin about the doll and fetches the feeding bottle. She sits down at the table again and says: "I want some coffee." Johanna pours the coffee and Elin makes herself comfortable with the doll on her lap. "Here Elin, Elin here", says Johanna and holds out the cup of coffee. "I can help myself", says Elin. She crawls under the table to pick up something that fell down on the floor. "Here, you can take this", she says holding out a mug to Johanna. "Thanks." Elin gets up from the floor. She drops the doll when picking it up from the floor and laughs. "There, there little baby", says Johanna. "Elin?" "Yes." "Would you like some more coffee?" "Yes." Johanna pours the coffee. "Here is more coffee."

It is interesting to note that when the children meet over a meal, they also drink coffee, which is an established custom in Sweden, that is, inviting people over for a cup of coffee. Another cultural aspect is that both boys and girls play in the doll corner looking after the babies and cooking food. Elin has just got a baby brother, and in her play with the other children, she is the mother caring for her baby:

> Elin stays at the table, feeding her doll. "Be quiet! Quiet! My baby is asleep on my lap and now I'm feeding her", says Elin to another child at the table. She fetches a pillow from the doll's bed and puts it on the chair, but immediately takes it away and puts it back in the bed. "Now she is awake", she says and lifts up the doll's eyelids. David and Johanna come forward to see. "Elin, she's tired", says David. "Hello. . . She's tired!" "No, she isn't tired. SHE ISN'T TIRED!" "A bit tired. . ." "No!"

Sometimes the children use pretend play on their own, sitting alone playing with animals and other figures talking to themselves, even though there are other children around. The teacher has an important part in children's play. Children do get help not only to continue to play but also to be part of the play when the teacher gets involved in their play:

> "Thanks for (not audible)", says one of the boys and takes something more from the table. "NO! AAH, THEY TOOK OURS. . ." Elin becomes angry and sobs and yells. "They took ours!" "But then you have to tell them not to, Elin", says the teacher from the other room. Elin walks over to the boys and says: "You cannot take ours." One of the boys gives her back a lid. "Can't they play together with you, Elin?", asks the teacher. Elin looks at the boys. "Of course they can", says Johanna.

However, the teachers seldom played with the children in pretend play. When they did, it was mainly outdoors in the sandbox, where the teachers both initiated an activity and played together with the children.

The teacher: "No, you can play with anything you want, Elin. Perhaps you would like to make some cookies here? Are you setting up a bakery?" Elin: "Mm. . ." "Here we have more of these baking-tins", says the teacher. Elin makes a sand-cake. "What kind of cake is that?", asks the teacher. "Strawberry", Elin replies. "Strawberry, mm, so good", says the teacher. "I would like a chocolate cake." "Mm." "Could you make a chocolate cake for me?" "Yes." Elin turns the tin over, finds a spade with which she bangs the cake making it come loose.

Becoming Independent and Engaged

In different ways, all the five target children give the impression that they are individuals who are competent and know what they want. "I can do this myself!" and "I managed!" are frequently heard. They think they have the right to different things and defend their rights. They are sensitive to obvious demands and expectations in preschool and are at the same time familiar with all routines and know what is expected of them. In preschool, many children come together, and this requires children to be able to both act together in a group and receive support as individuals (Williams & Sheridan, 2006).

In the following example, we can see how an individual child in the group is paid special attention, by being the one who opens the advent calendar for the day – a calendar made of gingerbread hearts. The teacher uses a Santa Claus hand-doll, Nisse, and talks through him. Linda is following. When it is time to cut out the heart of the day from the Christmas tree, Nisse cuts a paper heart on which the name Linda is written. Together with the teacher and Nisse, she goes into the dining room and Santa Claus takes down her gingerbread heart from the curtain. She shows the heart to the observer. Brings it back into the assembly where she sits down in her place again, starting to eat the gingerbread. All the children are given some fruit, and when they have finished eating, the assembly is over.

The next day it is another child's turn to cut out the heart of the day. Therefore, this example is also interesting from a cultural perspective as it mirrors an aspect of fairness. In Sweden, equity and fairness are extremely important, and every child is treated similarly and given the same opportunities. Hence, all children in the preschool have their turn to cut out the heart from the Advent calendar.

The children are also given encouragement in other situations. Hans is sitting cutting with scissors. The teacher passes by and says "How good you are at cutting Hans". He says "Mm", and nods. He cuts strip after strip and laughs. "Oh", he says, "oh, it fell down", when a piece of paper falls to the floor.

To be able to manage the daily routines at preschool is important. Daily activities such as dressing and undressing, going to the toilet, taking food from different bowls and eating without help, rinsing one's plate and sorting the cutlery after finishing a meal are chores that all the children are expected to carry out.

"Look what I can do", says Axel. He takes his plate and walks over to the kitchen sink, gets some help to get rid of the leftovers and puts the plate on the trolley. He then goes to wash his hands. He carefully checks where his card is, to make sure that he dries his hands on his own towel.

The children communicate their desires both verbally and non-verbally. Sometimes they get what they want, sometimes they do not.

When the book is finished Linda rises and walks over to the shelf. She comes back with a new book in her hand, approaching the teacher. The teacher and the other children are tidying up and putting things away. Linda holds up the book in front of her. The teacher answers: "Now we'll soon be having a snack."

Hans beats the dough and says angrily: "Eat this!", but the teacher says that he has already eaten too much dough. Angrily he repeats several times: "Eat this!" He looks displeased and raises his voice more and more. He is given a piece of apple instead, which he eats.

They also defend their rights even against the teacher:

Once again the teacher tries to push down a form in his dough, but he firmly says: "No!" and she accepts that. He has put dough into his mouth again. When the teacher gives the rolling-pin to another child Hans says: "It's mine."

The teacher has to achieve a balance between helping a child and letting him/her manage a task independently.

Once again, Oskar tries to put the dustpan back on its hook, but does not manage. "I can't do it", he tells the teacher, who helps him.

There is an open atmosphere and a close positive relationship between teachers and children. There are relatively few conflicts. Minor conflicts do appear among the children, which sometimes involve disputes about the possession of an object. The following illustrates one such dispute.

The teacher: "Girls, all blocks should be in the box." Elin: "I should put it in!", trying to take the block from Johanna. The teacher says: "It doesn't matter, Elin, if you put it in or not, you can take another block." Johanna looks at Elin and puts the block in the box. Elin gets cross and walks over to the sofa. She stands there watching the others tidying up. "But I want to carry it too!", she suddenly says and runs back. The teacher: "Yes, but give us some help here, we can all help together." Elin and Johanna help one another to carry back the box to its place. "Oh, how good you were now girls", says the teacher.

"No, I want this one!", says Axel. Elin says that she wants to have a motorbike, but Axel takes one in each hand and holds them behind his back. He just sits looking. He places the motorbikes far away from Elin.

The children show that they want to manage to do different things by themselves, but they also turn to the adults for support and help and sometimes in order to create an interplay, even if the latter is not very common (Johansson & Pramling-Samuelsson, 2006). In the following example, we can see how the teacher creates an interplay situation which allows Linda to take part in play where other children are also participating:

The teacher fetches a blue blanket, which she spreads over the table so that it forms a shelter under it. Linda half-rises from the sofa and touches the blanket. "You can pretend you have a shelter under the table", she says. Linda tries to squeeze herself down under the table from where she is standing between the table and the sofa. She does not succeed and the teacher asks: "Isn't there enough room for you?" Linda gets up and walks over to the short end of the table. She crawls in and the teacher says: "Here comes Linda too, Robin, Linda also wants to be in the shelter." Linda stays in the shelter for a while. She comes out and gets up. The teacher says: ". . . difficult to get room for the two of you?" Linda bends down and crawls in again. After a while the teacher says: "What do we have under the table? Is it a pussycat?" She lifts up one end of the blanket. Linda crawls out. The teacher who is sitting on the floor caresses Linda's hair and says: "Is it a pussycat?"

Friendship

Children's joy and togetherness in friendship, with other children in the preschool, are very obvious. All the children clearly show that they want to be together with other children. *Oskar* is doing all he can in order to play with other children. Sometimes Oskar is allowed to play with other children, at times he is not; but all the time he is looking for opportunities to get together with others. Most of the time, he seems unable to follow the conventions that will allow him entry into the ongoing play among other children and uses the wrong strategies to connect with others' play. However, sometimes he does succeed:

> Oskar is out in the yard, riding a tricycle. Isabelle is sitting on the luggage carrier. He asks her: "Come on now, push!" She jumps off and pushes, but as soon as they have gained some speed she jumps up onto the carrier again. After a while Isabelle gets fed up and climbs off the tricycle. Oskar stays on the bike for a while, just sitting there looking, but then he also climbs off the bike and lets it slowly drift away. He walks down a steep slope and climbs a big tree together with some other children. He climbs quite high and sits down on a branch, observing the older children.

It is obvious that Oskar needs support from the teacher to be part of the other children's play and to learn how to enter different play situations and involve himself in interplay.

Both the example above and the one below demonstrate that observing other children is part of young children's daily life. *Hans* is the youngest child, and he has only attended the preschool a few months, so he adopts a "wait-and-see" policy. He observes rather than involving himself in interplay with other children. However, he does sometimes enjoy and participate in the interplay.

> Hans sits together with Tilde in the painting room. He fetches a plastic box filled with crayons and picks up a few. "No, they are mine", he says when Tilde reaches for the crayons. He collects all the crayons and tells Tilde: "All of them – empty", holding up the empty box to show her. //. . .// Tilde throws all the crayons on the floor. Hans says: "Oh, all the pencils." He laughs and observes her. Says once again: "All the pencils." He bends down, looking under the table several times. Laughs, facing Tilde. Bends down and picks up all the crayons.

Here interplay and shared joy arise from a "mischief-activity", that is, something both children are aware that they should not do – throw crayons on the floor!

In play, children also guide one another. Elin and her best friend Johanna play together, and their relationship is based on mutual trust. Elin has a tendency to take the lead and tell her friend and other children what to do. However, when Elin goes too far, Johanna draws the line:

> David comes in with a doll in his arms. "This one is having a birthday", he says. "That many." He holds up his hand showing five fingers. Elin wants to take his doll. "I'm having

it", says David. "But I want it", says Elin. "No, now you have that baby", says Johanna. "But it's cold", says Elin. "I can get a blanket, wait here", says Johanna. Elin and David follow Johanna.

Axel has a best friend, called Elin. Most times of the day, when Elin and Axel are allowed to choose, they choose to be together. They spend most of the day together, indoors as well as outdoors. They build with Lego blocks, side by side, they play together in the "doll corner" and when Elin does not wake up after the afternoon nap in her carrier, Axel keeps checking if she is awake so that they can play. As soon as she is awake, they stay together at all times in the yard. They run around chasing each other, cook together in the playhouse and imitate each other and joke. It is obvious that this is no casual friendship but one that will last day after day.

> Elin and Axel are riding on hobby-horses. They run back and forth with the horses. "Here I am", says Axel. "Now we are going to sleep", says Elin. Both of them lie down on a couch together with their horses. They laugh and get up again.

Linda is the only child who plays on her own most of the time, or in parallel with the other children. All through the day, there are very few situations in which she has some interplay with other children. However, she does initiate contact with the adults. She prefers to be close to the adults and she often takes out books from the shelf and asks the teacher to read to her.

> ... picks up a book and hands it to Marie, the teacher, and says: "Can you read this?" Marie takes the book and Linda places herself on her lap.

Research has shown that friendship and social time together are important even for young children in preschool (see Dunn, 1991; Johansson, 1999; Løkken, 2000). Most children want to be included in the group of peers, even if they are younger than 3 years.

Children's Opportunities for Choices and Experiences in Preschool

There are many opportunities for children to make their own choices in preschool. In fact, it is mostly the structure and the organization that impose limits. At meal times, you have to sit down at the table. When it is time to go out, in most preschools you have to go out. Usually, the children are allowed to choose what to eat from the food that is served and how much. But all children do eat! Within the structural framework of preschool, children make their own choices when it comes to toys, what game to play and who they want to play with.

When children interact, they have new experiences. They both imitate each other and play well together.

> We follow Hans as he joins two older girls who are watching a video on the computer, a video showing themselves dancing. He forces his way in between them and stands watching for a while.

At one of the preschools, they keep chickens, which children, teachers and parents take care of together. Today it is Axel's and Gustav's turn and responsibility to help the teacher.

> They go out to the poultry-house. Axel: "They are awake?" Teacher: "Yes, they are awake. Good morning, good morning." They enter the poultry-house. Axel says again: "Yes, they are awake!" Teacher: "Let's see if they need some food." She takes out their food trough and water trough. She asks Axel to fill up the food trough with fodder and Gustav to throw out the water and fill up the trough with fresh water. But before they get started the teacher asks: "Should we check if there are any eggs? No, there are no eggs, they haven't laid any eggs, they're sly, aren't they?", says the teacher. She continues: "Now we must fill up the food anyhow." "They haven't finished their food", Axel tells the observer. He is scooping up cup after cup. Teacher: "Is there any food? Very good, you can add some cups." He shakes the trough. Continues to scoop. "Some more." Axel smiles at the teacher and says: "Now I'm done!" Teacher: "Do you think it's okay now? Yes, perhaps it is." He throws the cup in the fodder bin and says: "Now they have food." Teacher: "Yes, let's bring it in to them." They step in to the chickens. Axel: "Now I have done something." They step out again to find out if Gustav is managing his chore. The water has frozen to ice so they have to fetch some from the house.

Do children in toddler groups and sibling groups have different experiences? It is, of course, impossible to answer this question on the basis of the five children studied. But something often seen in sibling groups is that the younger children observe the older ones. They might not always take part in the older children's activities, but they carefully observe what they do. On the other hand, there seems to be a feeling of greater closeness between children and adults in toddler groups, that is, the teachers spend more time together with the younger children.

Communication and Interaction Are Important!

A close and warm relationship between children and adults is often observed. Children look for contact with adults and adults are often there for them, listening and encouraging them. They interpret children's actions and understand their intentions, and also help them to create a meaning in the world around them. Children also take any opportunity to practise their verbal skills and to develop ways of communicating. Here the teacher has a key role in helping them to extend their language. Below, we can see how Axel and his teacher chat with each other.

> They talk about Winnie the Pooh being dressed in a mackintosh and Wellingtons. "Are you going to climb down?" He does. He is asked to push back the ladder, which he does. "I can do it, I'm a big boy." Looks happy. He jumps. The teacher says: "Look what Elsa's found!" (the other slipper). He brightens up and starts jumping about. The teacher wants him to put on the slippers, but he says that he cannot. Teacher: "Yes, I know that you can, because you usually do." "No", he says. "Yes, no", he says. Teacher: "You said that you were a big boy, big boys manage." He puts on the slipper and the teacher says: "You managed!" Axel says: "Elin is still in the hut." Teacher: "Is she still in the hut?" Axel tries to put on the other slipper, but does not manage. Suddenly he stretches out his leg with the slipper dangling from his foot and says: "It won't!" "It won't?", asks the teacher, bends down and helps him

put it on. She reminds him to wash his hands and he walks over to the wash-basin, turns on the tap, pumps up some soap and runs away to dry his hands.

In the next example, we follow Linda as she walks over to the table, leaning on it. She is carrying a paper heart in her hand. There are other children around and she says something inaudible to one of the boys sitting around the table.

> She looks at one of the teachers, holds up her heart and says: "Me, uhh. . ." //. . .// She licks herself around her mouth and says: "Can't eat." The teacher answers: "You can't eat this. You are going to eat later. Do you know what we will have today?" Linda shakes her head. "We will have fish-balls and potatoes, you like that, don't you", says the teachers. Linda nods. She stays for a while, watching the other children.

Here we can study the interplay between the teacher and Linda in which they hover between the actual situation and what will happen later on, that is, the teacher goes beyond the "here-and-now-situation." Another example of how communication goes beyond what is happening here and now is when the teacher talks with Axel about his older sister who is ill, among other things.

> He is lying on his back, looking and pointing at Winnie the Pooh and his friends who are on the box on the nursing table. "How is Frida?" (She has chicken pox). They talk for a while about her spots. "Can you lift up your bottom?" asks the teacher, wiping him clean. He lifts up his knees and says: "Look how much!" Teacher: "Yes, have you fallen and hurt yourself?" "Yes", he responds. He points at both his knees. Teacher: "Lift up your bottom." Puts on a new nappy. When she lifts up his leg it brushes against a bell hanging from the ceiling. He starts to kick at the bell with both his feet deliberately. Teacher: "That's it, can you stand up, please?" She lifts him up, putting him down on the floor. "Here you are, your trousers." He sits down on the rug and touches it (the rug?). Elin comes in to the doorway and Axel sits watching her.

In the next example, we will follow a dialogue in which the teacher attempts to extend Elin's experience. She makes Elin aware that there is more to see, and she tries to interpret and put Elin's feelings into words.

> Elin is lying on her back on the ground. "The trees!", she says and points. The teacher: "Do you see the trees?" Elin: "Yes." The teacher: "What more do you see?" Elin looks around. "Do you see aeroplanes?" Elin lies watching for a while. The teacher says something (not audible) "the clouds that are a bit darker are moving, can you see that?" Elin nods: "Mm." The teacher: "Yes. But does it not make you dizzy in your head?" Elin laughs and shakes her head.

The teachers nearly always respond to children's interactions and sometimes also initiate them. The atmosphere is usually very good and very encouraging, and children are helped to master things by themselves. There are exceptions. Especially in the case of the observed children who spend a lot of time in preschool just waiting and are not always seen or listened to. In this preschool, some of the teachers do not seem to be able to take the perspective of the child. In other preschools, the teachers often put things into words and talk to the children continuously about both what is close and what is beyond a situation. They often comment on the children's actions, ask and are interested to know what children do. They joke with the children, and the atmosphere is cheerful.

Is it Possible to See the Intentions of the Curriculum in Preschool Practice?

In this study, we analysed the play in relation to Rogoff's three foci of analysis and found that many personal, interpersonal and institutional or cultural dimensions were being foreground in the Swedish centres. On the *personal focus* of analysis, we can see that teachers believed in children's independence and engagement in play activities as very important. Teachers foreground pretend play and believed it was important for the children to feel at home, and we have also seen how they do not intervene in the children's play. At the *interpersonal focus* of analysis, communication and interaction between staff and children were important and central for children's learning, also children building friendships was considered to be central. Finally, on an *institutional and cultural focus* of analysis, children were given opportunities to make choice and encouraged to express their thoughts and feelings, something stated in the Swedish curriculum. Gender equality is also actively examined in Sweden.

According to the National Curriculum (Ministry of Education and Science in Sweden, 1998), the preschool should be safe, joyful and instructive. The picture we get from both the parents and our observations is that the children "feel at home" in their preschool. They dare to say no when they do not want to do something, ask for help when help is needed, and challenge other's opinions by sticking to their own points of view. The atmosphere is positive and harmonious (Johansson, 2003; Sheridan, 2001). It rarely happens that children are passive. They are generally active participants in their own everyday life. They can make a variety of choices, and usually there are adults around who are ready to interact with them and give them support.

The preschool should make use of and develop children's ability to feel responsible and their ability to take social actions, so that solidarity and tolerance are founded at an early age (Ministry of Education and Science in Sweden, 1998). Here the goal is to become a strong and responsible individual. In the observations reported earlier, we have seen how children are given space and special attention as individuals in relation to the group and counted on as important members of a collective in which all have to contribute, for instance, cleaning up after themselves after having a meal (Williams & Sheridan, 2006). In an earlier study in which England, the USA and Sweden were compared, the Swedish preschool stood out as the one that best promoted the idea of collective responsibility (Carlson, 1993).

Furthermore, the curriculum states that "preschool should provide children with good pedagogical activities, where care, nurturing and learning together form a coherent whole" (op. cit., p. 8). In practice, this is achieved through educated teachers who engage themselves with the children and their ongoing activities. Care, play and learning, in particular, constitute an integrated/a coherent whole in children's interaction and togetherness. It is the close interplay and the communication that take place both in children's play and different routines that contribute to early learning. In their interactions with the children, the teachers communicate both about the near and the concrete and about things not found in the immediate surroundings. The communication with adults and other children provides the foundation for creating meaning, looking for new knowledge and being able to participate in social interaction. These children create meaning out of their everyday life in preschool. Even children's imaginative play is related to their everyday experiences, for instance, cooking and eating food, and no gender differences are apparent at this stage.

The curriculum (Ministry of Education and Science in Sweden, 1998) points out two goals to strive for, which become obvious in this study.

One goal is about parental co-operation, something which is known to be crucial for children's learning and development in preschool (Siraj-Blatchford, 2004). "Each and everybody who works in preschool should show respect towards the parents and feel responsible for the development of a trusting relation between the preschool staff and the children's families." What we found in the interviews with the parents is that they have great trust in the preschool staff. What does vary between the different preschools, however, is how much the parents know about ongoing activities and what their children do in preschool. Some parents are surprised and happy when they see their children in our video recordings, and suddenly they see things which they were not aware of.

Another goal to strive for is that children should "develop their ability to express their thoughts and views and thus have the opportunity of influencing their own situation" (op. cit., p. 14). Democracy and participation are central in all pedagogical activities in Sweden (Jonyniene & Pramling-Samuelsson, 2000; Pramling-Samuelsson & Sheridan, 2003; Pramling-Samuelsson, 2004). In the observations, we can also see how children have almost unlimited opportunities both to be included in a collective and to make their own choices and decisions even before the age of three. As far as possible, they choose what and how much they want to eat, and during a great deal of the day, they choose what they want to play and with whom. They ask the teacher for help or call for the teacher's attention when they want her to read a book or help them with something. Children's own initiatives appear to be central in preschool practice.

When it comes to the teachers' views on play and learning, they differ in theory, but in practice and interaction with the children, these differences are hard to distinguish. For the parents, this is more like a diffuse whole, even if play takes precedence. They also state that it is natural for children to play and children learn while playing. Many teachers seem to share their view, even though some of them have a more reflective way of looking at play and learning. From a theoretical perspective, they see how both play and learning are reciprocally interlocked with each other if children are given enough space (Johansson & Pramling-Samuelsson, 2006).

What could be considered is that we rarely see any of the adults taking the initiative or actively trying to influence children. Preschool practice is child-centred, and the adults guide children indirectly through certain rules or expectations. Could this lack of adult initiative be negative in some way? There are other studies that also show that the practice in preschool for children under the age of three mainly consists of free play (Loizan, 2004). What we fail to notice is any clear educational approach or learning orientation on the part of the teacher. How does that agree with both the curriculum intentions and personal experiences that children love, such as helping with every day activities such as peeling potatoes, vacuuming, weeding the garden etc? Is the teachers' way of acting conscious, or do they hold a takings-things-for-granted perspective, that maturity and development are the foundation for children's learning, despite knowing that the curriculum has a social, cultural experience perspective? This perspective conflicts with the development psychological perspective since children's experiences and social interplay are seen as the foundation for learning.

We have seen here how the social–political features of Swedish preschool are manifested in the everyday life of some toddlers. The teachers' professional competence is good, and the staff/child ratio is acceptable. It gives children room to choose activities and take the initiative. The picture that emerges is that "free play" is dominant, and that the teachers generally only provide the framework and intervene when it is necessary, in order to facilitate learning and help to solve conflicts among the children. The teachers want the children to become independent and take responsibility for their own learning, although the authors observed that the teachers could be more active in challenging and supporting children in their play, so that play could develop even further.

Gender questions have long been a subject of heated debate in Sweden. From an international perspective, we think that we have come a long way as there are few gender differences in the children's play with dolls, cars, etc. (you have seen Axel cooking, p. 140 and David playing with dolls, p. 144). However, from a national perspective, there is still a long way to go before equality is reached between both sexes in all areas.

These five children's days in preschool seem to be fairly positive. Does that mean that there is no room for improvement? We also have to bear in mind that it is a small study of five children only, but let us look at other studies.

Comparison with Other Nordic Studies

During the last few years, several evaluations of Swedish preschool have been carried out. Sweden was one of the 12 countries that the OECD (2001) evaluated in the project Starting Strong. One of their conclusions was that "democracy" could be seen even in the groups for young children, something which we have also found in our study. Today democracy and participation are seen as prerequisites for all kinds of learning at all ages. This can be related not only to the curriculum of preschool but also to the social policy that characterize it, low fees, accessibility and efforts to maintain good quality (Regeringens proposition 2004:05/11; Skolverket, 2005).

For children under the age of 3 years, learning in preschool is very much about acquiring a language and being able to talk about their world of experiences. Here the everyday life, with all its daily activities, constitutes a substantial content. Both parents and teachers point out how preschool can influence children's language development, even though studies from England have shown that there were very few dialogues between children and teachers in preschool (Wood, McMahou, &

Cranstoun, 1980). From our data, we are convinced that teachers could do more to promote children's language development.

Hännikäinen, de Jong, & Rubenstein Reich (1997) have followed children in preschool in the Nordic countries, with the intention of illustrating what quality means in a Nordic perspective. According to them, children's relations to each other is a central aspect of quality, Another aspect of quality is the teacher's respect for the child, something that requires the adult to take the child's perspective, in order to be able to judge the situation and decide whether to interfere or not. This is also obvious in this study.

Frode Søbstad (2002) has asked parents, preschool teachers and children about how they define quality in preschool. They believe that it is important to have a varied outdoor environment, to walk in woods and fields, to be able to interact socially and in play, giving school-preparation activities low priority. Finally, they emphasized parental co-operation and being sensitive to children's needs in the preschool world.

Sheridan (2001) studied pedagogical quality in 30 Swedish preschools and 10 German preschools from a national and international perspective. The core of pedagogical quality is in the interaction that takes shape and develops in the meeting between the child and the teacher and between the children. The educational approach of teachers in preschools of average quality can be described as democratic. This means that the teachers' attention is focused, and they make room for the child's contribution, confirm the child's experiences, respond sensitively, listen intently and let the child pursue his or her own line of reasoning. Time in preschool should also be characterized by both teacher- and child-initiated activities. The focus of the teacher is, however, more on the activity itself than on what is happening to the child, that is, what the child learns and understands from the activity, and on the child's emotional and social development.

In preschools of high quality, teachers also interact with the children in a democratic way. However, interaction here is characterized by mutual recognition and by the teacher meeting each child by using a reciprocal approach to find out what the child is interested in, why she or he approaches friends, activities and things in the way she/he does, that is, how she/he sees the world. This approach is distinguished by the teachers having a very clear aim as to what they want the child to learn and develop an understanding about. Activities are clearly directed towards learning, and the teacher focuses on the child's possibility of developing an understanding of various phenomena, and of developing basic skills as well as social competence. Characteristic of this teacher approach is that the overall learning goals are implemented in dialogues and communication with the children, and through activities based on children's interests, previous experience and knowledge (Sheridan, 2001).

We conclude that the content and activities in the preschools participating in our study are seldom learning-orientated and/or guided by the teacher from the democratic/educational approach described above. The results from the longitudinal study Effective Provision of Preschool Education embracing over 3000 children clearly shows that children benefit most from preschools where there is harmony between teacher-initiated and teacher-directed activities and child-initiated activities (Sylva, Melhuish, Sammons, Siraj-Blatchford, & Taggart, 2004).

Johansson (2003) studied the quality aspects of learning in Swedish preschool amongst toddlers, that is, children younger than 3 years old. Johansson followed the pedagogical activities of 30 teams at 20 Swedish preschools dispersed throughout the country. The aim was to provide a picture of the pedagogical work with younger children by studying teachers' attitudes, the content and organization of the activities, as well as following children's experiences of everyday life. The results can be summarized as follows: *Preschool content is constituted in the intersubjective learning encounters which teachers create.* This is the actual essence of the activity in early childhood education and, as such, a fundamental prerequisite of children's learning. In those work teams where the atmosphere and view of children are characterized by a common commitment, emotional proximity, candour and a fundamental respect for children, there often exists a view of learning where teachers to a large extent make a mental note of the child's competence, significant for its learning. Moreover, in the work teams where the atmosphere and the view of the child tend to be built on distance and the teacher's notion of being the only one who can determine what is best for the child, a view of learning emerges where the children have a more subordinate and passive role in learning. When the atmosphere can be described as controlling, a view of learning with behaviourist features can be discerned, where moulded learning strategies such as threat and/or commendation and reward are often expressed.

We conclude that the preschools in our study may partly be compared to Johansson's (op. cit.) example where there is an atmosphere characterized by allowing different standpoints, emotional closeness and a basic respect for children – although our teachers do not tend to take the initiative or challenge the children in their learning process.

Lindahl (1996) studied how ten toddlers aged between 13 and 20 months experience and learn in a new preschool world. She observed what she called the children's direction of awareness. The child's action was supposed to be related to its way of perceiving or making sense of a context. Lindahl's findings indicate an awareness of changes in the toddlers' learning process. Moreover, the children were able to keep to their intentions, but they needed to have an idea of a situation or of something they wanted to master before they acted intentionally and learning came about. Lindahl (2002, see also Palmérus, Pramling, & Lindahl, 1991 in a similar project) also studied the ability of teachers to understand a toddler's perspective. An intervention programme was carried out where special attention was paid to how children's initiatives, ideas or intentions were followed up and responded to by the educators. The effects on the teachers' learning were evaluated through interviews. Lindahl (2002) claimed that an increased understanding of the infants' intensity of activity and richness of initiative stimulates the educators to create a learning environment that offers children over the opportunity to influence their everyday activities in preschool. When teachers are aware of the competence of the child, the child also grows in his or her skills at handling everyday situations and being together with peers (Williams, 2001).

If we look at the three perspectives of Rogoff (1998), personal, interpersonal and community/institutional, on a personal level, we can claim that every child in Swedish preschools enjoys a great degree of freedom in which to act and react. We can also see from the observations reported that children are included in interpersonal communication and interaction with teachers and other children. However, the teachers could improve their approach by becoming more active and learning orientated without losing sight of the democratic goals set up in the curriculum. We can also see that Rogoff's third level concerning the overall policy of community and institution influenced the quality in the five groups we have followed. In our study, it became evident in the teachers' competence and education to implement the overall goals in practice and how they structured the physical, social and learning environment. Together, they influenced the learning and playing process in various ways, which we assume made a difference for the individual children's learning and well-being.

References

Carlson, H. L. (1993). Impact of Societal Orientations on Early Childhood Programmes and Parents' and Professionals' views of those Programmes: Sweden, England, United States. *International Journal of Early Childhood, 25*(1), 20–26.

Craft, A. (2003). *Creativity and early education*. London: Continuum.

Dunn, J. (1991). Young children's understanding of other people: Evidence from observations within the family. In D. Frye, & C. Moore (Eds.), *Children's theories of mind: Mental states and social understanding* (pp. 99–114). Hillsdale, NJ: Erlbaum.

Harms, T., & Clifford, R. (1980). *The early childhood environment rating scale*. New York: Teachers College, Columbia University.

Hännikäinen, M., de Jong, M., & Rubenstein Reich, L. (1997). *"Our heads are the same size!" A study of quality of the child's life in Nordic day care centres*. (Educational information and debate 107.) Lund University: Department of Educational and Psychological Research, School of Education.

Johansson, E. (1999). *Etik i små barns värld. Om värden och normer bland de yngsta barnen i förskolan*. Göteborg: Acta Universitatis Gothoburgensis.

Johansson, E. (2003). *Möten för lärande. Pedagogisk verksamhet för de yngsta barnen i förskolan*. Stockholm: Skolverket.

Johansson, E., & Pramling-Samuelsson, I. (2006). *Lek och läroplan. Möten mellan barn och lärare i förskola och skola*. Göteborg: Acta Universitatis Gothoburgensis.

Jonyniene, Z., & Pramling-Samuelsson, I. (2000). Swedish and Lithuanian students' experience of their rights. *Child Youth and Care, 162*, 81–107.

Lindahl, M. (1996). *Inlärning och erfarande. Ettåringars möte med förskolans värld*. Göteborg: Acta Universitatis Gothoburgensis.

Lindahl, M. (2002). *Vårda – Vägleda – Lära. Effektstudie av ett kompetensutvecklings-program för pedagoger i förskolemiljön*. Göteborg: Acta Universitatis Gothoburgensis.

Løkken, G. (2000). *Toddler peer culture. The social style of one- and two- year- old body-subjects in everyday interaction*. Trondheim: Norges teknisk-naturvitenskapelige universitet, Pedagogisk institutt.

Loizou, E. (2004). Humorous bodies and humorous minds: Humour within the social context of an infant child care setting. *European Early Childhood Education Research Journal, 12*(1), 15–28.

Ministry of Education and Science in Sweden. (1998a). *Curriculum for preschool. Lpfö 98.* Stockholm: Fritzes.
Ministry of Education and Science in Sweden. (1998b). Curriculum for the compulsory school, the preschool class and the after school centre. Stockholm: Fritzes.
OECD (2001). Starting Strong. Early childhood education and care. Education and skills. Paris: OECD. (www.SourceOECD.org).
Palmérus, K., Pramling, I., & Lindahl, M. (1991). *Daghem för småbarn. En utvecklingsstudie av personalens pedagogiska och psykologiska kunnande.* Göteborgs universitet: Institutionen för metodik i lärarutbildningen.
Pramling-Samuelsson, I. (2004). Demokratie: Leitprinzip des vorschulischen Bildungsplans in Schweden. /Democracy – guiding principle for the pre-school curriculum in Sweden./ In W. E. Fthenakis, & P. Oberhuemer (Eds.), *Frühpädagogik international: Bildungsqualität im Blickpunkt.* /Early childhood curriculum issues: international perspectives./München: IFP, Staatsinstitut für Frühpädagogik.
Pramling-Samuelsson, I., & Asplund-Carlsson, M. (2003). *Det lekande lärande barnet i en utvecklingspedagogisk teori.* Stockholm: Liber.
Pramling-Samuelsson, I., & Sheridan, S. (2003). Delaktighet som värdering och pedagogik. In E. Johansson, & I. Pramling-Samuelsson (Eds.), Barns perspektiv och barnperspektiv. *Pedagogisk Forskning i Sverige, 8*(1–2), 70–84, [Special issue]..
Pramling-Samuelsson, I., & Sheridan, S. (2004). Recent Issues in the Swedish preschool. *International Journal of Early Childhood, 36*(1), 7–22.
Regeringens proposition. (2004:05/11). *Kvalitet i förskolan.* Stockholm: Utbildningsdepartementet (www.regeringen.se/utbildning).
Rogoff, B. (1998). Cognition as a collaborative process. In W. Damon, (Chief Ed.) D. Kuhn and R. S. Siegler (Vol. Eds.), *Cognition, perceptions and language. Handbook of Child Psychology,* (5th ed., pp. 679–744). New York: John Wiley & Sons, Inc.
Sheridan, S. (2001). *Pedagogical Quality in Preschool. An issue of perspectives.* Göteborg: Acta Universitatis Gothoburgensis.
Siraj-Blatchford, I. (2004). Educational disadvantage in the early years: How do we overcome it? Some lessons from research. *European Early Childhood Education Research Journal, 12*(2), 5–20.
Sylva, K., Melhuish, E., Sammons, P., Siraj-Blatchford, I., & Taggart, B. (2004) The effective provision of pre-school education (EPPE) project: Findings from preschool to end of key stage 1. University of London: Institute of Education
Skolverket (2003a). *Uppföljning av max-taxa, allmän förskola, mm.*/Follow up of the max-tax-reform, compulsory preschool etc./Skolverkets rapport till Utbildningsdepartementet.
Skolverket (2003b). *Beskrivande data om barnomsorg, skola och vuxenutbildning.* [Discribing facts about the educational system.] Stockholm: Fritzes.
Skolverket (2005). *Allmänna råd och kommentarer. Kvalitet i förskolan.* Skolverkets allmänna råd. Stockholm: Fritzes.
Søbstad, F. (2002). *Jaktstart på kjennetegn ved den gode barnhagen. Første rapport fra prosjektet "Den norske barnehagekvaliteten".* Trondheim: Dronning Mauds Minne Høgskole for førskollæreutdanning.
Tullgren, C. (2004). *Den välreglerade friheten. Att konstruera det lekande barnet.* (Malmö Studies in Educational Sciences, No. 10). Malmö högskola: Lärarutbildningen.
Vanderbroeck, M. (1999). *The view of Yeti. Bringing up children in the spirit of self-awareness and kindredship.* Hague: Bernard van Leer Foundation.
Williams, P. (2001). *Barn lär av varandra. Samlärande i förskola och skola.* Göteborg: Acta Universitatis Gothoburgensis.
Williams, P., & Sheridan, S. (2006). Collaboration as one aspect of quality: a perspective of collaboration and pedagogical quality in educational settings. *Scandinavian Journal of Educational Research, 50*(1), 83–93.
Wood, D., McMahou, L., & Cranstoun, Y. (1980). *Working with under fives.* London: Grant McIntyre.

Chapter 8
Play and Learning in Wisconsin

Lenore Wineberg and Louis Chicquette

*Every child has the right. . .to engage in play and recreational
activities appropriate to the age of the child and to participate
freely in cultural life and the arts.*
(1989, U.N. Convention on the Rights of the Child, Article 31)

Introduction

The purpose of this chapter is to describe play and learning in the United States of
America, specifically through a representative population of five toddlers in child
care centers located in Northeastern Wisconsin. Qualitative data were collected in
five child care centers in the cities of Appleton, Oshkosh and Milwaukee. Videotapes
of five toddlers and interviews with their teachers and families were recorded and
interpreted by the two researchers.

The two researchers worked together for over 7 months to gather data. One researcher is a native of Chicago, an urban and cultural center of the Midwest. She
has worked in Wisconsin approximately 20 years and has gained familiarity with
the culture of the state. The other researcher grew up in a small Wisconsin village
and has a lifelong knowledge of the culture.

The researchers viewed and edited the videotapes to look for themes and patterns related to play and learning. Teachers and families then viewed the edited
videotapes and were interviewed by the researchers. The researchers also analyzed
and interpreted the data, which is reported in their findings and conclusions.

Definitions of play and learning will be described through current research, leading play theorists and standards (e.g., national, state). This theory base will be critical to key findings in the study and provide links to the videotapes and interviews.

Environment

The State of Wisconsin is bordered to the north by Lake Superior and to the east by
Lake Michigan. According to the general demographic characteristics provided by
the 2000 census, there were approximately five and a half million residents living

L. Wineberg
University of Wisconsin Oshkosh, Oshkosh, Wisconsin 54901, USA
e-mail: wineberg@uwosh.edu

I. Pramling-Samuelsson, M. Fleer (eds.), *Play and Learning in Early Childhood
Settings*, DOI 10.1007/978-1-4020-8498-0_8,
© Springer Science+Business Media B.V. 2009

in Wisconsin. The predominant ancestry of the population speaks to the American melting pot – German, Irish, English, Italian, Polish, French, Dutch, Norwegian, Swedish and Scottish (U.S. Census Bureau, Census 2000). In addition to major Scandinavian and European influences, Hispanic, African-American and Asian populations currently comprise the largest minority populations.

Additional demographic information reveals that approximately 342,340 children are under five. Around 179,386 participate in some form of licensed child care (group or family care), and of that population, 60% of the requests are for infant and toddler care, 25% preschool and 15% for school-age care. It is also interesting to note that in the population of children under five, 23% are cared for by a relative. There are 9,322 child care providers working in the state of Wisconsin, and the average income for full-time employment is $18,300 (NACCRRA, 2006 Child Care in the Sate of Wisconsin). Certification and training range anywhere from minimal (80 hours/Early Childhood I & II) to 4-year college or university degrees in early childhood and/or elementary education.

Background

In a broad stroke of the brush, the definitions and understanding of play and learning have been guided by theory and research across all 50 states. During the past century, American early childhood has been impacted by the works of John Dewey, Jean Piaget, Maria Montessori, Lev Vygotsky, The Waldorf School, Reggio Emilia and many others who created a melting pot of theory and philosophy. Over time, early childhood professionals saw the spotlight shift from Piaget to Vygotsky, as Vygotsky's work became more available in the United States. More recently, the emergence of Barbara Rogoff's research (based on Vygotsky (1978) and colleagues) has indicated how children's play is affected by culture (e.g., family members, community, educators) and how learning "is a process of people's changing participation in socio-cultural activities in their respective communities" (Ryder, Wright, Adams, & Jones, 2004, p. 1). Rogoff proposes three foci of analysis in helping to understand a socio-cultural experience: intrapersonal, interpersonal and cultural institutional. Though not an anthropological study, this chapter will provide the reader with similar lenses to observe play and learning within a socio-cultural context described in three cities (Appleton, Oshkosh and Milwaukee) representing Wisconsin's diversity and culture.

It is significant to note that as American early childhood theory and practice evolved, a unifying organization known as the National Association for the Education of Young Children (NAEYC) developed a series of position statements on developmentally appropriate practices (DAP). According to Copple and Bredekamp, "developmentally appropriate practice refers to teaching decisions that vary with and adapt to the age, experience, interests, and abilities of individual children within a given age range" (2006, p. 7). In the United States, the NAEYC DAP handbook illustrates appropriate and inappropriate practices, and it also guides early childhood educators who work with children from birth to 8 years of age.

To illustrate, in the area of recommended appropriate play practices for toddlers, DAP guides practitioners as follows:

Appropriate practice:	Inappropriate practice:
• "Adults engage in reciprocal play with toddlers, modeling for children how to play imaginatively; such as playing 'tea party.' Caregivers also support toddlers' play so that children stay interested in an object or activity for longer periods of time and their play becomes more complex, moving from simple awareness and exploration of objects to more complicated play like pretending" (Bredekamp & Copple, 1997, p. 84).	• "Adults do not play with toddlers because they feel self-conscious or awkward. Caregivers do not understand the importance of supporting children's play, and they control or intrude in the play" (Bredekamp & Copple, 1997, p. 84).

The above statements are only an example of the many appropriate practices presented in the DAP handbook. Other practices include adult–child relationships, curriculum, environment, health and safety, guidance, relationships with families and policies for staff.

However, given the controversial cultural climate in the United States, DAP position statements now give recognition to cultural context to inform best practices. According to Carol Brunsan Phillips (1994),

> Culture consists of sets of rules or expectations for the behavior of the group members that are passed on from one generation to the next. Cultural experiences are not limited to the artifacts or products of culture, such as holiday celebrations, foods or music. These products are what can be seen easily but they are not the culture itself, which is that set of underlying rules of custom or habit that yield or shape the visible products. Understanding culture requires an understanding of the rules that influence behavior, rules that give meaning to events and experiences in families and communities (p. 42).

To further illustrate, DAP guidelines for practitioners working with toddler parents include the following:

Appropriate practices	Inappropriate practices
• "Caregivers listen carefully to what parents say about their children, seek to understand parents' goals and preferences and are respectful of cultural and family differences" (Copple & Bredekamp, 2006, p. 3).	• "Teachers communicate with parents only about problems or conflicts, or they avoid difficult issues rather than resolving them with parents" (p. 3).

Teachers in the United States, as well as other countries around the world, are faced with many diverse cultural groups. The challenge is to develop a deep understanding of social and cultural contexts in practice.

The handbook on DAP has been widely accepted as common practice since its first publication in 1986. In addition to NAEYC, each state is guided by child care licensing requirements, as well as state standards and curricula designed for school age populations within the birth to 8-year-old population.

For the purpose of this study, it should be understood that early childhood is broadly defined by the National Association for the Education of Young Children (NAEYC) as any "early childhood program in a center, school, or other facility that serves children from birth through age 8" (Bredekamp & Copple, 1997, p. 3). In addition to the population of children served, the definition also includes administrators, early childhood professionals, families, policymakers and others whose decision making affects the lives of young children. Within the birth to 8-year-old population are categorical levels defined by ages and stages, such as infants (birth to 1 year), toddlers (1–3 years), preschool or prekindergarten (3–5 years), kindergarten (5- and 6-year olds), first, second and third grade. More specifically, this study will focus on five toddlers from 19 months to 3 years.

Play and learning are seen as driving forces in most early childhood programs as evidenced by the impact of NAEYC accreditation, DAP guidelines, current research, child development and increased understanding that learning begins at birth. A significant issue emerging from federal mandates and guidelines (e.g., *No Child Left Behind*) has generated the perception that play is frivolous and takes time away from learning. Mandates for older children have resulted in devaluation for play in the curricula.

What is Play?

Defining play is as difficult as nailing smoke to a wall. A scan of relevant play research would offer the following definitions:

- "Defining and articulating play are far from easy for at least two different reasons. First, play is abstract and fluid; it is not a concrete object, place of action...A second reason that play is problematic in its multiplicity of meanings. Play, like love, is a many-splendored thing" (Johnson, Christie & Wardle, 2005, p. 11).
- "Adults are instrumental in choosing the objects with which children work and play, their companions in learning and exploration, and the circumstances of their participations in activities" (Rogoff & Wertsch, 2003, p. 43).
- During a symposium at Yale University (PLAY = LEARNING, June, 2005), respected researchers in the field of play were asked to define play. Some responses included these thoughts:

  o "It is a means over the end" (Anthony Pellegrini, University of Minnesota).
  o "Play is relevant and meaningful. Play has many dispositions" (James Christie, Arizona State University).
  o "There are many kinds of play and it should not be driven to a consummate act" (Dorothy Singer, Yale University).
  o "It is learningful play" (Herbert Ginsburg, Columbia University).
  o "Play, learn and discover" (Deborah Weber, Fisher-Price, Inc.).

Play is also defined and described as multi-dimensional, when seen through the eyes of Jean Piaget and Lev Vygotsky. Piaget has become widely known for his stages of development theory (e.g., sensory-motor, preoperational, concrete operations, formal operations) and related work in cognitive development (Singer & Revenson, 1996). Piaget also formulated his theory of play around three main stages – practice play, symbolic play and games with rules, which are still seen as driving influences in the culture of American early childhood practices. However, that influence has had to make room for the work of Russian psychologist, Lev Vygotsky, whose work has finally reached a wider audience in the West.

Vygotsky's substantial collection of work remained largely unknown in the United States until the fall of communism in Russia. As more collaboration and collegiality was established with Western culture, early childhood professionals began to compare and contrast his theories with his contemporary, Piaget. For example, both men noted that play "characterizes language, artistic and literacy activities that develop during preschool years" (Berk & Winsler, 1995, p. 53), but differed in their views of imaginative play. Piaget regarded play as a "means through which children practice newly formed representational schemes" while Vygotsky "emphasized the development-enhancing, forward-moving consequences of pretense" (p. 57).

Another contrast was found in how the theorists viewed learning. While Piaget emphasized biological maturity as a condition for learning, Vygotsky disagreed, claiming that learning processes lead development (Berk & Winsler, 1995). Piaget's constructivist theory focused on intellectual development forming through play, whereas Vygotsky believed that a child's learning is assisted by others. An example of this is found in Vygotsky's zone of proximal development (ZPD), which is considered a major contribution to education. ZPD is described as follows: "A difficult goal is offered; the child receives orientation from an adult; he reaches that goal and another one is offered; he tackles it and solves it independently, if possible, with the help of the adult" (Blanck in Moll, 1990). The contrasts of these two theorists are echoed in the words of others who have struggled to define learning.

What is Learning?

Again, a scan of current research and theory leads us to varied definitions of learning. Consider the following quotations:

- "Learning, therefore, is simply the process of adjusting our mental models to accommodate new experiences" (Brooks & Brooks, 1993).
- "They (meaning infants and young children) advance their own development by using whatever resources and skills they possess to gain further access to learning experiences through involvement with people, materials, and activities. They are thus active participants in their own development" (Rogoff & Wertsch, 2003, p. 32–33).
- "Learning is the making of meaning" (Robert Kegan, in *About Learning* by McCarthy, 1996).

- "Learning can be defined as relatively permanent changes in behavior as a result of experience" (Roopnarine & Johnson, in *Approaches to Early Childhood Education*, 1993).
- "Learning is a process of building neural networks" (Wolfe, 2001).
- "We all learn best in our own ways. Some people do better studying one subject at a time, while some do better studying three things at once. Some people do best studying in structured, linear ways, while others do best jumping around, 'surrounding' a subject rather than traversing it. Some people prefer to learn by manipulating models, and others by reading" (Bill Gates, Microsoft CEO).
- "Learning how to learn is life's most important skill" (Tony Buzan, writer and researcher).

While it may be difficult to establish consensus on definitions of play and learning, perhaps it is more important to remember that both represent a broad and extensive body of research which suggests that early development progresses at a rate more rapid than any other stage of life. How children develop and absorb information to reach their greatest capacity is well documented by some of the leading contemporary scientists and researchers (e.g., *Eager to Learn [2000]* and *From Neurons to Neighborhoods: The Science of Early Childhood Development [2000]*). If we can accept the premise that (1) all children are born ready to learn, and (2) play helps construct knowledge, what does that look like in Wisconsin early childhood environments?

Five Child Care Environments

To understand play and learning in the United States, five children (three girls and two boys) who ranged in age from 22 months to 3 years were videotaped in their early childhood environments. These videotapes, which averaged approximately 2 hours, were edited to 15–20-minute tapes. The teacher and the child's parent viewed the video tapes and then were interviewed regarding play at school and at home.

The five child care settings selected are representative of the major early childhood programs in the United States. Four of the five programs serve predominately Caucasian children, while one program is representative of urban diversity. These centers include one family child care, two not-for-profit centers, one campus child care and one employer child care. The centers, located in Oshkosh, Appleton and Milwaukee, Wisconsin, were randomly selected from lists provided by Child Care Resource & Referral, Inc. (CCR&R) of Appleton. CCR&R provides technical assistance, resources and best practices to early childhood programs. There are 850 CCR&Rs in the United States, and eight are in Wisconsin.

All five of the programs are licensed by the state of Wisconsin, which signifies that they have met minimal standards for health and safety. Three of the programs have received accreditation from the NAEYC, signifying that they have met the criteria for high-quality early childhood programs.

The researchers found that most schedules were predictable and flexible. Four of the five schedules had similar activities spread throughout the day. Toddlers arrived at their respective centers and had play time until breakfast. Breakfast was generally followed by another play time that included outside play time when the weather permitted. Lunch was served 3 hours after breakfast, as specified by state licensing requirements. The toddlers took afternoon naps, were given a snack and then more play time until departure with their parent(s).

Observations in all five centers revealed that the teachers were sensitive to the needs of toddlers, meaning that not everything ran on a tight schedule but was dependent on the attention and interest of the children. Whether a prescribed curriculaum was followed or not, the teachers provided opportunities for children to play with toys, engage in short circle-time activities, sing, participate in art activities, and read books.

During one of the observations, a child arrived in time for breakfast, ate (and played with) her oatmeal, and then went to a housekeeping area where she took on the role of mom while rocking her baby in a child-sized rocking chair. She then moved over to an area where the teacher was half-way through reading a picture book to a small group of toddlers. When the story ended, she looked at a number of books before moving on to play with a container of musical instruments. She was intrigued by the sounds coming out of a small electric piano before moving on to some other instruments. Her play tended to be solitary, and little interaction was seen between the child and her teacher. After a play time outside, the child ate lunch and went to her cot for nap.

In talking with the teachers, the researchers found this to be a typical schedule for most children in their center, and not just the toddlers. In short, a toddler day had the possibility for endless play that was interrupted now and then for toileting, food and rest.

The following is a brief description of each child and their centers.

Family Child Care

K was a 22-month-old Caucasian girl, an only child from a two-parent family. She attended the program for 5 days a week, for approximately 6 hours per day. The teacher has worked in this family program for 9 years. Her education consists of a 2-year degree from a technical college.

This program, located in a home in a suburban setting with a population of approximately 63,000, has been in operation since 1997 and serves 18 children ranging in age from 7 months to 10 years, who attend the program at various times. The at-home program has not received NAEYC accreditation. There are two main play areas, indoors, for the children: living room and basement. There were many age-appropriate toys that were often out of reach or scattered about. Storage of materials was such that children could not put things away or reach materials. The outside area was spacious with swings and many wheel toys that were stored in the garage.

Not-for-Profit Program

D was a 3-year-old African-American boy from a two-parent family of five children, who attended the program 10 hours a day, 5 days a week. The lead teacher had a Child Development Associate certificate and had been with the center for 11 years. This program, located in an urban setting with a population of 600,000, has been in operation for 74 years serving 72 children ranging in age from 6 weeks to 11 years, and has received NAEYC accreditation. The center is located in a remodeled office building in a low socio-economic neighborhood. The toddler room, located in the basement, meets minimal standards for size. The room is divided into centers with mediocre materials. The outdoor space was designed for toddlers with minimal materials to engage children in play.

For Profit Center

L was a 22-month-old Caucasian girl, an only child in a single-parent family and attended the center for 6 hours a day, 5 days a week. Her mother worked at the center and was able to visit her daughter during the day. The teacher had been in child care for approximately 10 years and has a 1-year technical degree.

The classroom was located in a building near the commercial area of the city whose population was 63,000. The school had been in operation for 8 years and had 120 children ranging in age from 6 weeks to 6 years. There were 28 teachers in the program. The school has not received accreditation from NAEYC.

The room was seen as small for four toddlers and barely met the minimum requirements of space per child. There were few toys in this room where the children eat, sleep and spend approximately 11 hours. The outdoor space for 120 children was extremely small and cluttered with plastic climbing apparatus.

Campus Child Care Center

J was a 2-year-old Caucasian girl who attended the program 10 hours a day, 5 days a week. She is from a two-parent family and has a sister who is 5 years older. The teacher has a Bachelor's degree in early childhood education and has worked in this program for 3 years.

This licensed center, located in a city with a population of approximately 17,000, was surrounded by the main college campus and had been in operation for 30 years, providing services for students and faculty. The center had an enrollment of 68 children ranging in age from birth to 6 years. The center had received accreditation through NAEYC. The indoor and outdoor space was seen as child centered and developmentally appropriate.

Employer Child Care

A was a 2-year-old Guatemalan boy adopted into a two-parent family. He had a sibling who was 5 years older. He attended this program 10 hours a day, 5 days a week. The teacher's education included an associate degree (2 years) in occupational therapy and 1 year of study in a child care and development program from a local technical college.

This licensed center, located in a city with a population of approximately 70,000, was designed specifically as a child care facility. The center was located on the grounds of a large medical center which served the employees of the medical center. This employee child care program had been in operation for 12 years, and served 75 children who attended full and part time. The center had received the accreditation from NAEYC. The indoor and outdoor space was seen as child-centered and developmentally appropriate.

Overview of Environment

This brief description of the five programs demonstrates both good news and bad news about the quality of these programs. All of the programs were licensed and accredited and had staff who took great pride in their work. The areas of greatest need are insufficient supply of developmentally appropriate materials and space.

According to NAEYC, play and learning is supported by the following practices (Bredekamp & Copple, 1997):

- Opportunities for children to engage in many forms of play (e.g., parallel reciprocal, solitary and exploratory).
- Flexible schedules that accommodate individual children's needs.
- Environments that encourage and stimulate the whole child's development (e.g., cognitive, emotional, social and physical).

In the state of Wisconsin, the Model Early Learning Standards (2003) for play and learning are supported by eight guiding principles:

1. All children are capable and competent.
2. A child's early learning and development is multidimensional.
3. Expectations for children must be guided by knowledge of child growth and development.
4. Children are individuals who develop at various rates.
5. Children are members of cultural groups that share developmental patterns.
6. Children exhibit a range of skills and competencies within any domain of development.
7. Children learn through play and the active exploration of their environment.
8. Parents are children's primary and most important caregivers and educators.

A Typical Toddler Day

The following narrative is seen as a typical representation of play between teacher, the child alone, and among peers. D is a 3-year-old boy in Milwaukee and the observations reflect over 1 hour of play in his child care environment.

Structured circle time – The morning begins with five toddlers sitting in a semicircle on the rug with the teacher, who sings a welcoming song, "Everybody has a Name, Oh, Yes." The child says his/her name, which the group repeats while singing and clapping. When one child does not respond with his name, the teacher has the group sing his name. The teacher asks who is missing and when the group responds incorrectly, the teacher supplies the names of children not in attendance. Following attendance, the teacher expressively reads a story to the group about Santa Claus. She repeatedly asks questions such as, "Do you think they are going to give him a button? What is that? What color is Santa's suit?" The teacher asks D to name colors of the shirts worn by children in the group. After the story, the teacher asks D (and each child) "Where would you like to go?" D's response is "housekeeping."

Housekeeping area – D enters the small housekeeping area and holds a doll. Another boy and girl are in this area as well. D struggles to pull an adult dress off a hanger in the dress-up area. He places this dress on the child-sized red couch and proceeds to wrap up the doll. D sits with another boy and together they rock their dolls.

D goes to the teacher to get assistance as he struggles to don the adult-sized dress. He slowly walks back to get a pair of men's shoes and watches two other toddlers put on dresses and adult shoes. D takes quite a bit of time to put one foot in the adult man's shoe while keeping the dress on his body, which keeps getting in his way. He walks around the small classroom with his long dress and clunky shoes. Slowly, the dress comes off and the teacher says, "Hang up the dress." D responds with "I can't do it."

Play dough area – D walks over to the play dough area where Christmas music is playing loudly and observes three other children working with play dough. One girl gives him a cookie cutter and D proceeds for 20 minutes was to explore the play dough by pounding and stretching it. The teacher informally goes to the table to ask questions, "What are you making? How does that feel? Referring to the play dough, D replies, "Cold." D and the teacher share some more conversation and talk about what D is creating at the table. The teacher says, "You know it's time for us to put play dough away." Girl at table says to D, "Put it in there D." D shouts "NO!" and the teacher replies, "Let him put it in himself."

Pretend sweeping and mopping – Several children begin to use the mops and brooms located in the housekeeping area. D gets a broom and begins to sweep while saying "I clean the floor." The teacher jokingly says, "Give me a broom. Nobody will give me a broom. I can't help clean."

Book area – D picks up a magazine and sits on some soft cushions. Several children are in this small area. D sits next to a girl who is looking at a picture book. Both children talk to one another as they flip the pages. D does not return the magazine to the rack and the teacher asks him to put it away. D says, "No." The

teacher reaches her hand over to D and says, "D, can I have that book? Pick it up."
D picks it up as the teacher tells the children it is time to go to the washrooms and
then on to the large motor room in another part of the building.

Interviews with Teachers and Parents

A focused interview session followed the review of the edited video which lasted approximately 15 minutes. Two researchers and a college student recorded the teacher
and parent responses. Viewing of the video and interview sessions took approximately 1 hour. The following describes how the five teachers and the five parents
viewed play and learning.

Parent Interviews

The parent interview questions focused on

1. the child's play at home and what they were learning;
2. the child's activities at child care;
3. how parents viewed the child's play and learning at home and at school; and
4. comments on the video.

1. In response to their child's play at home and what they were learning, several of
   the parents noted that their children love to read.
   Play at-home:

   - "Loves being read to and will often choose to look at books on his own, taking
     time to look carefully at the illustrations on each page."
   - "She likes to play in the real and pretend kitchen. She also likes to play dress-
     up with old clothes that we keep in the play room."
   - "She is really independent when getting her stuff. Right now she loves
     blocks."

   Views on learning:

   - "Much learning has come from reading with family members."
   - "She seems to have learned more about language through the use of sign
     language as an infant...I think she picked up language earlier because of
     those experiences."
   - "In seeing this tape, he's learning independence. Either I don't know about it
     or I don't want to know about seeing him."

2. Several mothers stated that their child's activities at child care consisted mainly
   of playing with other children. Parents noted they learned about activities at child
   care by talking with the teacher and from the posted daily schedules. One mother
   worked in the center and visits the room during her break time. Some reported
   that they did not know what their children were involved in during the day, but
   said the children liked coming to child care.

A recurring theme regarding communication is represented in the following parent comments:

- "We have good communication 10–15 minutes a day in the morning to see what she is doing and what is going on."
- I think I know the most about her day though talking with her teacher each day during drop-off and pick-up".

Socializing with other children was noted as an important part of play and learning at school.

Mothers responded

- "...it is important for children to learn from one another ..."
- "Play at preschool is rougher. There are no other kids at home, no one to roll around with or goof off with except us. It is quieter at home."
- "At home play time is free time to do what you want."

When asked to comment on the video of their child, mothers said the following:

- "D shows me he's not a baby anymore. After looking at tape, I see him as a 3-year old. He is not the infant I rocked and fed and put to sleep. After seeing the tape "that's my big boy." The independence hits me with his book reading...shows you the impact we have at home with reading."
- "She is more quiet than at home. She is normally not that quiet. She knew something was different. She was more sensitive to things going on in the room."
- "The video was very consistent with what was expected. It showed A doing what he does best and that is play.
- "I kinda know what she does. She loves the swings. We don't have a swing at home because we wanted her to have different things to play with at home than here. She interacts well with other children and is very independent."

In summation, what do parents say about play and learning at home and school? At home, parents viewed reading and pretend play as integral parts of learning. They perceived socialization as key factors in child care. The mothers reported that they were informed of what occurs in child care, yet lacked specificity. After viewing the videos, three of the five mothers stated that the video was consistent with how their child played. Two mothers were surprised at the independence of their children. Overall, interviewees provided little information on their understanding of play and learning.

Teacher Interviews

The following data of the videotapes of the five children and interviews with teachers will provide information on how play and learning is understood. The teacher interview questions focused on

1. how the child plays at preschool;
2. how would you describe the child's day;

3. how the child plays and learns at home;
4. differences in play and learning between home and school; and
5. comments on the video.

Representative responses to the teacher-interview questions:

1. Tell about what/how the child plays in preschool.

   - "She loves playing outside. She will sit and read books for 15–20 minutes. She loves anything that you can stack or build with, or anything that makes noise. Right now she loves a popular cartoon character (Elmo), and she enjoys running through the mall (a pre-existing space used by a shopping center that is now attached to the child care center)."
   - "She plays with anything the boys play with. The boy things as well as with the dolls. I just started curriculum with her. She does about everything coloring, circle time, she loves to build things right now."
   - "She likes to read books and be read to."

2. How would you describe the child's day at preschool?

   - "It's very busy. He is actively engaged with kids or toys and is constantly looking for new ways to stay busy."
   - "She is very stuck on things being routine. If the routine breaks, it is the end of the world for her."
   - "It has a lot of structure and routine. The children follow the same schedule every day."

3. How does the child play and learn at home?

   - "His play is similar to that at school. However, he has an older sibling and will do whatever his brother is doing."
   - "I don't really know anything about home life. They both are very good parents. They work with her on a lot of different things. They are a family. They are very into her."

4. Are there differences between play and learning at home and in preschool?

   - "The only difference is, here we do curriculum. On home, it is one-on-one, otherwise it is pretty much the same as here."
   - "She can interact with other kids here and learn to share and take turns."
   - "There are lots of similarities. There are books and many manipulatives at school and home. He will look at books endlessly at home, which mirrors his activities at school."

5. Would you comment on the video?

   - "She was very well behaved that day. As long as we stay in routine, she's ok. She loves playing with the other kids. They wait at the door for each other every day. That video was typically her; there was nothing unusual about it."

- "To see the video, I think, "I should do more of that with my kids." It was an awesome video. You see them everyday, but it was different on the video. The imitation was amazing. I did something and she does it. She is more independent. She does things on her own, not really following what someone else wanted to do."

To summarize, it was felt that teachers saw the children as being actively involved in days that followed an established routine. The days were perceived to be full of activities that were developmentally appropriate and geared toward a child's interest. Play and learning seems to be viewed as similar when comparing home and school environments. Communication appeared to be positive and face-to-face during drop-off and pick-up time.

Findings

In reviewing collected data, the researchers found the following recurring themes:

- Connections between standards and play and learning.
- Developmentally appropriate practices were demonstrated in all five centers.
- Centers were of average and/or above average quality in terms of environment and activities.
- Characteristics of toddler play were observed (e.g., parallel, solitary).
- Teachers directed and provided resources to expand and facilitate play.
- Parents and teachers appear to provide minimal scaffolding.
- Oral language development was valued and encouraged through practices and materials.
- Children had free choice of play experiences and materials to engage in deep and/or extended play.
- Parents and teachers interview responses indicated a superficial knowledge of play and learning.

In drawing upon Rogoff's cultural – historical framework, the findings of this study can be grouped according to the three foci of analysis, as noted in the table below:

Focus of analysis	Summary
Personal focus of analysis	Teachers' knowledge guided by DAP, Piaget, and Vygotsky. Teachers modeled a belief in free choice play and provided resources to support play and learning. Teacher's knowledge of play and learning was found to be superficial.
Interpersonal focus of analysis	Minimal scaffolding was evident from parents and teachers. Oral language was valued by the teachers. Characteristics of toddler play were observed (e.g., parallel, solitary)
Institutional or cultural focus of analysis	Connections between standards and play and learning. Centers were of average and/or above average quality in terms of environment and activities.

Overall, play and learning were promoted in all five centers, in varying degrees of practice. While teacher and parent actions may be promoting play and learning, their responses and observations to the videos reflected a lack of understanding regarding the depth and complexity of play and learning.

Specifically, teacher interviews indicated that there is little comprehension of theory and pedagogy of play. To illustrate, teachers were unable to describe play and learning at home and school with detail and clarity. For example, this comment from a teacher reveals superficial information: "It's very busy. He is actively engaged with kids or toys and is constantly looking for new ways to stay busy."

Parents were equally unaware of the need for depth and understanding of play and learning development. Additionally, the connection(s) between school and home provides information but contains little substance, as evidenced by this quote: "I think I know what J is doing because I talk with the teacher each day during drop-off and pick-up." This reveals that the communication is more about activities than knowledge of child development.

"All researchers are affected by observer's bias. Qualitative researchers try to acknowledge and take into account their own biases as a method of dealing with them" (Bogdan & Biklen, 1982, p. 43). The researchers recognize that the introduction of the study constitutes a variable that cannot be controlled. However, the researchers worked in childrens' natural environments as a team, reviewed recorded observations, and repeatedly critiqued their findings, which minimized the effects of observer bias.

Conclusions

Our findings support the current thinking of Johnson et al (2005): "Defining and articulating play are far from easy for at least two different reasons. First, play is abstract and fluid; it is not a concrete object, place of action... A second reason that play is problematic is its multiplicity of meanings." A significant finding was the incongruous nature of play and learning being supported in practice, but not in understanding of theory. Specifically, is it understood that all of the child's play experiences are related to learning?

Some other questions have arisen during the course of this study. Do the observations and interviews truly reflect reality of play and learning, or are the observers seeing a "performance" of what the parents and teachers feel play and learning *should* be? The researchers' response to the observations and interviews would be that the findings provide an incomplete picture of play and learning in the lives of this population.

Another question centers on the culture of America and its impact on play and learning. The study focused on play and learning in five centers throughout northeastern Wisconsin where independence is highly valued, an attribute that is reflected by the culture of people in the Midwestern region and throughout the United States. The researchers question whether this drive for independence impacts how adults remove themselves from play with children.

As stated previously in this study, NAEYC standards suggest that adults engage in reciprocal play with toddlers to promote learning. Data collected would suggest that teachers and parents separate themselves from play, which according to NA-EYC is an inappropriate practice.

What education needs to take place in order to align parents and teachers with the need for reciprocal play? Comparing the knowledge bases of play and learning between researchers and teachers/parents reveals a disparity that needs further analysis. How do we bridge this gap between parents and teachers? The challenge for teachers is to collaborate with parents to provide experiences at school and home that reflect the theory and pedagogy of play and learning.

References

Berk, L. A., & Winsler, A. (1995). *Scaffolding children's learning: Vygotsky and early childhood education*. Washington, DC: National Association for the Education of Young Children.

Bogdan, C., & Biklen, S. K. (1982). *Qualitative research for education: An introduction to theory and methods*. Boston: Allyn and Bacon, Inc.

Bowman, B., Donovan, M. S., & Burns, S. (Eds.). (2000). *Eager to learn: Educating our preschoolers*. Washington, DC: National Academy Press.

Bredekamp, S., & Copple, C. (Eds.). (1997). *Developmentally appropriate practice in early childhood programs* (rev. ed.). Washington, DC: National Association for the Education of Young Children.

Brooks, J. G., & Brooks, M. G. (1993). *In search of understanding: The case for constructivist classrooms*. Alexandria, VA: Association for Supervision and Curriculum Development.

Brunsan Phillips, C. (1994). In S. Bredekamp, & C. Copple (Eds.), (1997), *Developmentally appropriate practice in early childhood programs* (rev. ed.). Washington, DC: National Association for the Education of Young Children.

Buzan, T. (1991). *Use both sides of your brain*. New York: Penguin Books.

Copple, S., & Bredekamp, S. (2006). *Basics of developmentally appropriate practice: An introduction for teachers of children 3 to 6*. Washington, DC: National Association for the Education of Young Children.

Johnson, J. E, Christie, J. F. & Wardle, F. (2005). *Play, development and early education*. Boston, MA: Pearson Education, Inc.

Kegan, R. (1996). In B. McCarthy, *About learning*. Barrington, IL: About Learning, Inc.

Moll, L. (Ed.). (1990). *Vygotsky and education: Instructional implications and applications of sociohistorical psychology*. UK: Cambridge University Press.

National Association of Child Care Resource and Referral Agencies. (2006). *2006 Child Care in the State of Wisconsin*. Arlington, VA.

Rogoff, B., & Wertsch, J. V. (Eds.). (2003). *Children learning in the "Zone of Proximal Development"*. San Francisco: Jossey-Bass, Inc.

Roopnarine, J. L., & Johnson, J. E. (1993). *Approaches to early childhood education* (2nd ed.). New York: Macmillan Publishing Company.

Ryder, D., Wright, J., Adams, C., & Jones, K. (2004). *Multiple voices and multiple layers of learning. New Zealand Ministry of Education*. Retrieved June 14, 2006, from http://www.minedu.govt.nz?index.cfm?layout=document&documentid=110288%indexid=8311&indexparentid=8303

Singer, D., & Revenson, T. A. (1996). *A Piaget primer: How a child thinks* (rev. ed.). New York: Penguin Books.

Shonkoff, J. P., & Phillips, D. A. (2000). *From neurons to neighborhoods: The science of early childhood development*. Washington, DC: National Academy Press.

United Nations Convention on the Rights of the Child. (1989). *Article 31*.

United States Census Bureau. (2000). *Unites States Census 2000*. Retrieved [November 15, 2006] from http://www.census.gov/main/www/cen2000.html.

United States Department of Education (2006). *No Child Left Behin*. Retrieved [November 15, 2006], from //www.ed.gov/nclb/.

Wisconsin Department of Public Instruction. (2003). *Wisconsin Model Early Learning Standards*. Madison, WI: Wisconsin Department of Public Instruction.

Wolfe, P. (2001). *Brain matters: Translating research into classroom practice*. Alexandria, VA: Association for Supervision and Curriculum Development.

Chapter 9
Commonalities and Distinctions Across Countries

Ingrid Pramling-Samuelsson and Marilyn Fleer

Introduction

For a child, being in an early childhood education setting is different from being at home, on a bus or at a public playground, and therefore play in this context is, and should be, different. From the countries covered in this book, it appears that all over the world, there are intentions to give children a good start in life, with opportunities for play seen as an essential component of this, even though the actual possibilities to participate in a programme of high quality differs. Early childhood education is purported, across all countries, to contribute to children's education and well-being in a way where care and pedagogy are mutual and dependent on each other (Siraj Blatchford, 2004). Play is therefore seen as a feature of such education as noted in the research reported by authors from Chile, Hong Kong China, Japan, Aotearoa New Zealand, Australia, Sweden, and Wisconsin USA.

In drawing upon cultural – historical theory, many of the researchers who reported their studies in this book sought to frame their research on play in relation to Rogoff's writings on sociocultural theory. As discussed in Chapter 1, Rogoff's writings inspired researchers to interview or gather data in relation to personal, interpersonal, and institutional or cultural dimensions. Whilst not all authors used the analytical framework for presenting their work, they were nevertheless inspired to use cultural–historical theory. In this final chapter, we seek to discuss the research presented in this book more explicit in relation to Rogoff's three lenses (see Chapter 1). The outcome of this analysis can be grouped in relation to personal, interpersonal, and institutional or cultural dimensions, as noted below.

Focus of analysis	Summary
Personal focus of analysis	
Interpersonal focus of analysis	
Institutional or cultural focus of analysis	

I. Pramling-Samuelsson
Göteborg University, Department of Education, SE-405 30 Göteborg, Sweden
e-mail: Ingrid.Pramling@ped.gu.se

I. Pramling-Samuelsson, M. Fleer (eds.), *Play and Learning in Early Childhood Settings*, DOI 10.1007/978-1-4020-8498-0_9,
© Springer Science+Business Media B.V. 2009

A discussion of these broad outcomes follows in this first part of this final chapter. It should be noted that only major themes from countries are summarized and discussed. The complexity and detail are provided in each of the chapters. Summary tables have been developed in relation to the data reported in the country specific chapters and cannot be viewed as representative, but rather as an indication or trend to be noted.

Cultural–Historical Analysis of Play Acitivity Within Australia

In Australia, it was noted that the institutional dimensions of play positioned what was possible within the centres. The theoretical beliefs about what is play and how professionals respond to or interpret play was hugely significant for determining what an individual could do within their play environment. For instance, the teachers predominantly used Parten's theory (1932) of play to guide them (personal focus of analysis) in relation to interpreting what children were doing. Similarly, the teachers took a nonactive role (interpersonal focus of analysis) as a result of their theoretical interpretations of Piaget's theory on learning. This meant that the focus of attention in play for children was in relation to the resources. Play was facilitated by the resources rather than adults suggesting or participating in young children's play.

The theoretical approach in relation to play (Parten, op. cit.) is consistent with what is taught to early childhood professionals with technical qualifications (see Table summary of Australia below). As such, how play was talked about, how children were supported in their play, and how play activity was observed and interpreted was governed by institutional factors – that is, what is taught about play and learning in the technical education institutions. Policy and regulations in Australia put technically qualified staff (rather than university educated staff) with babies and toddlers. The net outcome is a system for learning, where play is framed through the institutional sanctioning of a particular theory of play that was developed in the 1930s. Further analyses in the Australian context have shown that the staff struggled to use just Parten's and Piaget's theory, and that on many occasions the theories did not help them with their daily decisions, making some feel guilty for occasionally interacting "extensively" (as they defined it) with children during play (Fleer, Tonyan, Mantilla, & Rivalland, 2006).

Focus of analysis	Summary
Personal focus of analysis	Teachers used Parten's theory of play to guide them with their expectations of children.
Interpersonal focus of analysis	Teachers did not intervene in children's play, they actively took an observation role.
Institutional or cultural focus of analysis	Teachers used the environment, particularly the resources, for framing and planning for children's play. Parten's theory of play determined their observations and analysis; and interpretations of Piaget, determined their non-active role in children's play.

Cultural–Historical Analysis of Play Activity Within Aotearoa New Zealand

In *Australia*, social development of children and problem solving appear as key values which are promoted. This can be linked to the origin of early childhood education where social development is supposed to be the base for everything else. Problem solving, however, became central for pointing out the importance of the child's cognitive development.

In contrast, the findings reported by the Aotearoa New Zealand researchers showed a great sensitivity to relationships and to culturally specific ways of communicating, planning, and observing. Family and community were foregrounded (cultural focus of analysis), in order to better understand children individually (personal focus of analysis). Local understandings of curriculum were featured, rather than an institutional perspective sanctioning a particular theoretical approach, as was evident in Australia. However, it should be noted that curriculum theory has evolved in Aotearoa New Zealand as a result of bi-cultural partnerships and a keen attention to sociocultural theory, where cultural dimensions are foregrounded (Nuttall, 2003).

In *Aotearoa New Zealand* early childhood education, the maintenance and promotion of cultural values is seen as important in developing individual and collective identity. To this end, educators strive to maintain cultural diversity in a variety of ways, not least in the integration of multiple languages and cultural practices with emphasis on *te reo Maori* and *tikanga* (the language and protocols of Aotearoa New Zealand's indigenous population). Associated priority is given to the notions of equity and citizenship, with an overarching goal of future sustainment for Aotearoa New Zealand as a strong bicultural nation. For many in Aotearoa New Zealand, the child represents the intergenerational link between the past and the future and, as such, teachers place high value on the unique knowledge that each family brings to the early childhood education experience. Each child is promoted as a treasure (*taonga*), whose participation in early childhood education contexts enhances their opportunities to make a valued contribution to society and, in doing so, represent the hopes and dreams of older generations for future society.

Focus of analysis	Summary
Personal focus of analysis	Knowledge of children's development was viewed holistically and teachers showed great respect for infants and toddlers.
Interpersonal focus of analysis	The importance of relationships was made explicit.
Institutional or cultural focus of analysis	Family and community played a central role in curriculum planning and cultural communities were foregrounded at all times.
	Collectivity was seen as important.

Cultural–Historical Analysis of Play Activity Within Sweden

Like Aotearoa New Zealand, relationships were also featured in Sweden. Staff focussed on their relationship with children, foregrounding communication and interaction as central to understanding and planning for children. The researchers noted that the children's capacity and opportunity to express their feelings and thoughts were important in the Swedish context. Similarly, relationships between children were also seen as very important. Building friendships between children was fostered. Like the Australian context, the teachers did not intervene in the children's play. However, they supported and valued children's social pretend play. These values are made explicit in the Swedish curriculum, and as such the institutional dimensions shaped what was possible for children in their play.

The *Swedish* early childhood educators work consciously towards giving children opportunities to become involved, make decisions, and express their own ideas from an early age, something shown in the OECD evaluation, where it was stated that democracy was practiced even in toddler groups. So, here the child's perspective, equality, and participation are important aspects.

The researchers noted that the teachers had not only been influenced by their curriculum in what was featured in their centres, but had embraced the national curriculum as a central defining theme in their interpretations of the value of children's play.

Focus of analysis	Summary
Personal focus of analysis	Teachers believed children's independence and engagement in play activities were important. Teachers foregrounded pretend play and believed it was important for the children to feel at home.
Interpersonal focus of analysis	Teachers do not intervene in the children's play. Communication and interaction between staff and children were important and central for children's learning. Children building friendships was also important.
Institutional or cultural focus of analysis	Children were given many opportunities for choice and encouraged to express their thoughts and feelings – important curriculum outcomes in Sweden.
	Gender equality is actively examined.

Cultural–Historical Analysis of Play Activity Within Japan

The significance of play for supporting social relationships in Sweden was also evident in Japan. In Japan, great significance was placed on supporting children to become socialized into the Japanese values where harmonious relationships were viewed as the responsibility of the individual to the group. As learning and play could not be separated, play was used as the main pedagogical approach for creating time and space for optimizing relationships between children. Like Aotearoa New Zealand, researchers in Japan noted that the family and community values shaped how staff framed learning and play opportunities for the children.

Focus of analysis	Summary
Personal focus of analysis	Teachers believed play and learning were inseparable.
Interpersonal focus of analysis	Play is developed through social relationships.
Institutional or cultural focus of analysis	The children's play reflected the cultural contexts and values of Japanese community.

Cultural–Historical Analysis of Play Activity Within Hong Kong China

In contrast to Sweden and Japan, the researchers in Hong Kong China noted that play was not valued highly for free expression of feelings and thoughts or for exploring social relationships. Rather, play was viewed as an instructional tool for maximizing direct teaching. Play was included in the range of pedagogical approaches to supporting children's learning. Of significance was the researchers' elaboration of the differing roles adults played in their interactions with children during play. The researchers noted that the role of adults in children's play could be leading play, supporting play, providing free play opportunities, or interacting to maximize direct teaching. Play in Hong Kong China was linked to an instructional orientation, and teacher modes of interacting were more sharply differentiated than in other countries.

In *China*, the value of learning and knowledge formation is very strong, a perspective widely accepted in the world when talking about the Chinese learner as a strong academic person (Marton & Tsui, 2004; Rao & Pearson, 2006). It is interesting that the reputation of the Chinese learner can be seen already among the youngest children.

Focus of analysis	Summary
Personal focus of analysis	Teachers' knowledge of Vygotsky's theory, particularly the insights gained from understanding the concept "scaffolding".
Interpersonal focus of analysis	The role of adults in children's play, as leading play, supporting play, providing free play opportunities, or interacting to maximize direct teaching.
Institutional or cultural focus of analysis	Teacher beliefs about the importance of play as a pedagogical approach for learning was framed from an instructional perspective.

Like in Aotearoa New Zealand, researchers in Hong Kong China found that teachers drew upon sociocultural theory to inform their beliefs and practices. In New Zealand, the focus of attention was on relationships and cultural knowledge of children, whilst in Hong Kong China sociocultural theory guided staff with their planned scaffolding of children's learning.

Cultural–Historical Analysis of Play Activity Within Wisconsin, USA

Sociocultural theory has also been influential in Wisconsin, USA, where teachers' knowledge of Vygotsky has also shaped how staff interact with children. Like Hong Kong China, researchers in Wisconsin valued scaffolding of learning during play. The researchers noted that staff also drew upon both Piaget's theory and developmentally appropriate practices (DAP), which lie in strong contrast to sociocultural theory. As with Hong Kong China, the role of the adult in children's play was examined. In contrast to Hong Kong China, the Wisconsin teachers did not intervene much in children's play. This outcome is consistent with the interpretations of Piaget's work, where staff focus mostly on planning environments and not on interactions. The provision of materials which are seen as developmentally appropriate for children becomes the focus of attention. The focus on materials and the cultural belief that each child is going to become independent, and by doing so they are able to take initiatives and gain trust in their own competence, is foregrounded. What is foregrounded in Wisconsin is the institutional dimensions.

There is a strong emphasis in the USA on DAP and standards, both of which have shaped how children play in Wisconsin. The researchers note that in the USA, the depth and significance of play is often misunderstood by educators, families, and policy makers.

Focus of analysis	Summary
Personal focus of analysis	Teachers' knowledge guided by DAP, Piaget, Vygotsky. Belief in free choice play, Parten's theory of play, and a focus on providing resources to support play and learning. Teacher's knowledge of play and learning was not strongly grounded in research and theory.
Interpersonal focus of analysis	Oral language was valued by the teachers. Scaffolding was less evident, with the teacher's role less dominant. The materials suggested opportunities for children's play.
Institutional or cultural focus of analysis	Connections between standards and play and learning were important to staff and education authorities. Institutional demands were important and focussed staff attention on what mattered during children's play.

Cultural–Historical Analysis of Play Activity Within Chile

Whilst institutional dimensions were highly influential in many countries for shaping how play was framed and discussed, in Chile researchers noted that teachers' personal knowledge of child development was central to guiding staff expectations and analyses of children at play. For instance, staff expected infants under 2 years to be interested in playing with their bodies, whilst children aged 2–3 years would be more focussed on role play. This personal knowledge was further developed by close observations of children to find what inspired them. In Chile, researchers noted that the role of the TV and gender differences were areas they were particularly concerned about in relation to how children played. In addition to Parten's theory of play, constructivist theories guided staff thinking about play. Consistent with a constructivist view of learning, teachers did not actively intervene in children's play, but rather focussed on singing and dancing with infants as their main mode of direct interaction.

Focus of analysis	Summary
Personal focus of analysis	Teachers' personal knowledge of the play they expect for at particular age groups, such as 0–2 infants playing with their bodies, and role play for 2–3 year olds. Teachers' knowledge about what inspires children being gained through close observations of children at play. Teacher knowledge and use of Parten's theory of play for analysing children's play.
Interpersonal focus of analysis	The importance of singing and dancing for communication between children and between infants and adults.
Institutional or cultural focus of analysis	The role of TV in children's play (e.g. aggressive cartoons), gender differences established in routines (e.g. sorting children into boys and girls). Selection of play materials is linked to curriculum areas. Constructivist learning.

Chile has a special political background, which also colours the values of young children's lives in early childhood education. Respect for other's differences and dignity is what the teachers struggle to mediate to their children by working with global themes that are transversally crossed with values like empathy, self esteem, among others. The idea of working in an inclusive way, where each child is welcome, is something strongly promoted by the government policies and forms the training of the teachers.

The values visible in the empirical data can be placed on a scale; from a collective interpretation which emphasizes the group and associated relationships with others to an individual focus which promotes the benefits for the child as a learner. These values, seen in everyday life in early childhood education, are the same as we can see on the political agenda all over the world – a collective priority for a nation vs an individual priority for the child (Gonazlez-Mena, 1986). What we notice in these countries are organizational, curriculum, theoretical, and cultural values which have shaped how play is enacted in each of the countries reported in this book. Concepts of the role of staff in play, the enactment of play in institutions, and beliefs about "what counts as play" were clearly variable across countries – reflecting the cultural–historical context of early childhood education. A discussion of the similarities and difference in these areas follows. It should be noted that whilst it would appear that the outcomes could collectively depict play as being representative of all the activities of children (as also discussed in Chapter 1 about what appears in the play literature), a sociocultural perspective on play research begins to make visible the dialectics between the child and the cultural–historical context in which the child plays and learns. What follows points to both structural and conceptual outcomes, and collectively they demonstrate how play may be discussed as a universal construct across countries, but importantly, this book highlights how play is enacted in cultural–historical practice as a most specific and nonglobal construct.

Organization, Curriculum, and Staff

In most countries discussed in the book, early childhood education is organized by the social welfare sector. However, in Aotearoa New Zealand and Sweden the Ministry of Education is responsible for early childhood education and, in China nurseries come under the jurisdiction of the department of Public Health and kindergartens are overseen by the Department of Education. In Japan, day care centres are under the jurisdiction of the Ministry of Health, Welfare and Labour, and preschool/kindergartens come under the jurisdiction of the Ministry of Education, Science, Sports and Culture. Early childhood education in Aotearoa New Zealand and Sweden has also, until quite recently (over the past 10–20 years), been linked to the social service sector. This means that children were seen, more or less, as independent entities with their own rights, but always as part of their family (read mothers).

All over the world, it is difficult to talk about children without considering their close relationship to their mothers. In countries where women's liberation has been strong, therefore, equal opportunities for women are deeply connected with greater opportunities for young children to participate in early childhood education. Recent research (The Daily Yominri, 2006) also shows that it is not only the children who benefit from having educated mothers, but also the mothers who work outside the home have a better health at the age of 54 than mothers of the same age who have spent all their life at home with their children.

In the light of this, it is interesting to see the increasing trend for some countries in positioning early childhood education for children under the age of three as education, and not only as care. The associated standpoint of each country may also be manifest in national policies and practices, such as the type of guidelines developed for early childhood education and the youngest age-group therein. These guidelines are presented in four different ways across the participating countries. China, Aotearoa New Zealand, and Sweden have *national curricula*, although these are very different from each other. The Swedish curriculum consists of 16 pages, stating a perspective of learning and the goals to strive for (Ministry of Education and Sciences in Sweden, 1998). The Aotearoa New Zealand curriculum is based on four principles that guide and shape practice – empowerment, holistic development, family and community, and relationships; as well as associated strands and goals that support a pedagogical framework across ages from birth to school (Ministry of Education, 1996). China has issued both Regulations and Guidelines for Kindergarten Education practice which are influential in guiding practice. Chile and Australia have guidelines and frameworks for different levels of kindergarten education. In Japan, kindergarten practice's framework is indicated in "the National Curriculum Standards for Kindergarten Education" issued by the Ministry of Education, Science, Sports and Culture. Although practice at day care centres are guided by "the Guidelines for Day Nurseries" issued by the Ministry of Health, Welfare and Labor, the guidelines does not have validity of law. In other words, the guidelines is a guiding tool for practice rather than to fulfil the detailed items indicated in the guidelines. Finally, USA (Wisconsin) has the US National Association for Education of Young children (NAEYC) standards as steering instruments. The NAEYC standards are based on child development research and are supposed to give an objective picture of children.

One may think that these documents offer a cosmetic overview for practice in each of the countries, but our research reveals their provocative and powerful influence on pedagogy, and more specifically on the way play is conceptualized and actualized. However, we note a fundamental distinction between Guidelines which tell you as a teacher what you *ought to do* in early childhood education, and a curriculum which is nationally endorsed and sets out what you *must do*. Obviously, the NAEYC standards represent the US culture, although it is not expressed in terms of cultural values which are very strongly emphasized in the Swedish and Aotearoa New Zealand curricula. The Chinese guidelines not only reflect both traditional Chinese beliefs and values but also promote ideas about early development and learning which reflect western, scientific and democratic notions. OECD (2004), in their recommendations for pedagogy and curriculum, endorses the notion that early childhood education curricula should be based both on a combination of research *and* on cultural values.

The emphasis each country's government gives to early childhood education is evident in their treatment of early childhood education provision as well as curricula. By developing policies and practices that promote quality education, each country is making a very public comment on the status of very young children and the significant role they play in future society. A tangible aspect of such promotion is seen in the academic and professional qualifications required to work in early childhood education settings.

In Australia about 20% of early childhood educators are university educated, while the rest have a technical education. In China and Japan the 12% and 85% of early childhood educators, respectively, have a university education (though, Japan's university education includes 2- to 4-year college to earn a teacher/educator license). In 2005, in Aotearoa New Zealand, 54% of all early childhood teachers held a 3-year

diploma in teaching or higher diploma and over 50% of all teachers in early childhood services were registered (which means that those teachers have completed a
subsequent 2-year period of registration). These figures will already be significantly
increased as the intention of the Early Childhood Strategic Plan (Ministry of Education, 1996) is that *all* teachers will be educated and registered in 2012. In Chile
and Sweden 50% of the staff are university-educated teachers. In Sweden the other
50% have a senior high school education. In Chile the other 50% also have senior
high school with a short training in the field (1 year). Statistics however can cover
many truths! In Chile the figure 50% should be seen in the light of the fact that one
teacher is working with about 25 children together with the helper, while in Sweden
three staff [two teachers and one nursery nurse] work with a group of 14 children.
The largest variation between different early childhood settings within the studied
countries is in the USA.

There has been a wealth of evidence which indicates that staff qualification
(Gustafsson & Myhrberg, 2002) and the number of children in the group (Asplund
Carlsson, Kärrby, & Pramling-Samuelsson, 2001) are two key factors which determine the quality of early childhood education settings (Sheridan, 2001; Smith
et al., 2000). There is also an increasing body of research which suggests family participation is critical to the quality of education for very young children. Against this
background we now turn to the empirical data collected from the various countries.

Play in Early Childhood Education

Some general and joint perceptions of play in young children's lives can be seen.
Both parents and teachers share the opinion that play is the most important notion
for describing the experiences of children from birth to the age of three in early
childhood education. In their expressions lies the idea of play as an indication of a
good life for children. Play is the ultimate good! The participants seldom discussed
the discursive functions of play, and the associated issues of power or exclusion
(Gibbons, 2005), viewing it as either a nostalgiac utopia or desirable goal.

In some countries learning seems to be viewed as a contradiction to play. This
dichotomous view is understandable since long-held psychological paradigms view
play as an "activity" which takes place at the child's own initiative. Learning has
been viewed as something planned and initiated by the teacher with a passive child
acting in order to reach a correct answer (product). Even though contemporary
theoretical perspectives (e.g. Engeström, 1999; Vygotsky, 1986; Rogoff, 2003) position learning as embedded in the cultural context which includes play, such traditional perspectives do not loosen their pervasive hold on education since all adults
have the experience of a school-related learning (Pramling-Samuelsson, & Asplund
Carlsson, 2003). It is also obvious that many teachers as well as parents feel the
notion of learning strange to deal with when they talk about children under three.
One can also see how learning is a taken for granted aspect, or consequence of
play. Here, one can also sense the Freudian perspective – children play to act out

their experiences. Similarly, play was seen to have very much to do with children's emotions (Johnson, Christie, & Wardle, 2005).

Both teachers and parents viewed video recordings of the children and their comments showed that in some aspects they had similar reactions to these video clips. First of all, many become *surprised* when they realized how skilful children are socially, how they actually played together with other children, and the closeness of the relationships among children. Many of the parents (who saw their child as small and in need of support at home) were also surprised to realize that the child could do a lot of things in the preschool setting which they never do at home. Parents also believe that children can concentrate better at home, since there are so many children and so noisy in the early childhood education setting, but get surprised when they see their child concentrating on a particular task for a long time in the early childhood setting. The New Zealand parents, however, many of whom spent time in the centre, expressed their delight at seeing the play that was valued at home endorsed and promoted in the context of the early childhood education setting. For them, play was a mediating strategy between home and early childhood education and therefore a way of supporting their values and beliefs.

Not only do parents get surprised, but also teachers discover a single child's skilfulness within specific areas as well as the relationships and cooperation between very young children (Dunn, 1991).

From these experiences we would like to point to the great power of analysing video recordings of everyday practice, something which will help the teacher, and the parent, become aware of the children's competence, as well as his or her own involvement and role in children's learning and playing (Palmérus, Pramling, & Lindahl, 1991; Pramling, 1995).

The Function of Play and the Teacher's Role

Australia gives expression of perceiving the function of play as supporting learning and social development. The role of the teacher is not to interfere, but to observe and support when necessary. Here the perspective in Sweden is similar when it comes to keeping oneself in the background when children are playing. The function of play is also social, although relations became a key notion for the teachers working with young children. Also Japan and the USA see the benefit of play in terms of socialization, where Japanese teachers see their role as giving support and care, while the role of the teachers in the USA is to arrange the environment and arrange for appropriate play to take pace, that is what is typical play for each age group, respectively. Aotearoa New Zealand teachers in this study see themselves as facilitators of children's learning – through the provision of artefacts, environments and, most importantly, practices which are attuned to the child. The function of teachers in play is to promote relationships that respond to the buds of learning children exhibit through spontaneous and planned play. China and Chile are similar in that they both see the function of play as a way to mediate knowledge and learning. Chile, however, also expressed the view that the teacher's role is to provide enjoyment, which we, however, believe is a statement so evident that most teachers take it for granted.

Learning in Toddler Groups

There were cross-cultural differences in notions about learning in early childhood settings. Also here we can see differences. Australia points to the perspective of play *as* learning which Japan proves in their study. Aotearoa New Zealand has a similar perspective based on the notion of *ako* which suggests that learning and teaching are reciprocal processes and, as such, occur in direct as well as in indirect relationships with "people, places and things" (Ministry of Education, 1996, p. 11). China, on the other hand, is most specific when they give examples of how the teachers try to intervene in order to mediate notions to the children. Both Sweden and Chile talk about learning as making sense of experiences. In USA learning is also related to the notion of developmental appropriateness. But what are children supposed to learn in toddler groups?

Similarities Across Cultures in Beliefs About Play and Learning

Between parents and teachers there seems to be a vague understanding of the meaning of play and learning for development and how these two phenomena are related. Play is perceived across all countries as an essential indulgence of the very young child, while learning, a deliberate process of acquiring something new, is a necessary part of toddlers' lives. Why? We all know that the largest and most dramatic learning takes place during the earliest years. Yet such changes are often described as development, that is something biological and innate is happening and does so without intervention. The notion of "natural" development is a perspective that has permeated the field of early childhood education (Dahlberg & Lenz Taguchi, 1994).

Let us consider these notions against the title of one of Barbara Rogoff's (2003) books, *The Cultural Nature of Human Development.* The whole field of new theories of young children's growth and how they become citizens show us that culture mediates knowledge, values, and skills to the child. At the same time the child him or herself contributes to the interaction and by that influences the surroundings (Sommer, 2005a, b). The child is born as a social creature – acting and reacting according to his or her experiences. This means, if one sees "the competent child", that child appears. Then, of course, how the experiences are shaped in the early childhood education have a great impact on the child's life and basic education.

It is also interesting to note that everybody claims that children learn to become social in early childhood education. At the same time, new research says that children are born social, so what is it that they are supposed to learn in early childhood education? To adjust to become one individual in the group? Or to follow the teacher's instructions? The most important social skills must be to interact, communicate, and build relationships. Most babies who have lived their first year together with human beings who care are mastering these skills even before they begin early childhood education.

We can also state that the experiences children in this study get, in seven different countries, are culturally specific as well as generally "preschoolish". This means that there are certain features of a child's day in early childhood education that are similar across societies. Young children eat, sleep, are cared for, and play with remarkably similar kinds of toys. Children become friends and play together, which is a very important aspect of their daily life, also for the youngest children, which Japan has also noted. All children play and explore the world via toys and interaction with other children or with a teacher. We also see many rich examples of children's pretend play, although they are at an age in which we used to think of their capacity as developed enough for such sophisticated play.

The third general trend we can see is that there is a change in early childhood education in all the seven countries, although it might differ – sometimes being on the political arena, other times on the educational, but still being a similar intention of the countries, it seems like all the countries involved are looking for *new approaches* to early childhood education, taking the child with his or her rights and intentions more into consideration, or trying to make sense of the notion "the competent child". In China, for example, this means to give more space to the child's own initiative and play. In Sweden, Aotearoa New Zealand, and Australia the paradigm shift is attempting to overcome the stronghold of traditional Euro-centric Piagetian child developmental perspectives, where children are considered to be similar in a specific age group, towards seeing every child's strengths regardless of age, but more related to everyday experiences. The shift brings with it an emphasis on aspects of equity between cultural groups and services as a central question in Aotearoa New Zealand, while equality between boys and girls is more on the agenda in Sweden (SOU, 2006, p. 75). Aotearoa New Zealand and Sweden are perhaps closer to each other than the other countries. They both share value questions as central and critical to work on. In Australia they struggle with the notion of developmentally appropriate practice, which earlier was "a leading notion" there for early childhood education.

What Is Culturally Specific?

What have researchers in each country then found to be cultural specific? In Sweden children express the habit of drinking coffee which is focused on in children's pretend play, something they experience their teachers (and parents) do every day. It might also be a way to involve the teachers in their play, inviting them to a coffee party. But also a quite new but common occurrence can be spotted in the outdoor activities – walking with two sticks – a very popular way of exercising in the Swedish society today.

In Australia, play in early childhood education centres has been dominated by a belief that the adult should have a limited role in children's play activities. Developmental beliefs and a history of drawing upon Piaget's work have meant that teachers believe that children's play should not be interfered with and planning should focus on providing materials. Teachers have predominantly utilized Parten's (1932) theory of play for guiding their analyses of children's play activity. Teachers have enacted a play-based curriculum and analysis following Parten's theory, and the resulting programme features constant traditional materials (e.g. home corner using wooden or plastic child-sized furniture) with the addition of specific resources to supplement learning directions (clothing featuring community roles, such as nurses' uniform).

In Japan, the importance of play is stressed in the Guidelines of Day Nurseries issued by the Ministry of Health, Welfare, and Labour, saying that play is a strong agent to stimulate and enhance children's development. Thus, abundant free time play is an essential component for a daily life at any day care centre. Through indoor and out-door play, such as pretending play, folding origami, riding a bicycle, sand and mud play from early ages, children have initiatives to choose what to do. Free-play time gives every child the opportunity to develop a sense of autonomy as well as sociality. Thus, the role of teacher/caregivers is to set up a rich environment for children to engage in various types of play. Although teacher/caregivers interact with children directly, their roles are to foster and guide children's development rather than telling children what to play. Teacher/caregivers sometimes learn the trends of children's lives at home through observing children's pretending play, such as ways of using utensils and cooking, and characters of TV programmes. Then the role of teacher/caregivers to create an environment for children both enhance activities related to their homes and encourage the children to be away from violent animated character play. These kinds of direct/indirect interactions are considered to form the learning environment for children.

In China, like in other countries, children engaged in pretend play when they had a free-choice of activities. However, children had relatively little time to engage in genuinely free play. The role of the teacher during children's free play is particularly noteworthy. Teachers intervened during children's free play to transmit and reinforce basic concepts such as colour and shape. The teacher was also actively involved in the majority of children's non free-play experiences by either directing or supporting them. Hence the term "eduplay" is used to connotate the form of teacher-directed play-based education which is evident in Chinese kindergartens.

In Chile they use play imitating some TV characters which reflects one of the current aspects of the Chilean culture. But they also play some verbal and socio-dramatic games that are clearly related with some folkloric aspects that we can find in the legends of the country, like preparing certain foods, that are usually served at their homes.

In Aotearoa New Zealand there was a common element in the emphasis placed on the natural environment, the outdoor spaces, and cultural places where children could go to explore the real world or where the real world could be brought to them in the form of sand, water, and animals. Children were observed in daily rituals such as prayer (*karakia*) and song (*waiata*), and valued cultural practices of movement (e.g. poi), rhythm (e.g. drumming) and sport (e.g. rugby). The environment across all settings offered calculated levels of risk which invited the children to play in ways that extended them physically and tantalized their extended engagement. Of particular note was the consistent presence (and engagement) of parents who were intimately involved in the early childhood education experience of their child, and contributed in a wide range of ways to their children's play both at home and through their interaction at the centre.

Critical Questions to Work on for the Future

What then are the most critical questions for early childhood education in our seven countries? In Chile one main question is to increase coverage and quality. The USA questions how to bridge the gap between theory and practice in play. In China they want to see an improvement of pedagogy and play. A question Sweden has been working on in the implementation of the curriculum (Ministry of Education and Sciences in Sweden, 1998) is that play and learning should be integrated (Johansson & Pramling-Samuelsson, 2006). A question asked in the study by Johansson and Pramling-Samuelsson is: "Is it possible to integrate play and learning in a goal directed preschool?" (Pramling-Samuelsson, 2005). And, of course, there are preconditions for being able to let play influence learning and vice versa. In Japan there are concerns about the integration of education and care, which can be improved, something they probably share with many other countries. As young children learn in everyday life throughout the whole day, the teachers ought to be able to utilize all situations for children's learning. Aotearoa New Zealand's challenge is to ensure that such opportunities for play are available to *all* children – regardless of their circumstances. In the present era of early childhood education's increased status, which is highly celebrated, it is important that teachers do not become complacent about their interpretive role in the play experience. The cry for more "eureka moments" in teacher's lives remains a firm resolve for the continued improvement of early childhood education in Aotearoa New Zealand. This is seen as best realized in increased opportunities for teachers to critically reflect on their practice, since it is their ability to notice, recognize, and respond to learning that shifts play from a pleasant past-time to an educative opportunity.

There seems to be an assumption in some cultures that "play" is "what happens" in early childhood settings in the same way that "curriculum" can be viewed as everything that happens in ECE settings. We can see that socio-cultural perspectives can break down dichotomies between child- and adult-initiated activities and dialogues, but somewhere there is a cut-off point when the label of play no longer applies. More empirical studies are needed for studying the relation between play and learning. We also know that adults have more power than children, and a central question for the future is in what way the child's right can be recognized and give children a feeling of being a participant in their own play, learning, and everyday life in ECE? Probably it all comes back to the role of the teacher and their perspective of children and their own profession in guiding children into the future.

Conclusions

If we go back to the three levels of Rogoff's (2003), we can see on the *intrapersonal lenses*, that most children studied are enjoying their day in early childhood education. They are all actively engaged in activities that we as adults may call play, but for them it is something interesting or challenging they deal with and make sense of. It might, most probably, be something they learn/discover/experience whatever we call it. Children are playing and learning individuals (described by a NZ teacher and parent as "sponges") who try to make sense of the experience they are involved in (Pramling-Samuelsson, & Asplund Carlsson, 2003). Focussing on the *interpersonal* level, we can see that the different children are more or less involved in interaction and friendships with each other, partly related to their age. However, we also see strong cultural differences between the interactions between the teachers and the children. In some countries children are left to themselves to play and learn more than can be seen in other countries. This is not by accident, but by conscious strategies of different kinds. On the other hand, teachers in China take every opportunity to interact and mediate knowledge to children. In other countries, such as Aotearoa New Zealand, there is a deep respect shown for the play preferences of children with an associated requirement (and challenge) on the teacher to intimately know that child in order to strategically respond in ways that will promote learning. The level of skill and knowledge required for such involvement drives a high level of professional education which is reflected in national priorities that have yet to be realized for all services.

We believe that the teachers can never interact and communicate too much with the toddlers in early childhood education since there are so many children and few adults. This is where Vygotsky's (1966) theory becomes helpful. By being close to children in daily activities (play and learning situations) and with an intimate knowledge of each child as a unique individual within the group, teachers can support, inspire, and challenge children's meaning making (something children deal with in play as well as in learning), at the same time they need to understand the child's perspective (Johansson & Pramling-Samuelsson, 2003), because it is only when they take the child's perspective they understand their meaning making. We need active responsive teachers, not to teach in narrow predetermined ways but to engage with children and their play as dialogue partners and facilitators who desire to give children a good start in life.

Finally, on the *cultural/institutional* level, we can see the largest differences between the countries, since the conditions, in terms of the role early childhood education play, in different societies varies a lot. For example, the money allocated to early childhood education in each culture, which has consequences for the child–adult ratio, the education of the staff, the actual number of children in the group, the way it is organized (age specific or sibling groups) and, of course, the level of support given to parents who are recognized as the most important quality variable in any toddler's life.

References

Asplund Carlsson, M., Kärrby, G., & Pramling-Samuelsson, I. (2001). *Strukturella faktorer och pedagogisk kvalitet.* [Structural factors and pedagogical quality.] Stockholm: Fritzes.

Dahlberg, G., & Lenz Taguchi, H. (1994). *Förskola och skola – om två skilda traditioner och om visionen om en mötesplats.* [Preschool and school – two different traditions and a vision of a meeting place.] Stockholm: HLS Förlag.

Dunn, J. (1991). Young children's understanding of other people: Evidence from observations within the family. In D. Frye & C. Moore (Eds.), *Children's theories of mind: Mental states and social understanding* (pp. 99–114). Hillsdale, NJ: Earlbaum.

Engeström, Y. (1999). Activity theory and individual and social transformation. In Y. Engeström, R. Meittinen, & R. Punamaki (Eds). *Perspectives on activity theory* (pp. 19–38). Cambridge: Cambridge University Press.

Fleer, M., Tonyan, H. A., Mantilla, A. C., & Rivalland, C. M. P. (2006, July). *A cultural historical analysis of play as an activity setting in early childhood education: Views from research and from teachers.* Paper presented at the International Society Social Behavioural Development Conference, Melbourne, Victoria.

Gibbons, A. N. (2005). *The matrix ate my baby: Play, technology and the early childhood subject.* Doctoral thesis, Auckland University, New Zealand.

Gonazlez-Mena, J. (1986, November). Toddlers: What to expect. *Young Children, 42*(1), 47–51.

Gustafsson, J. E. & Myhrberg, E. (2002). *Ekonomiska resursers betydelse för pedagogiska resultat: en kunskapsöversikt.* [Financial resources" influence on pedagogical results: An overview.] Stockholm: Liber.

Johansson, E., & Pramling-Samuelsson, I. (2003). *Förskolan – barns första skola.* [Preschool – Children's first school.] Lund: Studentlitteratur.

Johansson, E., & Pramling-Samuelsson, I. (2006). *Lek och läroplan. Möten mellan barn och lärare i förskola och skola.* [Play and curriculum: Children and teacher meet in preschool and school.] Göteborg: Acta Universitatis Gothoburgensis.

Marton, F., & Tsui, B. M. (2004). *Classroom discourse and the space of learning.* Mahwah: Lawrence Erlbaum.

Ministry of Education and Sciences in Sweden. (1998). *Curriculum for pre-school. Lpfö 98.* Stockholm: Fritzes.

Ministry of Education. (1996). *Te Whāriki: He Whāriki Mātauranga mo ngāMokopuna o Aotearoa– Early childhood curriculum.* Wellington, New Zealand: Learning Media Limited.

Nuttall, J. (Ed.). (2003). *Weaving Te Whaariki. Aotearoa New Zealand's early childhood curriculum document in theory and practice* (pp. 243–268). New Zealand Council for Educational Research: Wellington.

OECD. (2004). *Starting strong: Curricula and pedagogies in early childhood education and care. Five curriculum outlines. Directorate for education.* Paris: OECD. www.SourceOECD.org

Palmérus, K., Pramling, I., & Lindahl, M. (1991). *Daghem för småbarn. En utvecklingsstudie av personalens pedagogiska och psykologiska kunnande.* [Day care for toddlers.] Rapport nr 8 från Institutionen för metodik. Göteborgs universitet.

Parten, M. (1932). Social participation among preschool children. *Journal of Abnormal & Social Psychology, 27,* 243–269.

Pramling, I. (1995). A mediational approach to early intervention: Upgrading quality of education in Swedish toddler groups. In P. Klein & K. Hundeide (Eds.), *Early intervention: A mediational approach on the cross cultural application of the MISC program.* New York: Garland Publishing.

Pramling-Samuelsson, I. (2005). Can play and learning be integrated in a goal-oriented preschool: Early childhood practice. *The Journal for Multi-Professional Partnerships, 7*(1), 5–22 Spring. www.earlychildhoodpractice.net

Pramling-Samuelsson, I., & Asplund Carlsson, M. (2003). *Det lekande lärande barnet – i en utvecklingspedagogisk teori.* [The playing learning child – in a developmental pedagogic theory.] Stockholm: Liber.

Rao, N., Ng, S. S. N., & Pearson, E. (2006). Preschool pedagogy: A fusion of traditional Chinese beliefs and contemporary notions of appropriate practice. (Unpublished chapter to appear in) In C. K. K. Chan & N. Rao (Eds.), *Revisiting the Chinese learner: Psychological and pedagogical perspectives.* The University of Hong Kong: Comparative Education Research Centre/Springer Academic Publishers.

Rogoff, B. (2003). *The cultural nature of human development.* New York: Oxford University Press.

Sheridan, S. (2001). *Pedagogical quality in preschool: An issue of perspectives.* Göteborg: Acta Universitatis Gothoburgensis.

Siraj Blatchford, I. (2004). Educational disadvantage in the early years: How do we overcome it? Some lessons from research. *European Early Childhood Education Research Journal, 12*(2), 5–20.

Smith, A. B., Grima, G., Gaffney, M., Powell, K., Masse, L., & Barnett, S. (2000). Strategic Research Initiatives, Literature Review, Early Childhood Education, Report to the Ministry of Education, New Zealand.

Sommer, D. (2005a). *Barndomspsykologi. Utveckling i en förändrad värld.* [Childhood psychology: Development in a changing world.] Stockholm: Runa.

Sommer, D. (2005b). *Barndomspsykologiska facetter.* [Childhood psychological facets.] Stockholm: Liber.

SOU. (2006:75). *Jämställd förskola. Om betydelsen av jämställdhet och genus i förskolans pedagogiska arbete. Slutbetänkande från Delegationen för jämställdhet i förskolan.* Stockholm: Fritzes.

The Daily Yominri, 2006-05-23.

Vygotsky, L. (1966). Play and its role in the mental development of the child. *Voprosy psikhologii, 12*(6), 62–76.

Vygotsky, L. (1986). *Thought and language.* Cambridge, MA: MIT Press.

Name Index

Subject Index

Printed in the United States
130327LV00002B/343-384/P